ACOUSTIC
SHADOWS

Mon Aug 11th 1862

Aug 11th left home to join
the 12th Ill. Inft. went
to Kewanee. took the cars
for chicago Arived there
at 6 P.M., went to the
Dearbourn House staid
there all night there was
6 in our co R. Holmes
S. T. Harding. M. Avery
J. Morris. J. Galley &
my self. we looked for
a recruiting officer this
evening but not finding
one returned to our
quarters

        Aug. 12th
Continued our search
for a Recruiting officer
but not finding one
we concluded to enlist
in the 72nd Ill. them

ACOUSTIC SHADOWS

Men at War and a Daughter Who Remembers Them

⟞◆⟝

BETSY L. HOWELL

Acoustic Shadows
Men at War and a Daughter Who Remembers Them

Rainforest Press
P.O. Box 659
Port Townsend, WA 98368

ISBN-13 978-0-9792716-0-1
ISBN-10 0-9792716-0-6

Library of Congress Control Number: 2007921564

Portions of this book appeared in the *Clackamas Literary Review*,
Spring/Summer 2003 ("Civil War Reenacting from a Woman's
Perspective") and the *South Loop Review*, 2006 ("River of Death").

I am grateful to O.C. Hood for permission to quote "Reload"
from his poetry collection *Millstream*.

Cover design by Mike Watters
Interior design by Kathryn E. Campbell

Printed in the United States of America
by Gorham Printing, Centralia, Washington

Portrait of Private D.W.C Arnold used courtesy of the
National Archives and Records Administration
(Arnold, D. W. C., private in the Union Army, number 111-B-5435)
Photos of First Lieutenant James Howell and James and
Betsy Howell courtesy of the author

The map of The Travels of James Darsie Heath, 1862–1865 and
the *Acoustic Shadows* Family Tree also by Mike Watters

All other photos also courtesy of the author

For my parents

CONTENTS

AUTHOR'S NOTE

Acoustic Shadows owes its structure and much of its soul to the content of my great-great-grandfather James Darsie Heath's Civil War journals, from which I draw heavily. I have chosen to reprint his words exactly as I found them without employing the word "sic" after every incorrect or unusual example of spelling, punctuation, or word usage. If I had done this, "sic" would have filled the quoted material to a degree that would have taken away from its original essence. Additionally, material quoted from other sources, most of it from nineteenth century writers, also contains numerous errors and I have chosen to use brackets only for clarification of information, such as distances traveled, dates of events, places visited, or people referred to, and occasionally to fill in missing portions of words.

THE ACOUSTIC SHADOWS FAMILY TREE

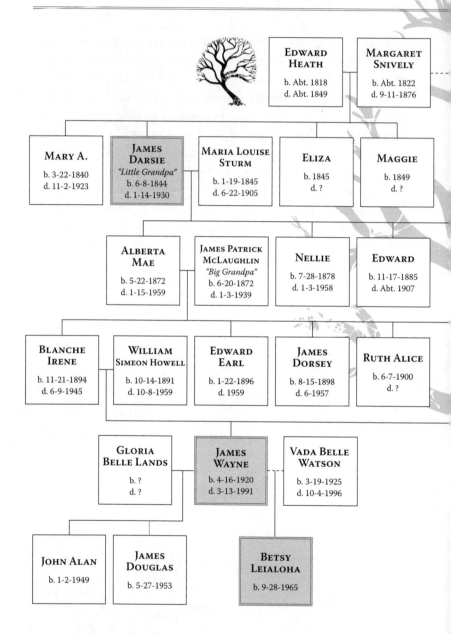

EDWARD HEATH
b. Abt. 1818
d. Abt. 1849

MARGARET SNIVELY
b. Abt. 1822
d. 9-11-1876

MARY A.
b. 3-22-1840
d. 11-2-1923

JAMES DARSIE
"Little Grandpa"
b. 6-8-1844
d. 1-14-1930

MARIA LOUISE STURM
b. 1-19-1845
d. 6-22-1905

ELIZA
b. 1845
d. ?

MAGGIE
b. 1849
d. ?

ALBERTA MAE
b. 5-22-1872
d. 1-15-1959

JAMES PATRICK McLAUGHLIN
"Big Grandpa"
b. 6-20-1872
d. 1-3-1939

NELLIE
b. 7-28-1878
d. 1-3-1958

EDWARD
b. 11-17-1885
d. Abt. 1907

BLANCHE IRENE
b. 11-21-1894
d. 6-9-1945

WILLIAM SIMEON HOWELL
b. 10-14-1891
d. 10-8-1959

EDWARD EARL
b. 1-22-1896
d. 1959

JAMES DORSEY
b. 8-15-1898
d. 6-1957

RUTH ALICE
b. 6-7-1900
d. ?

GLORIA BELLE LANDS
b. ?
d. ?

JAMES WAYNE
b. 4-16-1920
d. 3-13-1991

VADA BELLE WATSON
b. 3-19-1925
d. 10-4-1996

JOHN ALAN
b. 1-2-1949

JAMES DOUGLAS
b. 5-27-1953

BETSY LEIALOHA
b. 9-28-1965

------------ INDICATES A SECOND MARRIAGE

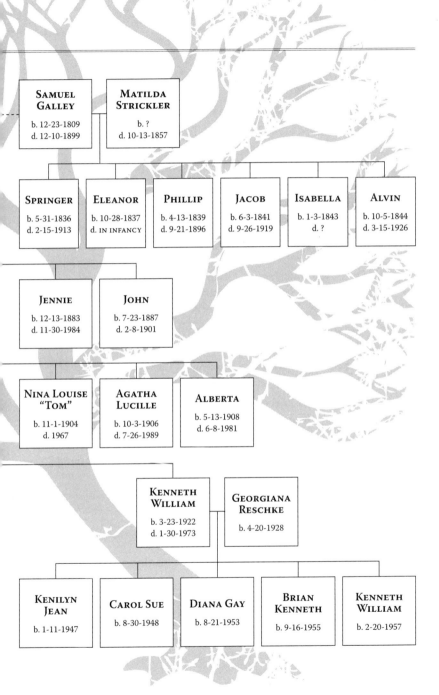

SAMUEL GALLEY
b. 12-23-1809
d. 12-10-1899

MATILDA STRICKLER
b. ?
d. 10-13-1857

SPRINGER
b. 5-31-1836
d. 2-15-1913

ELEANOR
b. 10-28-1837
d. IN INFANCY

PHILLIP
b. 4-13-1839
d. 9-21-1896

JACOB
b. 6-3-1841
d. 9-26-1919

ISABELLA
b. 1-3-1843
d. ?

ALVIN
b. 10-5-1844
d. 3-15-1926

JENNIE
b. 12-13-1883
d. 11-30-1984

JOHN
b. 7-23-1887
d. 2-8-1901

NINA LOUISE "TOM"
b. 11-1-1904
d. 1967

AGATHA LUCILLE
b. 10-3-1906
d. 7-26-1989

ALBERTA
b. 5-13-1908
d. 6-8-1981

KENNETH WILLIAM
b. 3-23-1922
d. 1-30-1973

GEORGIANA RESCHKE
b. 4-20-1928

KENILYN JEAN
b. 1-11-1947

CAROL SUE
b. 8-30-1948

DIANA GAY
b. 8-21-1953

BRIAN KENNETH
b. 9-16-1955

KENNETH WILLIAM
b. 2-20-1957

PEOPLE IN *ACOUSTIC SHADOWS*

1860s

The 72ⁿᵈ Illinois Infantry:

LIEUTENANT COLONEL JOSEPH STOCKTON (1833–1907)—author of *War Diary*

ADJUTANT GEORGE HEAFFORD (1845–1916)—author of *Chevrons and Shoulder Straps*, and the essay "The Army of the Tennessee"

CAPTAIN JAMES SEXTON, Company D—author of the essay "The Observations and Experiences of a Captain of Infantry at the Battle of Franklin, November 30, 1864"

LIEUTENANT RICHARD POMEROY, Company F—killed at Benton, Mississippi, May 1864

SERGEANT WILLIAM SPARKS, Company I—author of the essay "Reminiscences of Sergeant Wm. Sparks of the 72ⁿᵈ Illinois Volunteers"

PRIVATE BENJAMIN TALMADGE, Company B—died at Columbus, Kentucky, October 1862

PRIVATE ANSON HEMINGWAY (1844–1926), Company D—author of diaries written July 1862–December 1863

PRIVATE THOMAS SEACORD, Company E—died at Memphis, Tennessee, January 1863

PRIVATE WILLIAM METZGER (1846–1940), Company E

PRIVATE DAVID TEMPLE, Company K—killed in battle at Vicksburg, Mississippi, May 1863

Company A:

CAPTAIN ROSWELL MASON

FIRST LIEUTENANT WILLIAM MOHRMANN—author of memoirs written ca. 1880–1885.

CORPORAL THOMAS RUSSELL—killed in battle at Vicksburg, Mississippi, May 1863

PRIVATE MILES AVERY—deserted at Cairo, Illinois, August 1862

PRIVATE JACOB GALLEY (1841–1919)

PRIVATE SCEPTER T. HARDING—killed in battle at Vicksburg, Mississippi, May 1863

PRIVATE JAMES DARSIE HEATH (1844–1930)

PRIVATE ROBERT HOLMES

PRIVATE JOSEPH MORRIS—deserted at Cairo, Illinois, August 1862

1940s/2000s

The 82nd Airborne, 505th Parachute Infantry Regiment, I Company:

Second Platoon:

SERGEANT STANLEY KULIKOWSKI

PRIVATE WILLIAM H. TUCKER—author of *Parachute Soldier*

Third Platoon:

FIRST LIEUTENANT GEORGE CLARK

SECOND LIEUTENANT JAMES HOWELL

PRIVATE JACK HILLMAN

PRIVATE JOHN LEVITSKY

PRIVATE JOSEPH SCHWAN

The 101st Airborne, 502nd Parachute Infantry Regiment, C Company:

CAM ANDERSON

The 17th Airborne, 513th Parachute Infantry Regiment,
A Company:

PRIVATE KURT GABEL—author of *The Making of a Paratrooper:*
Airborne Training and Combat in World War II

2000S

The 19th Indiana Infantry, Company A:

CAPTAIN DANIEL O'HARA

SERGEANT/CAPTAIN CHRIS SCARANO

FIRST SERGEANT DERRICK STURDIVANT

PRIVATE JEFF BAKER

PRIVATE RICK FITZGERALD

PRIVATE NIELS FOLEY

PRIVATE BERTRAM HOWELL

PRIVATE BRETT WILLIAMS

People I Met on the Road Trips:

CATHIE BUECHLER—present owner of my father's childhood home
in Geneseo, Illinois

MARY JANE HALL—woman whose grandmother was a little girl
during the Civil War, College Hill, Mississippi

JOHN RUSKEY—river guide, Clarksdale, Mississippi

JEFF GIAMBRONE—historian, Old Court House Museum,
Vicksburg, Mississippi

BOB DUNCAN—historian/archivist, Columbia, Tennessee

BETTY WATSON—owner of the East Port Inn, Iuka, Mississippi

EDWARD COX—tour guide, Spanish Fort, Alabama

THOMAS CARTWRIGHT—director, Carter House, Franklin, Tennessee

DAVID FRALEY—historian, Carter House, Franklin, Tennessee

MAPS AND PHOTOGRAPHS

Maps

Photographs

THE TRAVELS OF JAMES DARSIE HEATH, 1862-1865

More than once during the Civil War, newspapers reported a strange phenomenon. From only a few miles away a battle sometimes made no sound despite the flash and smoke of cannon and the fact that more distant observers could hear it clearly. These eerie silences were called acoustic shadows.

—From Ken Burns's PBS documentary, *The Civil War*

PROLOGUE

October 2004, Spring Hill, Tennessee

CHARLIE LEMONS, captain of the Union Western Brigade's Third Company, looked at his troops through the haze of the autumnal Tennessee heat. Short, with a round face, Charlie spoke rapidly as his excitement grew.

"Gentlemen, it looks like we're going to be a part of Opdycke's Brigade. We are the reserve. *We*," he paused for effect, "will be pushing the Confederates back." The men cheered. I, too, felt the buzz of battle even as my blistered feet pleaded to stay behind.

"When they break through the line," the captain continued, "we are going to hit them at a dead run. I don't mean a double-quick either; I mean a *run*. This was the moment that saved the Union at Franklin, so when we hit them, we hit them hard." He looked pleased, as if we were being sent in on fourth and long, and he knew that one of us would make the game-winning touchdown.

Charlie trotted off to confer with the ring of Union commanders, and the soldiers of Third Company gathered around our first sergeant.

"Anybody have any concerns about doing this?" Harold, a firefighter and paramedic in his "other" life, asked. I had concerns but didn't say anything. The heat and dust, along with my exhaustion and aching feet, made me feel like I was floating in a dream. In the last twenty-four hours we had marched close to nine miles, slept on the campaign trail, gotten into two skirmishes, and fought three battles. This experience—the 140th anniversary reenactment of the Battle of Franklin, Tennessee—paled next to what my great-great-grandfather endured during the real Civil War, but it far surpassed my previous reenacting endeavors.

Less than a half hour later, the scenario that was to recreate the

battle for eighty thousand spectators fell apart. The Confederates—
who were supposed to break through at one narrow opening in the
Union line—flooded the entire east flank. An incoming tide of gray
rushed the machine-made trenches and pushed us bluecoats back
toward the audience.

"Third Company, *fall in!*" screamed Captain Lemons.

From that point on, everything happened at lightning speed. My
Yankee comrades and I ran to the last line of trenches and met the
Southern soldiers over the mound of soft earth. Soon bodies and
arms and weapons were swinging and the confrontation seemed as
chaotic as I had imagined real Civil War battles to be. Someone's
gunstock accidentally smacked my head, and a tingling sensation
oozed down my scalp like the contents of a broken egg. I fell over
one soldier and continued falling into another. Dark, Tennessee dirt
exploded around me as bodies fell into the trench. Peeking over the
top of the trench, I watched cavalry zipping up and down the battle
line, a "wounded" Confederate soldier waving a small banner atop
his gun, and smoke rolling in waves across the field.

As I fired round after round of black powder, my gun heated up
as if it had been lying in a kiln. I put it down.

"Keep shooting!" yelled the first sergeant. "Keep shooting! Ya
can't kill anyone if ya don't shoot!"

An hour later, only one-fifth the time of the real Battle of Franklin, we marched the mile back to camp. A small woman dressed in
a hoop skirt with a hat and shawl around her shoulders stopped us
as we left the field. "Thank you so much for your work," she said.
"I'm from Nashville and I had ancestors on both sides of the battle."
Though I appreciated her enthusiasm, my oozing blisters made me
want only to reach my dog (nowadays known as a "pup") tent and
get my boots off. Later that evening I limped out to the campfire. A
man named Tim was describing the Battle of Perryville, Tennessee,
where some of the troops never joined the fight because they didn't
get the order. I sat down carefully in the burr-infested field.

"And sometimes," I added, "the men didn't participate because
they never *heard* the fight, even though they were very close."

"That happened a lot because of topography," Tim replied. "It was called 'acoustic shadowing.'"

"Yeah," I said, "I know."

⚊⚊⚫⚊⚊

During the summer of 1998, after resigning from my job with the U.S. Forest Service, I began transcribing my great-great-grandfather's Civil War journals. I had seen them on many occasions, but had opened James Darsie Heath's two small books only briefly during my thirty-three years of life. That summer, eager to leave behind a life haunted by my parents' recent deaths, I finally had the time and desire to know exactly what the journals said. As I read, the details of my ancestor's experience as a Union private from 1862 to 1865 came to life—with the boredom, sickness, and fear of the experience of war laid out in a rainbow of words upon frayed, yellowed pages.

Using the Internet, I found a bibliography of writings on his regiment, the 72nd Illinois Infantry. Several members of the unit had published the journals they'd kept during the war or essays they'd written years later. After obtaining copies of *War Diary* by Lieutenant Colonel Joseph Stockton, *Chevrons and Shoulder Straps* by Adjutant George Heafford, and the diaries of Private Anson Hemingway and First Lieutenant William Mohrmann, I was able to piece together a more complete picture of those years than what I had learned from my great-great-grandfather's often fragmented record. This spurred me to attempt a trip retracing James Darsie Heath's footsteps during the war. The path was clear: from western Illinois across to Chicago and then down to southern Illinois; south along the Mississippi River, with stops in western Kentucky and Tennessee, to Vicksburg, Mississippi; then northeast to central Tennessee; and finally to southern Alabama. *Why* I suddenly wanted to learn about the Civil War and my long-ago relative seemed less obvious, but I hoped the answers would come as I ventured further into the past.

And so the summer of 1999 and the fall of 2000 found me traveling the highways and rivers of Illinois, Kentucky, Tennessee, Mississippi, and Alabama. More letters from regimental members turned up along the way, and I met historians and others who made me think about the impact of past events on present-day lives. I had never paid much attention to the Civil War, but I soon began to grasp my personal connection to it. James Darsie Heath had survived. His journals told me, however, that his experiences had cost him. He'd never forgotten what he'd seen and done, and this was the legacy passed down to me.

During this process, while trying to imagine the life of a Civil War soldier, I joined a reenacting company. Over the course of the two trips I had accumulated several notebooks worth of material, but as I began writing a narrative of James Darsie's life, picturing the military culture proved challenging. Becoming a soldier—albeit a theatrical one—seemed the path to understanding. Yet as I delved deeper into my research, I realized that James Darsie Heath wasn't the only soldier whose experiences had affected me. My father's life and our complicated relationship surfaced in a focused way that told me this quest was really about understanding him. *His* wars—World War II and Korea—had seeped into my childhood via his stories, his drunken behavior, and his nightmares, the shouts from which I could often hear from my bedroom. I requested my father's military papers, read narratives about his unit, the 505th Parachute Infantry Regiment, and interviewed some of the surviving members of his company. The trauma of battle, too large to remain one person's experience, had formed the background for the person I had become.

Acoustic Shadows, a narrative that moves in time between the 1860s, the 1940s, and my life, from 1965 to the present, is about my evolving awareness of war's far-reaching effects. It is also about forgiveness and how learning about the people I came from has helped me understand myself. This book is dedicated to my father and great-great-grandfather.

—BETSY L. HOWELL

February 2007

The Ship of State

Still sail thou on, O Ship of State!
Sail on, O U~~~~~ ~~~~~ and great!
Humanity with all its fears,
With all its hopes of future years,
Is hanging breathless on thy fate!
We know what Master laid thy keel,
What workmen wrought thy ribs of steel,
Who made each mast, and sail and rope,
What anvils rang what hammers beat,
In what a forge and what a heat
Were shaped the anchors of thy hope!
Fear not each sudden sound and shock,
'Tis of the wave and not the rock,
'Tis but the flapping of the sail,
And not a rent made by the gale!
In spite of rock and tempests roar,
In spite of false lights on the shore,
Sail on, nor fear to breast the sea!
Our hearts, our hopes, our prayers, our tears,
Our faith triumphant o'er our fears,
Are all with thee — are all with thee!

H. W. Longfellow

PART I:

Marching

march, verb

1. to walk with regular, steady steps of equal length, usually in a group or military formation.
2. to go or advance steadily.

Vada and James Howell, ca. 1960

Chapter 1

9302 Snowberry Circle

We understand death for the first time when he puts his hand upon one whom we love.

—Madame de Stael, writer (1766–1817)

October 1996, Tacoma, Washington

TWENTY-SEVEN YEARS after moving to my childhood home, I sat in front of my family's fireplace with a grocery bag full of loose papers. A fire roared, nourished with appliance instruction manuals (yellowed and dating back to the 1970s), old bank statements, and credit card bills—all of which my parents had saved but no longer needed. The tongues of fire licked the soot-encrusted chimney walls, reaching beyond my sight through the damper's opening. After the long, fireless summer, I hoped there were no rats' nests in the chimney.

The phone rang, interrupting my fire tending. The caller was my father's cousin, Patti.

"Hi, hon. How are you doing?"

"Fine," I said, trying not to slur my speech. I squinted at the fireplace bench to see how much beer I'd had. Four bottles. Not so many. I should be able to sound sober. Not that it mattered; Patti was used to talking to drunken relatives.

"Well...*what* are you doing?" she asked awkwardly.

"I'm burning piles of papers that Mom and Dad kept. Trying to work my way through their stuff."

There was a pause. My anger felt palpable: I could count on one hand the number of times Patti had called my mom to see how *she* was doing after my dad died five years ago. My father's unexpected illness and quick demise had revealed people's true natures. Some friends and relatives drifted away from my mother and me, unable to make room for his absence. Others came to the fore.

"I'm really sorry about your mother," she said.

"Yeah, me too."

"It was so...so sudden."

"Not really. Mom hadn't been well for some time."

"Not being well" was a euphemism in my family. What it meant was too much smoking, too much drinking, too much of a life that beats a body down. I stretched the phone cord and grabbed another beer from the fridge. The cap snapped off with a hiss.

"So, you're...you're staying there...at the house by yourself?" Patti asked.

"Yeah."

"Aren't you afraid?"

"No."

"We're worried about you," Patti said, and I felt bad for not letting her in. She was trying. And she was right to worry, but not because of ghosts or other images she had conjured of a young woman staying alone in her parents' home after their deaths. If Patti had known more, maybe she would have worried about the bitterness eating me alive—and the drinking that I hid far better than my parents ever had. About the collapse of my spirit as I contemplated a life without my family. About the questions beginning to form surrounding who I was and whom I'd descended from. Questions, all of which seemed answerless, that came from a time snarled by alcohol, pain, and regret.

———◆———

Without either of my parents there, my childhood home seemed like a museum, a place to visit but not to stay. My entry into many rooms felt deviant, like slipping under a thick, velvet rope while a security guard turned his back, and I felt comfortable only in certain parts of the house. Memories clawed at me to relive the past, then pushed me away again.

In my parents' room, a 1940s painting of my mother looking like a Hollywood starlet watched over me as I listened to her answering machine. I sat on the edge of her bed and hit the "greeting" button over and over just to hear her voice. Looking at the painting, I marveled at the way even ordinary secretaries looked like glamorous actresses back then. Long, curly red hair fell down below her neck, and her face turned back over one shoulder to look at the artist. Her delicate eyebrows, like the gentle slant of a roof, stood out dark as night against her creamy skin. Her curved upper lips, neither smiling nor frowning, resembled a bird with outstretched wings. "Why did you leave me alone?" I asked my painted mother. No reply. My finger pressed the button again. "Hi. We're not here to take your call. Please leave a message after the beep."

Likewise, the painting offered no clue as to the combination of my parents' strongbox in the closet, which contained their wills. I used a hammer and screwdriver to break it open, the metal twisting reluctantly. My mother's eyes followed me and I remembered how she had protected me in this room from nightmares. Now the quiet of her absence settled like a snowfall that has fallen softly, yet weighs many tons, on a steep, avalanche-prone mountainside. Finally, I pulled out the wills of James and Vada Howell. Everything went to me, their only child.

My old room looked much as it had when I left thirteen years before to attend college. Yellow walls. Framed pictures of friends. A poster of a cat wearing glasses, with the caption, "Everyone has a right to my opinion." My father had moved a television and his *National Geographic* books into this room after my departure. A water bed had replaced my old twin bed, which had long since been moved into my father's den.

The den, the smallest room, still exuded the essence of the ex-soldier I'd grown up with. A bookshelf held books on history and warfare, as well as the Civil War journals of my great-great-grandfather, James Darsie Heath. Framed prints of soldiers hung on one wall. On another, a beer can collection stretched the length. One Christmas in the late 1970s, my mom had given my dad a plastic panel that would hold one hundred beer cans, thus turning the empty castings of a disease into art. In time, he bought three more panels. I helped with the collection by memorizing the cans already acquired, and tallying those that were still needed. Some undoubtedly are collector's items now: "Billy Beer," "M*A*S*H" beer, and a can commemorating the Armed Forces Day Celebration at Fort Lewis, Washington.

Dad's small desk rested beneath the window and still contained his handwritten notes from more than five years ago. It was outside below this window, next to the arborvitae, where my cat, Tiger, had died during my senior year in high school. As a teenager, I had often traded off between sleeping in Dad's den and my room. I would just settle into one bed, when nightmares of confusion and helplessness would begin. Having little perspective to understand or fight them, I coped by changing beds. In those years, my mother often never knew where to find me in the morning. I'd been sleeping in the den when Tiger crept below the window and breathed her last. We figured she had somehow known I was in this room. Later, my father had hammered together a box, lined it with old scraps of carpet, and we buried her where she lay.

After I finished roaming the vacant rooms and the fire died down, I went to bed on the couch in the living room. I dreamt that my parents were standing over me. Their presence felt authentic, as if only a thin membrane separated us, but *they* were not there. Just like the painting and the voice on the answering machine, the two images above me belonged to another time. Feeling in limbo between wakefulness and sleep, I tried to ignore them. This interaction was a far cry from those that awaited me in the morning, when I would meet with a lawyer, a real estate agent, and a U-Haul clerk who would sell me the boxes into which I would place my mother and father's worldly possessions. *Go away*, I finally pouted to my parents' images. *You can't help me now.*

The next evening I built another fire. I fed it more papers and drank more beer. Warming my back against the flames, I noticed burn marks from long-ago flying embers that had scarred the linoleum floor—the remnants of the many fires I had shared with my parents. Later I went to bed on the couch again, but I couldn't get away from my memories: the weeks my dad virtually lived on the sofa during his illness, us watching TV together as a family, the many parties my parents had hosted. Recalling these moments made me search for a space in the house that seemed neutral. I moved onto the floor and laid out a sleeping bag. Sleep finally came, but this battle with my memories was only the beginning; for the next several years, the past would become more important to me than the present.

One weekend morning when I was eleven, I entered our dining room and found my dad affixing a five-by-eight-foot map of the world to the wall. In three sections, he pasted Asia, Australia, and half of Alaska next to the Americas and Greenland, followed by Europe and Africa. Big, black letters at the bottom of the middle section read, "THE WORLD." This particular map, based on a Mercator projection, did not define land mass accurately. For example, Greenland, in reality several times smaller than South America, appeared nearly as large as Africa—but it was a distortion that we learned to live with. The map covered most of a wall that my mother had painted orange, and the improvement in this regard was immediate.

Later that day, after playing in the woods with my friends, I returned to find Dad pinning lengths of yarn to the map. Dark red, light red, and yellow strings connected continents and states.

"What are you doing?" I asked.

"I'm documenting my travels as a soldier and our vacations as a family. See," he said as he pointed to a dark red string reaching from West Virginia across the Atlantic Ocean to France and England, "this was during World War II. And this was during the Korean War." His finger traced another string that ran from California over the Pacific to Korea.

"What is light red?"

"That's military travel during non-wartime. And the yellow strings are where we've been as a family."

One yellow string stretched from Tacoma to various locations including Honolulu, Montreal, Los Angeles, and Colorado Springs. Next to each string, Dad had pinned a small paper flag with each journey's date. The earliest date on the map was 1941. This dark red string made a shape like a scythe, cutting from Chicago south to Fort Worth, east to New Orleans, then southeast to Panama City.

"You've been a lot of places," I said. My father looked at the strings.

"Yeah, I guess I have. We're a little heavy on the Northern Hemisphere though."

That night my father opened a gallon jug of Carlo Rossi red wine. After dinner, Mom washed the dishes while Dad and I looked more at the map and talked about traveling. He wanted to go to Argentina and find some long-lost relatives; I wanted to go to Africa and live on the plains with the lions and leopards.

As the wine jug emptied and my father became more unsteady, he sat down and crossed one leg over the other. Soon his head drooped forward. I put more logs on the fire, petted Tiger, and only peripherally observed his arm waving and his voice mumbling as he sunk lower and lower into his alcoholic stupor.

———•———

My last night in the house at Snowberry Circle, I drank a dark beer and studied the map. I took notes on the dates and places for each string. *1944—Norfolk, West Virginia→ Birmingham, England → Normandy, France→ Birmingham, England→ Groesbeek, Holland → Reims, France→ Magdeburg, Germany. 1945—Paris, France→ Gibraltar→ Azores Islands→ Boston, Massachusetts.* Soon the house would be sold, and the map would probably be painted over. The real estate agent hadn't been impressed with my dad's creation, saying that people wanted blank walls.

Later, I sat by the fire and looked at James Darsie Heath's Civil War journals. I had held them back from the U-Haul boxes, wanting them easily accessible. Five years before, just after my father's death, I had taken the journals to my home in southern Oregon for transcription, but I had never opened them. At that time, the present, though altered and painful, still held my attention. My mother had still needed me. Eventually I had brought them back to the bookshelf in my father's den. Now, however, no one needed me, and the present was excruciating. Something called me into the past, and it seemed the voice came from these two small books.

As I held them and gently turned the crisp, yellowed pages, I felt the weight of my aloneness. Not the kind of alone where your partner leaves for the weekend and you suddenly have the house to yourself, or how you feel when the last guest from your party has departed. This wasn't even the aloneness I imagined must come to parents after their children leave for college. No, this physical separation from nearly every member of my family, including aunts and uncles, cousins, and my two half brothers, either through death or estrangement, closed like a vise grip around my soul. My mother's departure had severed the last connection. This was *it*. I would be the next to die. I imagined myself floating atop a small square of wood on a vast, dark ocean, or drifting away into space and, my life support connection broken, tumbling ever backward into the endless night. In truth, I wasn't alone, but I *felt* alone. I was a chalice of memories for three people, holding remembrances that no one else shared. The responsibility seemed too great. I drank more.

This solitary existence sliced even deeper because of my unanswered questions. While he lived, I never wondered about my father's drinking and repeated withdrawal from our family life. While my mother lived, I never questioned her moodiness and the silent treatment she often imposed on my father and me. What had made them this way? I realized now, too late, that I did not know who my parents had truly been. I was thirty-one and I had never even seen a picture of either of them as a child. My mother, a private, reticent individual, almost never spoke about her childhood. And when she had, I had not listened well. My dad shared more: his fragmented war stories floated through my mind, but they were without context.

An anxiety attack began to envelop me. It made my limbs feel light as forest breezes, as if they were vanishing into the clouds. The fireplace, the rectangular yellow house that had been my childhood home, the woods where I'd played, and the elementary school I'd attended down the street all seemed to fan out below me as I left the earth. The "good old days"—the past that my parents and I had shared but experienced differently—seemed to be chasing me farther into the stratosphere. In the five long years, since my father's death, I had thought that the past wasn't important because I couldn't change it; in fact, with both my parents now dead and my being forced to live an entirely new existence as an adult orphan, events from long ago were suddenly becoming crucial.

Not knowing the past now made me feel like a stranger to myself, and I began to realize that I wouldn't know who *I* was until I knew who *they* had been. *They* comprised many people: four grandparents, eight great-grandparents, sixteen great-great-grandparents, and on and on. Yet only one of them had left me a connection. Changing the direction of my life to follow an ancestor off to war seemed as drastic a departure as I could imagine from my career as a wildlife biologist and part-time writer, yet I *knew* the experience of battle was one aspect of my history. And, sometimes it's best to go back to the beginning.

Chapter 2

The Legacy

[Saturday, April 8, 1865, Spanish Fort, Alabama]

I believe nothing anymore until I have seen it. I often see things which I am very unwilling to believe. Now why am I keeping a journal? I skarcly know why. not for myself I'm sure: for God knows if I am ever spared to return home I shall only be to glad to forget all of the scenes and hardships of The Three yrs is it for anyone else? is there any one who would spend time in looking over it? A Glance at it would show him or her it is not interesting enough to peruse.

—From the journal of Private James Darsie Heath,
20 years old, 72nd Illinois Infantry, Company A

ONE MILE from where I grew up the land drops hurriedly away into a feeder stream of Washington's Puget Sound. Chambers Creek at this point has little time to be a creek, turning quickly into an estuary and mixing with the saline waters of the Sound. For decades the flow widened beneath the belching smoke of a paper mill. Now the mill is closed. The creek moves beyond the empty factory, hesitating closer to train tracks that skirt the inland ocean.

Chambers Creek Road snakes down from the flats of my old neighborhood to a small bridge over the stream. My parents and I must have driven this path a thousand times or more during my childhood. It took us through the town of Steilacoom out to Fort Lewis, the local army post.

Yet long before my parents and I moved to this land on Puget Sound, the Steilacoom people lived in six camps along Shilacum Creek, later renamed Chambers Creek. There they hunted game and fished for salmon. They made their clothing, canoes, and longhouses from the drainage's abundant cedar trees. Eleven years before my great-great-grandfather questioned in writing why he was keeping a journal, the Steilacoom tribe participated in the Treaty of Medicine Creek. Expecting a huge influx of white settlers into the Steilacoom area, the Indian Office in Washington, D.C., recommended against a reservation for the area's native people. They would have to go elsewhere. The prime timberland, salmon streams, and access to Puget Sound would go to the white people.

The greater area surrounding Shilacum Creek became a military stronghold during the late nineteenth and early twentieth centuries. Fort Steilacoom, established in 1849 to monitor and control the activities of Native Americans, lay just over a mile southeast of the creek and farther south, Fort Nisqually had been constructed in 1833 near the present town of DuPont, Washington. In 1917, Camp Lewis, later renamed Fort Lewis, enveloped 68,000 acres of lowland prairies, which became littered with names from American military culture: Argonne Forest, Marne Forest, 91st Division Prairie. The complex would eventually grow to 87,000 acres and thousands of soldiers in the coming decades would serve at Fort Lewis.

In the late 1960s, developers cleared a section of forest above Shilacum Creek, leaving a few stringy fragments of forest, and built several dozen one-story, three-bedroom homes. Cul-de-sacs and curving avenues spider-webbed the land into order. They christened the neighborhood Bristonwood and named the streets after native flora: oxalis, deer's tongue, madrone. In June 1969, my parents and I moved into our yellow, rectangular home in Bristonwood. Our cul-de-sac contained a dirt center like the red middle of a bull's-eye. The developer had used his backhoe to deposit two large stones, shaped like miniature mountains the size of lawn chairs, in the sandy loam. Planted around the rocks were the cul-de-sac's eponymous flora, snowberry bushes.

For me, a four-year-old and only two and a half feet tall, the trees in this wild landscape reached to the sky. The forest the developers had spared harbored imaginary wolves, panthers, and the occasional shipwreck, along with its subsequent story of survival. My friends and I became denizens of these woods, building forts with scrap plywood, "killing" each other in pretend battles, and bringing each other "back to life" with water and reassuring words. In the backwoods, our stories were compact and always concluded with a happy ending before dinner.

For all my bravery on the battlefield, however, I worried a lot as a child. Our house creaked and made me jump with its unpredictable noises. Many nights I thought I heard a hammer pounding. I imagined ghosts with oversized heads that stuck out from walls.

"It's just the new house settling," my mother assured me. But it wasn't settling that regularly rattled the windowpanes and sent shudders through the walls. It was the nearby military rifle range. The acoustic reverberations of gunfire quickly became background noise for our family life.

The world was suddenly expanding too quickly for me. I began to have chaotic nightmares about a tangled ball of string that plagued me. I could not undo the snarl, nor could I make it leave. Trapped in a situation in which I had no control, I felt unable to breathe, unable to escape. Upon waking, I'd run into my parents' room, and crawl into bed with my mom. My father would still be working swing shift at the post office, a job he'd taken after he retired from the military. My mother would stroke my head and the feelings of confusion and helplessness would eventually pass.

The tangled ball of string image arrived only at night. The rest of my life was full of pleasant activities with my parents and new friends. In the evenings my family and I watched television. Sometimes I played barber while we tuned in to *The Wonderful World of Disney* or *The Brady Bunch.*

"Dad, can I work on your hair?" I would ask.

"Of course," came the reply, followed by, "Do you think it needs it?"

"Yes, definitely."

I'd get out a clean hand towel, one of his small black combs, and a bowl of water. Sitting behind him on the back of the couch, I'd go to work. At forty-nine, my dad seemed very old to me, especially as I made friends in the neighborhood whose parents were in their twenties. Dad's black hair had wisps of gray at the temples, but as I look at photos now from those first years in Bristonwood, I see that my father looks young for his age. He is slim though not tall. His thick, short hair, trained from twenty years of military cuts and rarely with a strand out of place, is brushed back tightly from the widow's peak above his forehead. His nose is prominent but not obtrusive, and his lips are thin. My father's skin is soft, flawless and golden hued. A few lines radiate from the corners of his eyes, but his face is not tight with the worry that I've seen accompany others as the years pass.

After watching television during the warm summer months, Dad and I often went out to the circle of snowberries. The stars seemed to float down from heaven and touch the top of my head while we talked, sitting on the anomalous river stones. He pointed out the Big Dipper.

"See, Bets, when the dipper is tipped up," he explained, "it means it's going to rain. If it's level, then the water will stay in the pan." My dad was pretty smart; it rained the next day.

Our house was the only one in the cul-de-sac with a fireplace. Its red brick stretched from floor to ceiling, and it had a wide, open mouth in the lower middle big enough to roast a pig. A white stone shelf served as a bench. My dad built a fire on nearly any evening with a chill, which was often around the moist Puget Sound. In the early years at Snowberry Circle, Dad cut wood from nearby land owned by the New Tacoma Cemetery. On Saturday mornings, he would load up our powder blue VW Bug with an axe, small chain saw, jugs of oil and gas, and gloves. Sometimes I tagged along. Mom would zip up my coat and hand me a plastic bag filled with cookies.

"To eat *after* you've cut a bunch of wood," she'd smile.

We would drive two blocks along Oxalis Street to the cemetery grounds. My dad waved at the neighbors. Many soldiers, retired and still serving, had moved their families to Bristonwood because the commute to Fort Lewis was short. Men in uniform waved back, looking sharp in pants with creases like knife ridges and shoes that hurt my eyes with their glare. Retired soldiers like my father still had the frames of hardened warriors, but some areas squeezed outside boundaries enforced by the military culture: a few extra pounds in the middle regions, hair curling around the ears.

"I'll bet I could get up early one Saturday here and blow a bugle, and fifty old soldiers would fall out of the trees," he laughed one morning.

I giggled. "That's silly, Dad. What would they be doing in the trees?"

"You never know with old soldiers." We laughed more.

In the woods Dad drove the Bug a short distance on an old dirt road. We stepped into a forest made ghostly by low clouds and strands of fog curling around the trees. Dad unloaded the saw.

"I'll pick up sticks for kindling," I announced.

"Just don't go far."

The chain saw's noise cut through the conversations of robins and crows. We never saw other people, but there was ample evidence of human presence, including old tires, abandoned appliances, and long, twisted and rusting chains. I soon became bored looking for sticks, though, and instead embarked upon an adventure in the wilderness. Keeping my dad in sight, I jumped over logs, searched for "clues," and escaped from "bears." My blond, nearly white, hair framed my face in a boyish, two-tiered cut. Bangs covered my forehead, and the rest hung straight to my shoulders, the locks flying into my mouth as I ran.

Dad loaded the Volkswagen with logs and we headed home. On the drive back he asked me if I was happy with my new cat, Tiger.

"She's a good cat," I said. "I can tell."

"How can you tell?"

"Well, she was washing herself when we bought her. So, she'll be clean."

"Good point. And I'll bet she'll like sitting by the fire too. Cats like to be warm."

"Yep." Dad and I agreed on most things.

My parents went to work making the yellow house on Snowberry

Circle their home. Mom planted a garden. Dad installed a thirty-foot flagpole. Mom painted the walls in the dining room orange, which contrasted sharply with the green linoleum and appliances. Dad painted the mailbox red, white, and blue. The Christmas before we moved to Bristonwood, Santa had brought my father tools for his woodworking hobby. Now Dad cut out stars from a thin sheet of plywood, painted each one banana yellow, and nailed them to the garage in the shape of the Big Dipper and North Star. He built bookshelves for his library. With a jigsaw, he carved out a gun rack for his shotgun and two rifles. And for many weeks he worked on the "Sore Thumb Tavern," an L-shaped bar that went into the dining room.

I don't remember the first time I saw the journals. They seemed always to have been there, as much a part of my young existence as my parents or our home. Throughout the years, the journals sat tucked away on the homemade bookcase in my father's den—the smaller, black journal atop the larger, brown one. My dad would bring them out to show guests.

"These are my great-grandfather's," he'd tell them proudly. "His name was James Darsie Heath, and he wrote them during the Civil War."

People regarded the two small books as if the answers to their deepest questions might lie within. They opened their hands and received them like communion. They turned the pages slowly, absorbing the past from the crisp paper and the delicate marks of the fine pen that had recorded thoughts from more than a century before. "Such treasures," people told my father. "You are so fortunate." He would smile and agree, then return the journals to their resting place.

I would like to think I learned about the diaries, and my great-great-grandfather, while sitting on the rocks in Snowberry Circle. Dad and I spent many nights outside that first summer looking at the stars. It was *somewhere* that I heard bits and pieces about James Darsie Heath that are now my memories. It could have been under the night sky, where the echoes of ancestors faded skyward with each passing minute.

"My brother Kenny and I called him 'Little Grandpa,'" Dad told me.

"Why? Was he little?"

"He was by the time he came to live with us. That's what happens to old people, you know, they shrink. But we called him 'Little Grandpa' because we also lived with our grandparents, and my grandfather was 'Big Grandpa.' Little Grandpa was old and sick when I knew him. He couldn't walk and stayed in his room most of the time."

"Did you ever talk to him?"

"Not really. I was about your age now. Little Grandpa seemed mean and grouchy to me, but Kenny and I were mean to him too."

"Really?" I couldn't imagine my father being mean. "How were you mean?"

"We had these big, heavy metal toy trucks. They clattered across the wood floors in our home like the thundering of a hundred horses. We'd roll them toward Little Grandpa's room, on the first floor next to the stairs. He hated the noise." Dad paused. "It's funny because I don't think he could hear much. Anyway, the trucks rumbled through the living room and smashed into his door. He'd get so mad!"

"What happened to him?"

"He died in his sleep when I was ten. He was really old by then."

"Like a hundred and fifty?"

Dad laughed. "Well, not that old! People don't live to be that old. But Little Grandpa was in his eighties, which was pretty old back then. Especially for a Civil War vet."

"Do you have a picture of him?" I asked.

"No. All I have are his journals from the war. And his powder horn."

"What's that?"

"It's a metal container to keep black powder for firing a pistol."

I knew about pistols and had been wanting a Lone Ranger double-holster pistol set. This, I was sure, would make me more successful in shooting my friends when we played gunslingers and war.

Dad and I sat for awhile in the dark. Only the porch lights diluted our view of the sky. Stars fell and, if we were lucky, a satellite blinked a greeting. This was the summer of the *Apollo 11* moon landing. I wonder now if that's why we spent so much time looking at the stars. I don't remember that event but I can imagine the impact it had on my parents—it was a moment in history that would send a man outside on a starry summer night with his daughter to impress upon her the possibilities of tomorrow. Little did my father know that from the beginning I would be more drawn to the past than the future.

"I like hearing about when you were little, back in the 'good old days,'" I told my dad, adding the phrase I'd heard him use many times. He laughed.

"You know what, kid? The 'good old days' weren't really all that good."

"Really?"

"Really. And you know what Grandma used to say?"

"What?"

"'We were put on the earth to suffer.'" Then Dad tilted his head back and laughed a laugh so deep that a piece of the sky seemed to open up to make room for the laugh, and I thought maybe the whole world would hear him. Dad's laugh made me want to laugh too, but I didn't get it. What was funny about suffering? I knew about suffering at night when the nightmares came. That was never funny.

"Was she kidding?" I asked.

"It was hard to tell with Grandma." But in the shadows created by the porch lights I could see my father smiling.

———

Chapter 3

The Prairie Peninsula

[Monday, August 11, 1862, Toulon, Illinois]

left home to join the 19th Ill. Inft. went to Kewanee.
took the cars for chicago Arived there at 6 p.m. went to
the Dearbourn House staid there all night there was 6 in
our co R.Holmes S.T Harding, M.Avery J.Morris-J.Galley
& myself. we looked for a recruiting officer this evening
but not finding one returned to our quarters

—From the journal of James Darsie Heath, 18 years old

James Darsie Heath was born on June 8, 1844, in Connellsville, Pennsylvania, to my great-great-great-grandparents Edward Heath and Margaret Snively, and came into the world trailing one sister and leading two. Connellsville, a town in the southwest corner of the state, was founded along the Youghiogheny River and became a center of activity for the nineteenth-century coal and coke industries. I don't know where Edward Heath came from, but it's possible that in Connellsville he was a miner. Working in a coal mine or a coke oven may explain his early death at age thirty-one, when his son was just five years old. For the next ten years, James lived with only his mother and sisters. Margaret Heath was a schoolteacher and, presumably, she alone supported her family for the next decade.

In 1859, however, Margaret packed up her children and moved "across the country" to western Illinois. The next February she married Samuel Galley, a widower with one daughter and four sons who had moved to Toulon, Illinois, in the mid-1850s where, in 1857, his first wife had died. I assume that Margaret and Samuel must have known each other in the East, since most mid–nineteenth century widows probably didn't move six hundred miles just because they wanted a change of scenery. It's likely that the Heath family packed their personal items in large trunks and traveled via steamship across the Great Lakes. Getting off in Chicago, they would have taken the Chicago, Burlington and Quincy Railroad, the most direct route to Kewanee, a town thirteen miles north of Toulon.

Toulon, the Stark County seat, fell within a land designation known as the "Military Tract," 5.4 million acres in between the Mississippi and Illinois rivers, south of what is now Interstate 80. Two-thirds of this landscape was deemed suitable for cultivation and set aside as "bountied land," to be paid to volunteer soldiers who had served during the War of 1812. In many cases, the soldiers themselves were not interested in the potential wealth of the West and would sell their "land warrants," certificates entitling the veteran to a certain number of acres, to other individuals. Samuel Galley, born in 1809, could not have participated in the War of 1812, but perhaps he had bought bountied land.

In the 1860 Stark County census, I found Samuel's profession recorded as "farmer." After Illinois became a state in 1818, the federal government had wanted farmers to populate the land. The preface to *Illinois in 1837; A Sketch*, a publication created to inform and encourage potential immigrants, stated:

> *This state is undoubtedly the richest in soil of any in the Union, and of course holds out the greatest prospect of advantage to the agriculturist. Here is ample room for farmers, there being still vast quantities of first-rate land extending in every direction, uncultivated, which may be had not only at a reasonable but a cheap rate, and one acre of which will in a majority of cases produce at least twice as much as the same amount of land in most of the eastern states.*

And what had the landscape looked like in 1859, when James and his sisters and mother arrived in Stark County? The land of the Military Tract fell within a plant community known as the "tallgrass prairie," an ecosystem characterized by grasses as tall as a horse's back, frequent drought conditions, and spectacular wildfires. The tallgrass prairie covered Iowa, the southern half of Minnesota, the northern half of Missouri, and the eastern edges of the Dakotas, Nebraska, Kansas, and Oklahoma. The portion stretching across northeastern Missouri, Illinois, and some of Indiana and Ohio was known as the "Prairie Peninsula." Among this prairie habitat were forests, comprised mostly of hickory and oak trees, which disappeared as the settlers traveled farther west, leaving the gentle ground to undulate only slightly with grasses such as big bluestem and Indian grass.

The Prairie Peninsula, because it had more annual precipitation than the grasslands to the west, was ideally suited for growing corn, a domesticated tallgrass. Over several centuries the prairie grasses had died and rotted, providing a ten-inch layer of rich, dark soil that eventually would instigate monumental migrations of people from the shallower soils of the East. Of course, the wild plant species would not turn loose of this ground without a fight. Because of factors such as wind, unreliable rainfall, and fire, the grassland community had evolved with a large amount of its biomass located underground in complex root systems. When the pioneers turned their wood and iron plows into the western soil, clods of humus stuck tenaciously to the metal. In the 1830s, a young man named John Deere, making frequent repairs on the plows people had brought with them from the East, constructed a "cast-steel plow," the cutting part of which came from the steel of a broken saw blade. The sticky soil fell away from this metal like sand slipping through fingers.

With John Deere's new plow and the completion of the railroad from Chicago to the Mississippi River in 1854, James Darsie Heath and his family arrived in 1859 to an Illinois metamorphosing from a wild, unmapped landscape into tame, straight-line plots and grids. Yet, not until the arrival of the railroad did settlers opt to live in the prairie uplands. By then locomotive transport could supply lumber that before had been obtainable only along riverbanks where such species as cottonwood, American elm, and green ash grew. Five years would not have been enough time to completely eradicate the tallgrass prairies where cattle could only be seen from horseback and mothers worried about children vanishing. But the transformation had begun.

———

Summer 1969, Tacoma, Washington

"We lived in this two-story farmhouse," Dad told me one day as he raked the dirt in our yard. Short stems of grass had begun to fuzz the brown earth of Snowberry Circle into a light green. I'd been instructed to stay off the exposed soil and to keep Tiger away as well. She thought this a poor plan and scampered out of my hands, leaving small kitten tracks that pushed the young blades out of sight. Dad had been digging holes beside the curved cement path to our front door. Four round arborvitae shrubs, looking like globes of the earth without the oceans, waited nearby with plastic bags around their roots.

"What color was it?" I asked.

"White. It had a big, covered front porch that stuck out like a nose on a person's face. Then above the nose was a triangular forehead where the roof peaked into a sharp point. It had to be really steep up there so all the snow would slide off." Dad stopped digging to take a break. Sweat stained his white T-shirt under the arms and on his chest. He lit a cigarette and sat on the front step, taking drinks from his can of Olympia beer. I sat beside him. Tendrils of smoke curled in the air between us. Dad sucked on the Lucky Strike and I could hear the fire eating at the paper.

"It snowed a lot in Illinois, huh?"

"You bet your sweet bippy it did!" Dad said, using a line from the TV comedy *Laugh-In*, because I always laughed when he said "bippy." "Hey, it snowed so much that Kenny and I hated going to the outhouse at night, so we'd pee out the window." Dad laughed. "Big Grandpa would be really mad in the morning. He hated yellow snow."

"Do you want to move back to Illinois?" I asked.

"Hell no! The winters will kill you."

"I like snow. I wish we got more snow here."

"You wouldn't if it stayed for six months and you never saw the ground."

I thought about this. "Six months" didn't mean anything to me. Six months ago we had lived in an apartment in another part of Tacoma. But who cared about where I used to live? I lived on Snowberry Circle now. Six months from now it would be Christmas. That might as well be an eternity.

"Did you have a lawn at your house, Dad?" I asked, throwing a fir cone I'd collected from the woods for Tiger to chase. She ran after it, stuck out a paw to bat it around, danced sideways around her "prey," and finally darted off to hunt a bug.

"We had a lot of grass that Big Grandpa cut with his tractor. Tall maple trees grew in the yard and made the house cool in the summer. Then all around were cornfields. See, Big Grandpa was a farmer. He harvested the corn."

Growing up on a farm sounded cool to me. I wanted a horse and a lot of cats and land that stretched out into more land, like the endless days of the six months until Christmas.

"I'd like to live on a farm," I told my father.

"A farm is a lot of work, Bets." He stubbed out his cigarette and finished his beer. "And we couldn't go on vacations like we do now. We'd have to stay at home all the time and take care of the crops and animals."

Staying at home all the time didn't sound so good to me. "Maybe I could just get a rabbit and a dog," I said. "Tiger should have some company."

Dad smiled. "I suppose."

The days of that first summer in Bristonwood crept into autumn. A solitary oak tree behind our house waved to us with one bare branch at its midriff. The round top without its leafy "hair" looked like a picture I'd seen of a brain, with blood vessels snaking every direction. It tilted back and forth on stormy days. My worries extended to this tree that had stood for decades.

"What if it falls on us?" I asked my mom.

"I don't think you should worry about something that hasn't happened," she replied, an answer that brought me little comfort. Because nothing bad had actually happened in my as-yet short life, all I had to worry about was imagined catastrophe. It was clear Mom didn't understand what it meant to worry.

Four miles east of Toulon lay Spoon River, a sinewy waterway flowing southwest for another seventy-five miles or so before joining with the Illinois River. Northeast of the town, and feeding Spoon River, were Jack Creek and Jug Run Creek. An 1873 plat map of the landscape shows "S. Galley" written next to a forty-acre parcel of land just south of Jug Run Creek. Here, amid the slow-moving water and rolling landscape, James Darsie Heath spent the last years of his youth.

Jacob Galley, Samuel's third son, was three years older than my great-great-grandfather. For a boy with only sisters, to suddenly have four brothers must have been like piling on extra blankets on a cold night. I have imagined days of them plowing fields, going on fishing and hunting forays, and watching clusters of stars as big as explosions in the clear, prairie nights. I have imagined bonds being forged among the young men, who would first become siblings, then soldiers.

In 1860, Margaret and Samuel had nine children between them, ages eleven to twenty-four. The house at Jug Run Creek must have been large. A year after beginning my research on James, I received a photograph from a Galley descendent. In it, a two-story, clapboard farmhouse sits on gently sloping ground, enshrouded in mist. Five windows stretch across the second floor, bookended by two chimneys extending from either side of a sloping roof. A portico hangs over two of the four downstairs windows. A woman, possibly Margaret Heath Galley, stands next to a picket fence. Outbuildings, more fence, and wraithlike trees surround the family's home.

In June of 1861, Samuel's two oldest boys, Springer and Philip, joined the 19th Illinois Infantry. Like most recruits during the first months of the Civil War, they were probably excited to help put down the insurrection before it ended. Few thought the conflict would last very long. Springer's and Philip's enlistments would have been for three months. More than a year later, however, they would still be soldiers—and Jacob and James would leave home to join the war effort as well. The illusion of a quick fix would have passed.

As I continued examining the plat map, I found the property of Hurlburt and Julia Harding across Jack Creek, a mile and a half northeast of the Galley land. They owned forty-one acres of land and had four children. In 1862, Hurlburt and Julia's oldest boy, Scepter T., was twenty-one. The map also shows the Holmes and Avery properties near the Harding and Galley plots. These must have belonged to the families of the boys who left with James for Chicago in August 1862. Because the young men of a community often joined the same company, whole towns suffered when that company experienced heavy casualties during battle. In this case, of the six who left that August, two deserted, one died, one was sent to the notorious Confederate prison in Andersonville, Georgia, and two fought until the war's end.

Chapter 4

918 South Oakwood

*"One of the main reasons that it is so easy to march
men off to war," says Ernest Becker, is that "each of them
feels sorry for the man next to him who will die."*

—Annie Dillard, American writer (1945-)

June 1999, Geneseo, Illinois

THE HOUSE WAS STILL WHITE. The porch stuck out like a nose. Towering maple trees hid much of the building, and trim grass carpeted the ground. It had not been hard to find my father's childhood home. Number 918 was one of the first houses along Oakwood Avenue, a north-south arterial that extended like an arrow from Interstate 80 into the heart of Geneseo, Illinois. My arrival this summer day corresponded with a city project to widen Oakwood from two lanes to four. Mounds of dirt discouraged but did not prevent me from driving over the top of them and onto the driveway that bordered the house's south side. I didn't know who lived here now or what kind of reception I could expect.

It had taken me four days to drive from spring weather in the Pacific Northwest to the already sweltering summer of the country's belly. My car was packed full: camping equipment, a backpack full of clothes, a cooler, one box of food, another box of notebooks, a stapler and three-hole punch, and several books on the Civil War occupied the backseat. Beside me up front were photocopies of James Darsie Heath's journals and my transcriptions of them, and they kept me company as I drove east through the Cascades, the Rocky Mountains, and the Great Plains on my way to western Illinois.

The journals had not taken long to transcribe, which surprised me. One of the reasons I had not endeavored to read them shortly after my father died was because I had assumed the writing would be too illegible. I had opened them and perused their pages then, but I couldn't focus enough to see the actual words. This time, however, the journals seemed like newly blossomed flowers, and the words emanated easily from the pages like insects that have gathered nectar.

The books' corners were curled, and the threads holding one together had begun to ravel. The first journal, a three-by-seven-inch black book, common during the 1860s, described James Darsie Heath's first year of military service, from August 1862 through July 1863. The second volume, from October 1864 to April 1865, was larger (five by eight inches), light brown, and emblazoned with the letters "J.D.H." on the cover. The first few pages included lists of letters, written and received: *Apr 2 received a letter from Mollie; Apr 10 Wrote to My Mother*. At the top of page five, James had written only four lines, enclosed in quotation marks:

> *Trust no Future how'er pleasant,*
> *Let the dead Past, bury it's dead,*
> *Act, act, in the Living present*
> *Heart within and God o'erhead.*

H. W. L.-

This stanza, part of a Longfellow poem entitled "A Psalm of Life," contained ideas that seemed as far away as the stars. For me, the past was not dead and the dead not buried, at least, figuratively speaking. In the journal's first entry—Monday, August 11, 1862—my great-great-grandfather described leaving western Illinois for Chicago. Therefore, my first stop would be the landscape where my father grew up, where James Darsie Heath had died, and where both had left for war.

The Illinois heat gathered force even as the clock still indicated morning. Dad had hated the winters here; perhaps the summers drove him away as well. As I got out of my car I saw a young teenage boy standing on the screened-in back porch saying goodbye to a friend. Big Grandpa's cornfields had been supplanted by houses on three sides. Traffic streamed along Oakwood on its way into Geneseo. The noise of suburbia—lawn mowers whining, car doors slamming, dogs barking—transcended the heat.

"Hi!" the boy said to me. He was dark-haired with soft-looking skin and a frame just on the verge of sprouting into manhood. As he galloped down the steps, I asked if his parents were at home.

"No, it's just me."

"Well, this might sound odd," I began, tentatively, "but my family used to live in your house many years ago. I, uh...wondered ..."

"How many years?" he interrupted, wrinkling his forehead.

"About sixty."

"Wow!" the boy shouted. "There are old things in the basement! Maybe they belong to your family! We don't go down there too much because it's dark and creepy, but I can show you if you'd like."

Visions of more journals and pictures of my faceless relatives made my heart beat faster with excitement, yet I wasn't sure about traipsing around someone's home with neither parent present.

"Would your mom mind you letting a stranger into your home?" I asked.

"Nah, we cleaned it up. Come on, it's this way." He started for the back of the house and said his name was Calen. I followed him and decided not worry about trespassing since cleanliness in the Midwest seemed more important than the possible danger of allowing a stranger in one's home.

The "old things" in the basement were in a small room with a disappointingly empty closet and an abundance of cobwebs. Broken pieces of a wooden desk lay scattered on the floor, but it was too dark to discern much else. Calen's trepidation permeated the musty air as he hung back in the dim light of the basement's main area.

"Do you have a flashlight?" I asked.

"Sure, I'll go get it." Calen ran upstairs and returned in seconds with the light. I looked at the desk. Paper had been chewed into fragments by the resident mice, and none of the scraps contained writing. I shined the light around the walls. My father had never told me any basement stories. Perhaps, as a boy, the dark interior here had scared him as much as it did Calen. *If Dad were here, he could tell me,* I thought.

"I'm pretty sure this house is haunted," Calen said as we walked back to my car.

"Really?"

"Yeah. I sleep upstairs and I can hear footsteps in the attic at night, and also, hangers in the closets move around for no reason. I've even seen a man with dark hair and a business suit on, and he's got bleeding cuts all over him."

Having experienced my own childhood nightmares and worries over resident ghosts, I decided *not* to share with Calen the fact that James Darsie had died in his house.

That afternoon I made a second trip to 918 Oakwood to talk with Calen's mom. Cathie Buechler—who appeared to be in her early forties, with straight auburn hair and clear skin like her son's—was hanging a plant in the screened-in porch when I drove up.

"Come in, come in!" she said. "Calen told me about you. The house is a mess, but you're welcome to see it."

My images from the stories my dad had told me about his childhood didn't match what unfolded now before my eyes. Conjuring the 1920s, I had imagined oil-burning lamps and squares of sunlight shining through small windows onto the floors. Winter scenes filled my mind because my father had frequently described those opaque months, and in those mental landscapes, cold air had swirled from room to room and settled at night like a blanket of ice. Dad told me he had shared a bed with his brother Kenny when they were young. I had imagined homemade quilts and nightstands scattered with books and half-empty glasses of milk. I pictured frosty breath as two boys dressed hurriedly for school in the morning, and saw the window where they peed out to the snow below. Over the years, pieces of my father's story had transformed into long narratives of places and faces and events created in my imagination, which probably only superficially resembled reality.

His stories had painted for me a dark home with dark walls. But those tenebrous walls had been replaced—if they'd ever existed at all—with painted blue rooms, blue wall hangings, and blue and white curtains. Light poured in from every direction. The cool air inside felt welcome on my already overheated skin. Cathie led me through the kitchen and into the living room at the front of the house. A stairway rose to the second story. The room on the other side of the stairs must have been Little Grandpa's. My father's voice, drawn from my own memory, narrated the tour.

We had these big, heavy metal toy trucks. They clattered across the wood floors in our home like the thundering of a hundred horses. We'd roll them toward Little Grandpa's room, on the first floor next to the stairs. The trucks rumbled through the living room and smashed into his door. He'd get so mad.

"Did you used to have wood floors?" I asked Cathie as my feet sunk into thick blue carpet.

"Yes. We carpeted and tiled all the hardwood floors a year ago. I was so sick of sweeping." She sighed. "Now I'm just as sick of vacuuming."

French doors opened into the room at the foot of the stairs, now Cathie's bedroom. A cat slept curled up on her bed. Clothes lay scattered. A plethora of items—earrings, brushes, books, papers, bracelets—cluttered the dresser top. What I had envisioned, however, was an austere room. A bed, a bureau, maybe a nightstand, and an old man, becoming smaller as his life ended. I wondered if James Darsie's uniform had hung in a closet here. Had he kept it all the years after the war? And what of the journals? Had they sat on my imagined nightstand? Had he looked at them again while he lived here? Had anyone?

When I began transcribing the journals, they had seemed too fragile for repeated handling, so I photocopied each page, magnifying the size to help me read them. On page 69 of the second volume I had found an old, very brittle piece of adhesive tape that was losing its seal on the margin. I peered closer at the writing next to it: *taken from my mustache at the age of 54 yrs.* One black whisker—

two inches long, with the root attached—had somehow survived 101 years of travel, storage, and handling.

The first volume contained short, succinct entries. James Darsie Heath left western Illinois to join the Union army with Jake Galley, Scepter T. Harding, and three other friends. They signed up with the 72nd Illinois Infantry, and on the "Muster and Descriptive Roll of Company A" that I sent away for during the transcription process, young James Heath was characterized as a five-feet-six-inch farm boy with hazel eyes and dark hair and skin. The 72nd was sponsored by the Chicago Board of Trade, which had been founded in 1848 by city merchants and was designed to address the chaotic marketing situation that occurred every year when crops were brought to the shores of Lake Michigan to be sold. Farmers and their grain came by wagon, rail, and barge to Chicago. Yet without a central trading facility, roads and canals quickly became congested with each person trying to get the best price for his goods. Many farmers were forced to dump the fruits of their hard work into Lake Michigan when buyers could not be found during the overabundant harvest season. James Darsie wrote of meeting Company A's Lieutenant Joseph Stockton, a businessman who had joined the Board in 1861, and of going to dinner at a saloon. The August 15, 1862, entry read:

Drew our uniform in full today. we have nothing to do except attend roll call. the day is usually warm and pleasant we have ice all we want and good cool lake water we get leave to go to the lak [Lake Michigan] to bathe

As I transcribed, I learned that words with "ss" were written in script that resembled "fs"; for example, "passed" was written as "pafsed," or "dress parade" as "drefs parade." Words truncated at the end of a line were not indicated with a dash, so I found in one case "wa" on one line and "nt" on the next. Random words, based on what James Darsie seemed to deem important, were capitalized in the middle of sentences. For example, the August 16 entry read:

> *we are invited to town to take Dinner at the Sherman*
> *House We donned our best went and paraded through*
> *the streets until 1 PM when we were taken to the Board*
> *of Trade Rooms had a glafs of Lemonade and a few*
> *crackers—*

For me, the vocabulary didn't always make sense even if I understood the individual words. What was "drefs parade" anyway? And "battalion drill"? I circled "pickits," "ague," "vidette," "fatigue duty," and "skirmishers"—all legible but from a time that was not mine.

At one point during that first day of transcribing, I stopped on page 3 where Joseph Stockton brings the new recruits their $60 bounty checks. I was savoring every detail but I also wanted to find out how the journal ended. I turned to the last page where the young soldier had written:

> *This is an abridged account of my soldiering. Let no one*
> *see It I present this to you my mother*
> *J. Darsie H*
> *Co A 72nd Regt Ill Inft*

> *P.S. I commence another one on the first of this month of*
> *[August 1863] I can if I ever get the chance delet many*
> *things from memory*

After reading that entry, I began to think of my great-great-grandfather as "Darsie." "James" had not fit him for some reason, perhaps because I knew my father by that name. Around the same time I was transcribing the journals, I received James Darsie Heath's 1871 certificate of marriage to my great-great-grandmother. It referred to the groom as Mr. J. Darsie Heath. The 1862 teenager, a recently sworn-in private in a new wool uniform on the shores of Lake Michigan, became to me "Darsie Heath."

———

Cathie and I stood in her living room and I thought of another story my father had told me, of a Christmas during the Great Depression.

"We didn't have much," he had said. "Big Grandpa farmed and my mother taught school, but there wasn't any money in those days. One Christmas I came downstairs and found two presents waiting for me: a book and an orange."

"Didn't your dad work?" I had then asked him, thinking his father must have made money to buy presents. Dad sneered.

"Who knows? He left my mother when Kenny and I were very young. I never saw him again and only heard from him once after I left home—when he called me needing money."

I wondered now if that memorable Christmas happened during the time Darsie lived here. He had first moved to Geneseo in 1926, four years before his death at the age of 85. In my father's genealogy files, I had found an affidavit from the State of Illinois, County of Henry, dated December 9, 1926, which read:

> [Dr. Arthur Parsons] *states that he found James D.*
> *Heath to be quite infirm with age, quite deaf and slightly*
> *demented; that, since July 15, 1926, said James D. Heath has*
> *been confined to his bed except when his daughter helped*
> *him to a chair near the bed and that both of his lower limbs*
> *are paralyzed; that said James D. Heath is totally and*
> *permanently helpless to care for himself without the daily*
> *personal attendance of another person and has been so*
> *since July 15, 1926; that said James D. Heath is now in the*
> *care of his daughter, residing at No. 918 South Oakwood*
> *Avenue, in Geneseo, Illinois, and this affiant believes*
> *that said James D. Heath is entitled to the full amount of*
> *pension due a totally helpless soldier of the Civil War.*

We walked around Cathie's one and a half acres, comprising mostly lawn and an august willow tree that seemed to protect the property with copious amounts of shade. I tried to imagine the place in the 1920s, with cornfields laid out as far as the eye could see and few neighbors. Cathie pointed to a newly painted red barn that stood off to one side.

"That barn has been here forever. A few years ago some people wanted to buy the lot that it is on, but I just couldn't sell it. I don't know why. Since my husband and I separated, this place is really too much for me, but I just couldn't do it. I love the house and this little spot of land. I'll probably have to give it up sometime, though I don't look forward to that."

Cathie walked me to the driveway. I told her about Calen's claims of ghosts and that Darsie Heath had died here. She laughed.

"The house is definitely not haunted. If your great-great-grandfather's ghost is around, it is a very peaceful one, because I've had nothing but warm feelings ever since we've lived here. In fact, you can look at the outside and tell it's old and a bit run-down looking, but whenever people come inside, they really like the atmosphere."

On Friday, January 17, 1930, Darsie Heath was buried in Annawan Cemetery. He had lived most of his life in Annawan, Illinois, a rural community fourteen miles east of Geneseo. The *Geneseo Republic* wrote that Darsie was the "last Annawan veteran of the Civil [W]ar and a retired painter and decorator. He served as police magistrate for about twenty-two years, and took the township census in 1880. He also was a notary public." Survivors included "a number of grandchildren and great-grandchildren."

My father, Darsie's oldest great-grandson, started his first job three years later at the age of thirteen.

"I worked for Mrs. Waterman next door," Dad had told me one Saturday morning during our second summer at Snowberry Circle. We were in the backyard, Dad digging up grass he'd planted the year before and me playing with Gray-Gray, my new rabbit. Gray-Gray had fur as silky as cream, a twitching nose that made me laugh, and legs as long as my forearm. She would nibble on the new lawn, look around quickly, then hop away. Tiger and Big-Boy, my terrier pup and also a recent addition, didn't quite know what to make of this jumpy animal with eyes on the sides of its head. After Gray kicked them both for getting too close, Big-Boy trotted after Tiger in a game of chase. I petted the soft spot above Gray's nose and watched Dad shovel plate-sized chunks of grass and turn them over. He was clearing a circle for an aboveground pool for me.

"What did you do?" I asked.

"Yard work. That was the only job a kid could find back then. She paid me ten cents a day."

"Who did?" asked my mother. She walked up with a beer for my dad and a glass of lemonade for me.

"Mrs. Waterman. I was just telling Bets about my first job."

"I remember her," Mom said to me. "We visited her on a trip back to Illinois. She served us coffee and cookies, and the cookies were perfect circles. Round like a half-dollar and as light as air. They melted in your mouth."

At the mention of light, round cookies, my mouth started to water. Dad popped the cap off the bottle of Lucky, put the cap in his pocket, took a big drink, then talked more about the good old days.

"I worked for Mrs. Waterman for six years. After I graduated from high school, she paid for my college tuition at Iowa State."

"Why'd she do that?"

"We didn't have any money and she had a lot, and I guess she thought I had potential. Never finished though. Studied engineering for two years before the war broke out. Next thing I knew, I was a soldier."

"What did you do as a soldier?"

"I was a paratrooper. I wanted to be a pilot but they wouldn't let me 'cause I was color-blind. They said I could be an engineer on the plane, but I said, 'To hell with that. I'll jump *out* of planes instead.' I did that fifty-one times."

"That sounds scary."

"It was. But you have a parachute and as long as it opens, you're usually okay."

As a five-year-old, this sounded interesting, but not enough to captivate my attention for long. I wandered off and played with my animals. My father's soldier stories had nothing to do with me, I thought. They had nothing to do with the life we lived now.

———

The village of Annawan sprouted up in the 1840s on land once known as the Great Willow Swamp, a vast marsh area in western Illinois. This wetland blanketed the low areas between the Mississippi,

Rock, and Green rivers—a paradise for wildlife, a bane for white men. Early settlers believed that miasma, the noxious vapor escaping from stagnant water, caused a host of diseases and ill health, though in reality, mosquitoes likely caused most of their problems, including malaria. Settlers avoided areas that remained wet year-round until 1865, when drain tiles were installed to draw water away. Until then, however, the immigrants descended on the upland sites and used John Deere's cast-steel plow to tame the prairie.

Though Darsie spent the last three years of his youth, from 1859 to 1862, in Toulon, Illinois, twenty-five miles south of Annawan, it would be to the north that he settled after the war. Named after a Winnebago chief, Annawan today sits at the intersection of a "T" of highways: Interstate 80 streaming west-east and State Highway 78 running north-south. With a modest population of eight hundred, this rural town has no need for stoplights. At the public library, from the 1895 List of Taxable Lots and Blocks, I learned that a home belonging to "JD Heath" had existed on Lot 3 of Block 1. I walked the five blocks from the library to this spot, hoping to find a welcome similar to my experience in Geneseo. Instead, I found no house at all. "Edna Jo's Hair Care" greeted me, a cracker box of a building, dwarfed by Victorian homes on either side. The house I sought was the only one absent. (Later I would learn that it had burned down some years after Darsie's death, while his daughter Jenny was living there.) Disappointed, I moved on to my last stop in western Illinois.

One-quarter mile south of Annawan sits the town's cemetery. Once perhaps secluded by the hickory and oak forests of the Prairie Peninsula, this five-acre ground now stands out like a sentinel, completely surrounded by the legacy of John Deere's revolutionary invention. The precise, angled boundaries of the croplands extend to where the cemetery begins its slight incline toward the wide-open sky. Grand American elms lined the cemetery on the north and south sides, while eastern red cedar and Norway spruce trees provided shade in the interior. Chipping sparrows, crows, and robins flew from tree to ground to tree again, and a hairy woodpecker worked one of the elm trees. Except for the avian life, I was alone.

The dainty, pointed tracks of a deer, like the leavings of a ghost, stood out in the soft earth of the tilled field next to my car.

It didn't take long to find Darsie's grave. The inscription on the flat stone slab simply read:

FATHER
JAMES D. HEATH
1844-1930

Next to the headstone was a five-point metal star stuck in the ground, which read: *GAR 1861–1865*. The Grand Army of the Republic, an organization begun in 1866 in Decatur, Illinois, and devoted to the preservation of friendships among soldiers who had fought for the North, became a haven for men returning to a society that had little understanding of their combat experiences. Local chapters quickly formed across the country. The GAR organized national reunions, pensions for veterans, and Memorial Day, a holiday to honor fallen comrades. Darsie participated in Annawan's GAR post as adjutant commander and was its final surviving member. The star, now crimson with rust, had stood watch over this site for nearly seventy years.

The afternoon slipped into evening as I sat by Darsie's grave. The chipping sparrows, with their cinnamon caps, trilled and flitted about the trees and shrubs, while crows cawed various messages of concern. A sinking sun behind me generated elongated shadows.

I thought about a book I'd read several years before called *Touching the Void* by British mountaineer Joe Simpson. After a climbing accident in the Peruvian Andes where he breaks a leg, Simpson then falls into a crevasse, landing upon a small ice shelf where he spends a long night fighting panic and despair. In the morning, sunlight pours through the opening at the top, but Simpson, with his broken leg, cannot climb up. He writes in his memoir that he knew he also could not spend another night upon the ledge waiting for death. So he chose the only other alternative, illogical as it was: go *down* into the crevasse. It was dark and deep, and once he began he wouldn't be able to change direction. Ironically, what Simpson found was another shelf and, in the angular way of crevasses, a shorter, less steep path to the surface. He had found a way out by going in deeper.

As I learned more about Darsie and began to feel closer to him, I wondered how the young soldier and, later, the old man fit into my world. Scattered images of my father, memories I had worked hard to forget, filled the spaces between Darsie's life and mine. At the outset of my journey, I was aware on some level that traveling to know a man I'd never met was really about remembering someone else, but just how that was to happen, I couldn't imagine.

Fifty years after my father left Geneseo to join the army, he died of colon cancer. The terminal diagnosis had arrived on New Year's Eve, 1990, and within two and a half months he was dead. One morning in February 1991, after I'd returned to Snowberry Circle from my home in Oregon to spend time with him, the two of us were alone in the kitchen. My father, wearing a brown bathrobe, with his hands clasped behind his back, stood in front of the window, staring out at argentine skies, frosted vegetation, and the skinny oak tree that had watched over us for so many years.

He had spoken little since the diagnosis. Finally, without turning around, he shared a part of himself that reached back decades, maybe even generations.

"It's a good thing I was a soldier."

"Why's that?"

"Because a soldier is always ready to die."

Chapter 5

The Junior Jumper

It doesn't matter who my father was; it matters who I remember he was.

—Anne Sexton, American poet (1928-1974)

Early to mid-1970s, Tacoma, Washington

THE MAY SATURDAY had arrived with hope. A gray veil had lifted from the Puget Sound lowlands and the sun stretched long rays down to our damp world. No season is more gratefully welcomed than spring in this part of the country. Seemingly endless rain curbs enthusiasm over the long winter months and causes many residents to enter a kind of torpor until a brighter time of year arrives, which can usually be expected by April or May. People raised here, or transplants who appreciate cause and effect, know the cycle can be no other way. The lush, green landscape would not exist without the rain; the spring light would not be cherished without the darkness.

My parents and I drove to Fort Lewis early this weekend morning in 1972 to attend Armed Forces Day, an annual celebration begun after World War II to commemorate all branches of the military. For me, it was like attending the state fair, minus the farm animals and agricultural displays. Helicopters, tanks, and planes, scattered across Gray Army Airfield, had been opened up for us to walk through. Soldiers gave tours and answered questions. Demonstrations at mock field hospitals coincided with combat assault re-enactments. Music from a military band made the gathering seem like a country dance, while the smell of grilling onions and frying burgers reminded me of Fourth of July parties.

After walking around "to get our bearings," as my father put it, we arrived at the Junior Jump Tower. This event allowed kids under twelve to get an idea of what being a paratrooper was like. The setup consisted of a wooden box, approximately one hundred feet in the air, accessed by stairs that zigzagged skyward like a lightning bolt. Out of the top, a ninety-foot cable extended to the ground. From below, the descent seemed gentle. We watched kids jumping from the tower, attached to the cable via a harness. With arms stretched above them, hands grasping the webbing material that linked their bodies to the cable, and legs splayed as if they were riding a horse, the jumpers swayed like giant bugs. They descended to the ground with rosy cheeks and toothy smiles. This looked better than all the rides I had seen at the state fair.

First I had to be fitted with a parachute harness. Big metal buckles snapped together across my chest to secure the vest, and two straps—each as wide as my dad's ties—snaked through my legs, connecting back to the vest around my torso. The weight settled heavily on my small body. I looked up at the tower that now seemed to disappear into heaven. Suddenly, my knees started shaking and my stomach began churning. I must have looked scared. Dad patted me on the shoulder.

"You can do it, Bets." I started climbing the stairs.

As I went higher, I saw kids popping out of the tower like kernels of corn in a hot skillet. Reaching the top, I looked down at my parents. Mom waved. They seemed only inches tall, like my plastic cowboy figures at home.

"Hold on to the straps above you," the attendant instructed, hooking me up, "and pull your legs up as you get closer to the ground." I nodded. Jumping out of a tower, like my paratrooper dad, was the scariest thing I had ever done. At the signal, I took one big leap.

Nothing in my short life could compare to stepping off into air. Slicing through the seeming emptiness pushed my blond hair against my scalp. Gravity pulled at me but I didn't feel out of control. I didn't *know* for sure that the equipment would work, but I trusted it and somehow settled into a faith that the harness and cable would hold me. Gliding to the ground, breathless but jubilant, I asked my mom for another quarter, the cost of jumping, and did it again.

After "hitting the silk," as the military referred to jumping, a second time, the man on the ground removed my harness. Smiling, he handed me a junior jumper certificate, signed by Fort Lewis's commanding officer, and plastic paratrooper wings, just like my dad's silver ones.

We spent the rest of the afternoon watching the air show and looking at the planes and tanks. I walked with my parents up a metal ramp into a plane that seemed bigger than our home. "It's a C-5," my father said. "They can transport a tank in here." At first, I didn't believe him, but then I heard a man in uniform saying the same thing. The man also said the tank could drive in from the back of the plane and out the front. My mom had been looking around and hadn't heard this. She said it was a big plane. "It's a C-5," I explained.

Away from the military vehicles, long, deep rows of soldiers stood at attention, their feet together, hands at their sides. For hours, while we walked around and I jumped from the tower, they stood. Once I watched them closely for any out-of-place movement, but soon became bored. They looked like machines.

My father's silver paratrooper wings sat on a shelf in his den. The homemade bookcase, orange and green, my parents' favorite colors it seemed, occupied one wall of the small room that faced our front yard. Dad's library included books such as *The Two Ocean War* by Samuel Morison, *The Campaigns of Napoleon* by David Chandler, and *Grant Takes Command* by Bruce Catton. Two golden, hexagonal medals—pinned against blue-black velvet backgrounds and protected in clear plastic cases—were displayed in one corner. An eight-inch silver knife with a black handle, mounted on a brass plate, sat in another. Darsie's Civil War journals moved around this bookcase. Sometimes they lounged atop the books on war and history. Sometimes they fell behind and vanished for a time. Then, when my father wanted to show them to someone, they'd appear again.

Above the bookcase, four 5 x 7 photos hung in a diamond formation:

two of my father and one each of my half brothers, John and Jim, all in their military uniforms. The boys, my father's sons from his first marriage, were twelve and sixteen years older than me. They never lived with us and I never got to know them well. John had a military career like our father; Jimmy left the service after two years.

In the top photo, Dad wore a beige dress shirt with a blue cord draped around his left shoulder and another two cords around his right, a green one and a red one. Eleven colored bars sat above his left breast pocket, as well as a silver rifle set against a rectangular blue background of blue. Pinned on the pocket were Dad's paratrooper wings, a silver parachute with the wings of two eagles on either side. Above his name tag on his right side was a rectangular box of darker blue surrounded by a gold leaf design. The bottom picture, apparently staged, showed my father about to leap out the door of an airplane, carrying his paratrooper equipment.

My own plastic jump wings have vanished into the ether of time. I don't know what happened to them or to the certificate I earned. Perhaps they rested for a time next to the war veteran's silver wings.

"You did great jumping out of the tower," my father told me that night as he built a fire. Just because the sun had appeared again didn't mean the temperature had changed much. Crackles and pops filled the air as the yellow-orange flames wrapped around the fir logs from the cemetery land. Tiger jumped onto the bench and watched the fire, as still as a statue.

"Thanks. It was fun. I liked falling."

My father nodded as he poured two glasses of wine. My mother took one and returned to the kitchen table to read the paper. Dad sat in a dark green cushioned chair across from the fire. Tiger sensed his movement and left the fire for an accommodating lap, curling up on Dad's gray pants. He sipped the wine.

"It never felt like falling when I jumped. It was more like the earth was coming up to me."

"Were you scared?"

"Sure, sometimes. One time I jumped and my chute came out but didn't expand. See, the parachute on your back is attached to the plane and when you fall a certain distance, then it automatically opens. There I was, falling fast, the earth coming up, and no parachute."

"What did you do?"

"I had to pull the whole thing back in, then release the reserve chute, which is bundled in a pack on your chest, before hitting the ground."

"That sounds scary."

"Of course, it was scary! Life is scary. But being afraid doesn't mean you don't do what you must."

This idea meant little to me. It would only become relevant years later after I began delving into my father's military career and understood better what "doing what you must" meant. As a child, however, I absorbed his actions more than his words—primarily, the moments when the brave man I worshipped vanished, and the drunk, an unpredictable man and someone who embarrassed me, appeared.

One afternoon in the mid-1970s, I decided to start reading my father's books and pulled *A Stillness at Appomattox* by Bruce Catton off the shelf. The title appealed to me. I liked its quiescence and the long word that sounded like my mouth was driving over speed bumps when I spoke it. The blue and white flyleaf with a cannon silhouetted on it indicated that the book had to do with war. My father had been in two wars. I opened it up and sat on the den's green and white hide-a-bed couch.

The first chapter, "Glory Is Out of Date," begins at a ball, held in an army camp along the Rapidan River in Virginia. Catton describes the ballroom, held not in a tent but in a building hastily constructed from nearby pine trees by the enlisted men. There were Chinese lanterns and regimental flags, and women arrived in army ambulances wearing hoop skirts. Officers, even though they would be dancing, wore spurs. The crowd strove for gaiety, fully knowing that many of the gentlemen attendees would soon be dead.

It wasn't until page 4 that I found a scrap of dialogue. Major General William Sherman explains why he wants Brigadier General

Judson Kilpatrick with him on his march to the sea: "I know that
Kilpatrick is a hell of a damned fool, but I want just that sort of man
to command my cavalry on this expedition." Well, I didn't know
who Sherman or Kilpatrick was. I didn't know what the "march to
the sea" was. And I couldn't appreciate the idea of pretending that
events were not all that they seemed. I closed the book.

At that age, I liked just being in my father's den. Something
about being near so many books felt good. I dreamed of having a big
library someday in my own house with shelves that traveled to the
ceilings, filled with old tomes and maps, and a big, thick wooden
desk near a small window that looked out over a garden. A chessboard would sit in one corner and a globe of the world in another.
My library would be dark except for a lamp that would cast a pool
of light onto a book as I read.

My father's den, by contrast, was small and illuminated. Afternoon sun bronzed the room until every corner became unshad-
owed. The light relaxed me. Years later when I experienced my first
series of anxiety attacks during high school, I would take refuge in
this room.

But on that day, with *A Stillness at Appomattox* closed and the
sun making me sleepy and daydreamy, I studied the soldiers on the
wall. My father had framed and hung four color reproductions of
a series of paintings entitled The American Soldier. One showed
an artillery officer, a first grade officer, and an infantry detachment
from 1786. The artillery officer wore shiny black boots up to his
knees, white pants and shirt, and a dashing coat of blue and red that
hung down to the middle of his thighs. The infantry marched behind him, but they didn't have cool boots. Instead, they wore what
looked like black slippers and white stockings that covered their
feet. One soldier walked a lone beat at the top along the frame, his
gun held high on his shoulders.

The painting of the 1805 soldiers showed little change in the officer's uniform and the enlisted men wore "fatigue clothing." They
dug trenches and built a pathway with long, thin boards. The officer
held a rifle with a spear attached to the end of it, and he gazed into
the distance as one who ponders questions of life might.

The last print I remember was the American soldiers from 1814. An officer with black, handsome boots gazed seriously at the ground where a map of rivers and dots lay. This man's coat was now short in the front with thick golden epaulets on each shoulder. His gleaming sword hung at an angle and touched the grassy field where his group had stopped to look at the map.

I didn't want to be a soldier when I grew up, but I liked the look of men in uniform: the swords, the boots, the long coats. And the wilderness settings depicted in the paintings fueled my fantasies of outback survival. In the woods behind our house, I pretended to wear a coat that fell to my thighs and gleaming black boots that came up to my knees and made me look taller. In my imaginings I always triumphed. I thought about endurance and I endured.

Despite its homage to the war experience, the den offered a neutrality not found in my bedroom, where I suffered nightmares, or in my parents' room, where my father shouted and thrashed in his sleep. The medals, journals, photos, and books reflecting battle all gave rise to an unlikely environment of equanimity.

In another part of the house, a very different ambience prevailed. The bar my father had built rested against a wall in our dining room. He tacked a heavy black material to the front panel and affixed a bronze plaque to its center. The plaque consisted of a fist with a bandaged thumb extending upward, with the words "SORE THUMB" hanging above the swollen digit, "TAVERN" below. The bar's top counter was one foot wide and four feet long. Behind were narrow shelves for glassware and one broader one for mixing drinks. Four round, orange barstools stood like sentries around the perimeter.

Behind the bar, on the orange-painted wall, Dad hung a long cloth print of a Spartan warrior, the bottom of which read "Servicemen Welcome." A dartboard was installed on the door to the garage, next to the bar, and when I was nine we got a miniature pool table. Swinging wooden doors dividing this area from the living room completed the saloon feel.

I became the bartender. I liked organizing the bar accoutrements—the corkscrews, glasses, and toothpicks. On the counter was a black lamp, rotating within a clear shade, that announced, "Bar is Open," when turned on. I'd flip the switch and go to work. The bottles of scotch, rum, and gin needed sorting, labels facing outward. Square, white cocktail napkins had to be arranged like fans. Shot glasses needed to be dusted. Around the Spartan warrior, I'd hang my own signs that announced special bargains such as "Happy Hour, 2 for 1," or "Why not have some Vodka, Bourbon, Vermouth? 4 Glasses, $5." I'd fill the ice bucket and wait for customers.

On Sunday mornings my parents drank Bloody Marys. I fixed their drinks in glasses etched with an "H" on the side. A shot and a half of vodka, tomato juice to fill, a splash of Worcestershire sauce, some salt, and a celery stick. The kids' version of this was simply beer and tomato juice. I made my drink by snapping open a can of Coors, filling the glass one-third with beer, adding the juice, and topping it with salt. This came as a welcome, savory combination after the sugary sodas and milk I'd had throughout the week. I couldn't drink the beer and tomato juice slow; it tasted too good.

My dad, gone during most meals throughout the week at his post office job, would make a big breakfast of scrambled eggs with vegetables and cheese, hash browns, and sausage. Mom made biscuits, the kind that came in a cylinder that exploded upon opening. I'd always eat at least three or four of these, slathered with butter and homemade jam. Life didn't get any better than being with my parents on Sunday mornings. After the morning drinks and breakfast, however, Sundays could be unpredictable, especially if the drinking continued.

To me, childhood is an ironic experience. At a time when one is least able to put behavior and events into perspective, everything happens. If I'd been older, if I'd known and understood more of the past, the present would have transpired within context. It probably would have been just as painful, but it might also have been comprehensible. Instead, life works almost backward: we are thrust into circumstances without any maturity. We must survive without being entirely sure that survival is possible. My relationship with my parents felt like I'd been given answers without ever having asked any questions.

If it was summer, my mother puttered in her garden on Sunday afternoons. Dad read the paper. I'd skulk around the house, playing with the cats but mostly bored and resentful of the enforced peace and quiet. Toward afternoon Dad would usually drink beer and sit in the backyard. He might take the long net and scoop dead bugs and twigs out of the swimming pool. On such a quiet day, the past could seep into the present.

"I'm getting a little big around the middle," Dad said to me one Sunday, sucking in his stomach and patting it at the same time. "Gotta go on a diet."

I gave him a playful punch. "You're not fat, Dad!"

"Plump then." He reached the net across, skimmed the water's surface, and dumped the contents onto the grass. "When I was a soldier, I didn't have this gut. You couldn't! We ran ten miles every day and did PT for hours."

This sounded terrible to me. Running around in the woods was fun, but anything organized, like calisthenics at school, grated on my nerves. I didn't like being in competition with other kids. Dad kept cleaning the pool, but I wanted to hear more about the good old days.

"Tell a war story, Dad."

"You can't just *tell* war stories," he said, a reply that made no sense to me.

"Please ..."

Dad put the net away and sat down. After awhile he finished his beer and asked if I'd get him another. Finally, he started talking.

"One time I fell asleep while marching. We'd been fighting for days. My legs kept going, but my brain shut off."

"Was it like sleepwalking?" I couldn't believe anyone could fall asleep while standing up.

"Not really. I woke up immediately, probably from stumbling. A little later, I'd drop off again. Then wake up again. This is how it went for awhile." Dad took a sip, then looked at the beer can and changed the subject. "You know, my brother could drink an entire beer in one gulp. He knew how to open his throat and leave it open." He took another sip. "Anyway, one morning my platoon was on patrol in Germany. We were walking along a gravel road. Suddenly there was a Nazi ahead of us, far enough that we couldn't distinguish him well. Everybody fired."

Another sip.

"When we got up to the body, we found it wasn't a German soldier at all. Just some old woman. She carried her possessions, maybe everything she owned in this world, tied to her back."

In the ensuing years, my father would tell the German woman story many times. Always after drinking. Always the same details—no more, no less.

"So, you killed someone?" I said, as if it were suddenly a surprise that this was what soldiers did. He shrugged.

"It was a war, Bets. You do what you have to do."

As he became more drunk that day, my father's head fell forward, then jerked back. He waved his arms like he was being held up, then became quiet. I petted Tiger and watched the oak tree weaving gently. Suddenly, Dad yelled, making my heart jump.

"Sieg Heil!" he shouted. Then he put his hand to one side of his mouth, leaning toward me as if whispering a secret. "In case we lose ..."

I always laughed at this, and "Sieg Heil! In case we lose ..." became a household phrase. I never understood until many years later its irony or how it must have been an attempt at humor by men who were worried about the outcome of the war.

Dad yelled again. "Sieg Heil!"

"In case we lose!" I shouted back. He laughed.

"That's right, kid. In case we lose. Hey, did I ever tell you about the North Korean that almost got me?" I shook my head.

"That bastard! He snuck up on me. I turned around just in time to see him going for his grenade. But I was faster! Got mine out, pulled the pin, and threw it right at him." Dad looked at his empty can. "Yeah, I got him."

This also became a repeated story in the years to come. It came from my father's memory with strength and regularity, like a wave crashing on shore. But what did the North Korean look like? What happened after my dad threw the grenade? These were not details my father ever shared.

As I got older, my hunger for war stories grew. I *wanted* to hear about the danger and the killing and the survival, and hear I did, but the cost has been that now I am the caretaker of these memories. I didn't kill the German woman and I didn't throw the grenade at the North Korean, but the events are cemented in my mind as if I must always remember them, maybe because there is no one else to do so.

War stories are not what they appear to be. For a young girl who dreamed of adventure, they represented peril, uncertainty, and, in my father's case, ultimate survival; at least he walked away. For one who wants to be tested, an experience in combat stresses the mental and physical fitness of a person to his or her limits. For the person who wants to do one good thing in the world, provided he or she believes in the cause, there is no greater sacrifice.

Yet, if valor and praise were enough to comfort the surviving soldier, the resulting haunting would not stretch across decades. It would not seep into relationships shared with a spouse and child. It would not trickle in and out of memory like a virus. The war story creates a myth. Tim O'Brien, a Vietnam War veteran, wrote in his book, *The Things They Carried*:

> *If at the end of a war story you feel uplifted, or if you feel that some small bit of rectitude has been salvaged from the larger waste, then you have been made the victim of a very old and terrible lie.*

My father's life as a soldier and his war experiences shaped my childhood. My own interests focused on the wild, natural world and on animals, but it was often war that expressed itself in my art and play.

For example, one autumn day after school I began a project. My father found me at the kitchen table, surrounded by a box of toothpicks, a bottle of Elmer's Glue, a blue marker, a square piece of plywood, piles of rocks and pebbles, and leaves in varying degrees of discoloration.

"What are you doing, hon?" he asked.

"I'm building a fort out of toothpicks."

"I see."

"Yeah, it's for art. We can build anything we want, and I want a fort. Kind of like the one at Fort Nisqually." Dad nodded. My Blue Bird troop had just visited a replica of Fort Nisqually, the first European settlement on Puget Sound, now a living history museum near our home. I'd been very impressed with the tall, pointed perimeter fence and lookout towers.

On the plywood I colored in a blue river that would flow through the fort, then poured the glue over the top of its sinewy body, and stuck rocks and wood in the glue. By the next morning, the glue had dried clear. My troops, not yet arrived to their outpost, would have clean water to drink. This was the easy part. The fort itself proved to be a huge amount of work. Each building required painstaking attention with its need for varying lengths of toothpick. The fence protecting the interior, a uniform height of one toothpick, was easier. I glued yellow and red oak leaves around the fort's grounds and crumbled a few loosely to be whooshed up as my plastic soldiers walked by.

"How's it going?" my mother asked on the second afternoon. The river looked great. Some buildings looked great. The rest needed a lot of work.

"Fine," I said cheerily, but exhausted from the huge task. "I think I'll go outside and play for awhile though." I went to my room, grabbed my guns and coat, and headed for the back woods to meet the boys.

By 1973, my blond hair had grown to nearly my waist and was the only feature about me that could be considered girlish. I usually had my mother pull it back into one ponytail, my bangs flopping around on my forehead. Though I sometimes wore dresses to school, usually I had on Converse high-tops, blue or brown jeans, a button-down shirt, and a vest, like my father.

The boys living on Snowberry Circle and I played "war" and "cowboys and Indians." The backwoods behind the cul-de-sacs provided the perfect realism. We took up sides and demarcated territory. Fir cones became grenades. Stacked branches served as fort walls. For either Christmas or my birthday one year, I had finally received the Lone Ranger double-holster gun set I'd been wanting. Having my own guns, instead of just sticks, made a difference. The boys respected authenticity and "died" more readily. With the "grenades," however, arguments broke out. Once, Timmy, an older boy with a hair-trigger temper who looked for any excuse to hit someone, disputed my shot. I'd nailed him with a fir cone, but he claimed he wasn't dead.

"It was a glancing blow!" Timmy cried, and kept throwing cones at me. I'd never heard of a "glancing blow" but acted as if I had.

"That's stupid!" I yelled back. "If I hit you in the head with a grenade, you're dead!"

"No, I'm not! It bounced off before exploding!"

"Listen, Timmy, a grenade does not just bounce off. It blows your head off. It might blow all of you to bits. That's it. You're dead."

But Timmy wouldn't die. He didn't understand. He had never heard my father's story about the North Korean, but since Dad only shared part of his war stories, I didn't really know what I was talking about either and never knew what killing does to the people who die as well as to those who survive. I dropped the issue and let Timmy live—getting punched for being right wasn't worth it.

During the early months of 1991, as my father was dying, I had pleaded with him to write down his stories. He refused.

"My hands shake too much," he had said.

"Maybe you could talk into a tape recorder?"

"No."

From this parrying I learned another myth about war stories: contrary to popular belief, the teller doesn't really want to tell them. Sober, my father shared nothing difficult about combat. When he was drunk, fragments escaped. What I have decided, however, is that his reticence didn't shield me from the pain of his experiences. In fact, knowing might have helped me understand him better. And it might have helped me understand myself.

Chapter 6

Little Egypt

[Sunday, August 24, 1862, Cairo, Illinois]

reached Cairo at 6 P.M. got off the cars and camped all night near the Barracks. and slept out in the open air for the first time.

—From the journal of Private Darsie Heath,
72nd Illinois Infantry, Company A

Cairo, Illinois, at the state's southern tip, juts like a defiant chin into the swirling waters of two great rivers. Flanked on the west by the Mississippi and on the east by the Ohio, less than half a mile at the point, the location had once been ideal to those who wanted to control the waterways. It had also proven a scourge to the town's founders as they tried to live and prosper in the resulting swamp. Investors came and built. The rivers flooded and destroyed. Residents lived with perpetual mud and sickness from the mosquito-infested waters. In 1842, Charles Dickens visited Cairo and wrote about the land in his travel chronicle, *American Notes for General Circulation*:

> *A dismal swamp, on which the half-built houses rot away; cleared here and there for the space of a few yards; and teeming, then, with rank unwholesome vegetation, in whose baleful shade the wretched wanderers who are tempted hither, droop, and die, and lay their bones; the hateful Mississippi circling and eddying before it, and*

*turning off upon its southern course a slimy monster
hideous to behold; a hotbed of disease, an ugly sepulchre,
a grave uncheered by an gleam of promise; a place without
one single quality, in earth or air or water, to commend it;
such is this dismal Cairo.*

Dickens felt such loathing for Cairo that he based the hell town, Eden, in *The Life and Adventures of Martin Chuzzlewit*, on what he saw between the watery legs of the Ohio and Mississippi. Still, the town itself shouldn't be blamed. The energy of two "super rivers" kept Cairo constantly in flux, making the land disagreeable, deadly, and unpredictable.

In August 1862, the 72nd Illinois arrived at Fort Defiance, the Union's defense against Confederate attack, situated on Cairo's southern end. The fort's cannons sat atop a thirty-foot levee, designed to keep the water from intruding. Now it also acted as a barrier in the war between men. Below the levee, sheds built to accommodate six or seven men, along with canvas tents, had been erected for the regiments. Hay soaked up the percolating water table and ever-flooding rivers. Cooking fires pockmarked the fifty acres like measles on a feverish body.

Cairo served as a transfer point. A few regiments stayed to guard against invaders, but most either headed south down the Mississippi River toward Vicksburg, Mississippi, or east up the Ohio River into western Kentucky and Tennessee. On the parade grounds, south of Second Street, the recruits learned the business of soldiering. They marched and drilled and were issued Springfield and Enfield rifles. They stood guard duty, participated in dress parade, received their monthly pay of $13, and awaited orders.

Joseph Stockton, the lieutenant who had bought Darsie, Jake, and Scepter dinner at the saloon in Chicago and delivered their $60 bounty checks, had become captain of Company A. Stockton, twenty-nine-years-old when he signed on with the 72nd, had been born in Pennsylvania but moved to Chicago in the early 1850s. In less than ten years, he owned part of a successful teaming business. After joining the regiment, he was offered the rank of adjutant, assistant to the commanding officer, but, according to *War Diary*, his memoir, he "declined the same, not having experience for such a position." Stockton's intelligence and popularity with the men, however, would leave him at war's end with the rank of brigadier general.

War Diary, a narrative based upon letters to his wife, recounts Stockton's Civil War experience. When Darsie's writings left me wanting for details, Stockton's, as well as those of others in the regiment, filled in the gaps. The captain of Company A did not mince words about the conditions in Cairo:

> *This Cairo is a miserable hole, the barracks are in*
> *a terrible state, filled with rats and mice and other*
> *creeping things. I prefer to sleep outdoors to sleeping in*
> *my quarters. Our time is taken up with company and*
> *regimental drill, weather very hot, no excitement except*
> *the passing through of regiments. We were ordered here to*
> *relieve the 11th Ill., who go to Paducah [Kentucky]. Men*
> *are getting sick and I am anxious for marching orders.*

June 1999, Cairo, Illinois

I drove into the southern half of Illinois on State Highway 51 and arrived in Cairo on a quiet Sunday evening. The streets were empty of people, and yellow barricade tape lay draped, like cravats, around four homes that had been condemned. The downtown offered more promise with its iron archway above Eighth and Washington streets announcing "Historic Downtown Cairo," glowing streetlamps, wrought-iron benches, and newly planted flowerpots. However, out of twenty buildings on one block, only six appeared to have functioning businesses. The flapping pigeons settling into the upper stories of boarded-up buildings, and large white placards posted beneath those buildings that read "For Sale," made the town seem as if it had just let out a long sigh.

Time has not been kind to Cairo. It has never risen above its watery location, and though once linked to Chicago via the Illinois Central Railroad and now connected to Kentucky and Missouri via bridges, it is still little more than a ghost town. That night in my motel room on Second Street, two blocks from where Darsie had trained and slept, I read more of Cairo's history. Doubt as to its livability prevailed from the beginning when Father Louis Hennepin, the seventeenth-century French explorer and missionary, noted, before traveling farther south along the Mississippi, that

the banks of the river are so muddy and so full of rushes and reeds, that we had much to do to find a place to go ashore.

A century later, General George Rogers Clark wrote to then-governor Thomas Jefferson that the area would be ideal for keeping an eye on the Spanish and added,

but the misfortune is, there's not an acre of ground nearer the Point than four miles rise the Ohio, but what is often Ten feet under water.

Likewise, William Oliver, an English traveler who wrote *Eight Months in Illinois*, an 1843 treatise for European immigrants, stated,

No doubt a town might be built, but the whole point is composed of an alluvion so very friable, that if the Mississippi, in one of his ordinary freaks, were to change his course, the whole affair might be swept away in a few days.

Despite the obvious limitations, people arrived with enthusiasm and more than a little hubris that they could control both the Ohio and the Mississippi and make the town a success. Levees helped keep the rivers' intrusions to a minimum, but the sopping ground and limitless mosquito population never allowed the city's residents and visitors to forget they were in a swamp.

The next day I rode my bike to Fort Defiance's parade grounds, now a grass field bordered by mini–storage units, a Budweiser distributing center, and a wastewater treatment plant. To see something where there was nothing proved a challenge. I tried to imagine the pole sheds, the mud-splattered men, the new guns. The feeling of another time washed over me, but not the view.

Likewise, looking at something where there should be nothing also obscured my insight into long ago. When Darsie stood atop the levee where I now stood, he saw the Mississippi, twice the size of the Ohio, splitting apart to encompass Cairo Island, then joining up with the smaller river to travel south. But all I saw was a tangle of southern jungle. Flashes of red and blue caught my eye as Northern cardinals and blue jays flew within the forest.

Puzzled, I went to the Cairo Library. There I found an "Official Souvenir Program" from 1896 describing the Civil War sites of Cairo. The author wrote:

> *Gaze down into the deep excavation* [from the levee], *and you will see the site of the old "Fort Defiance." On this spot was mounted the first hostile gun of the great war between the sections. Pass up the Mississippi levee. Where is that mighty river you looked upon in your boyhood days? Gone. In its stead you gaze on a forest of cottonwood. The channel of the river has changed. From sweeping close around the point at Fort Defiance it cut off Cairo Island to the south, Bird's Point* [Missouri] *directly opposite. As these localities crumbled into the river on the Missouri side, land was made on the Illinois side.*

A century later, the southernmost tip of Illinois land is located one mile south of where it was in 1862.

The yellow and green grass of the parade grounds once held, like a nest, the emergence of the new soldier. As I sweated in the still heat, I wondered what Darsie thought during those days. He didn't write about becoming a soldier, but William Mohrmann, a German immigrant and corporal in Company A, described in his memoirs the regiment's stay in Cairo and its metamorphosis from an assemblage of individuals into a unit of soldiers:

Upon our arrival at Cairo we were ordered into some
barracks which had been newly whitewashed, but our
Col. would not occupy them until he had inspected them;
he therefor bivouacked us amongst a lot of jim-son weeds
(stramonium) and thereby brought on the very thing he
desired to avoid, next morning half of the command was
sick. Having shelter, our lines and a numerous camp
guard was established and then came the school of the
company. Neither were wanting the customary capers
when the civic chrysalis tries to transform itself into the
military butterfly.

This new life as a soldier clearly wasn't for everyone. A few days
after arrival and before the regiment left to travel up the Ohio River
to Paducah, Kentucky, Darsie wrote beneath his August 28 entry, *M*
Avery And J. Morris Deserted at Cairo. Now, only four Toulon boys
remained: Darsie Heath, Jake Galley, Robert Holmes, and Scepter
Harding.

Chapter 7

Bertram Howell

What the archeologist and the superintendent discovered [in February 1934] *was an overlooked and unrecorded mass grave from the Battle of Shiloh. Judging from the buttons, they concluded that the soldiers were Union. Finding a Civil War mass grave seventy years after the war was enough to secure a place in the papers, but what made headlines was the determination that one of the dead soldiers was female.*

—From *They Fought Like Demons: Women Soldiers in the American Civil War* by DeAnne Blanton and Lauren M. Cook

Spring 2000, western Oregon

Battalion drill. Dress parade. Company and regimental drill, Springfields, Enfields. I still couldn't attach images to these words. During my travels, I had amassed more letters and diaries from soldiers that spoke of a world I didn't understand. I realized that my connection with Darsie, or my father, would never progress unless I better understood the soldier's experience, and to that end I needed to do more than just read. After returning from my first trip to the Midwest tracing Darsie's path, I learned about the 19th Indiana, a Civil War reenacting company based out of Portland, Oregon. I contacted them and asked about joining. They welcomed me with one directive: to "look like a man." After all, women had joined the ranks of North and South during the war, but in disguise.

With a list of necessary supplies, I went shopping. To look like a soldier, I bought a dark blue wool frock coat as well as the shorter sack coat (for hotter weather), sky blue trousers, brogan boots, a cotton pullover shirt, and a Hardee hat made of heavy felt, resembling more a cowboy hat than the well-known kepi. To fight like a soldier, I purchased a replica 1861 Springfield musket, leather cartridge and cap boxes for my belt, and a bayonet and scabbard. A rubber blanket (useful as a poncho or sleeping mat), a mattress tick for stuffing hay in case we found an abandoned barn, and a wool blanket would keep me warm. I added a canteen; a knapsack; a haversack to carry my belongings; a sewing kit, known during the Civil War as a "housewife"; a wooden toothbrush; coffee beans in a cloth "poke sack" with drawstring; reproduction 1862 Union playing cards, with a colonel as the king, the Goddess of Liberty the queen, and a major as the jack; and an ink bottle, powdered ink, and a quill feather. I bought a new leather journal with hand-sewn pages and a leather tie for keeping it closed. On the front page, I wrote my reenacting name, Bertram Darsie Howell.

The Springfield musket, made of a walnut stock and a one-piece steel barrel, came up to my shoulder. It seemed longer than the rifles my dad had owned. And heavier. I shot a real bullet out of it once into a tree, and the impact nearly spun me around. Fortunately, during reenactments, we would put only black powder into the barrel.

Another female reenactor told me about a theatrical company in San Francisco that sold facial hair. They made beards, goatees, and mustaches from real hair, each strand individually tied to a fine piece of lace. I bought three blond mustaches and one chin beard. To attach them, the company recommended a substance called spirit gum. The first time I pasted on my new face, a memory surfaced that I'd almost forgotten.

My father had never had a beard or mustache. He shaved every day, yet surprisingly the harsh action didn't mar his skin, which looked and felt as soft as Tiger's fur. A canister of Colgate shaving cream sat next to two razors on one side of the medicine cabinet in our bathroom. On the other side were my mother's makeup, lipstick, eyebrow pencil, and fingernail file. Sometimes I'd join my dad in the bathroom as he got ready for the day. As a six-year-old, my height did not yet reach to the mirror.

"Can I shave with you, Dad?" I would ask as he pressed the top of the Colgate can and filled his palm with the airy cream.

"Sure. Do you think you need to?"

"Yeah." I climbed onto the sink counter where my head popped up next to his in the mirror. Like him, I spread shaving cream across my cheeks and chin. While Dad's razor made a rasping noise across his face, the metal nail file I used swept up the white foam in silence. Finishing, we toweled our faces and Dad splashed Skin Bracer after-shave on his neck.

Thirty years later, the blonde mustache and beard transformed me, though my soft cheeks and narrow eyebrows belied this new-found masculinity. I looked a little like my half brother John. I looked a little like no one I had ever seen before.

Next I visited a hair salon. Using a picture of a Confederate general as a guide, I told the Laotian woman that I wanted a similar style. She looked puzzled.

"I need a man's haircut," I explained.

"You sure?" she asked through a thick accent.

"Positive." Although I had never had such short hair, I wasn't worried. My father had always said the difference between a good and a bad haircut was about two weeks, and I knew short hair, very unusual for a nineteenth-century woman, was the main way in which women soldiers had passed as young men, since they didn't have fake mustaches and beards and spirit gum. "You see, I'm a Civil War reenactor," I continued, "I need to look like a soldier."

The woman smiled at the word "soldier," and began to cut with enthusiasm. After she finished and I had about an inch of hair left, she asked if I liked it. The fuzz that moved back and forth under my hand shocked me more than the facial hair.

"Well, it is different." I didn't look as handsome as the general, but I did seem more boyish.

"You have do for your job," she consoled me. "It great you going help people."

With surprise I realized that she thought I was joining the modern-day military.

Before my first reenactment, I attended a workshop called "The Complete Impression and School of the Soldier." Daniel O'Hara, captain of the 19th Indiana, led us through the manual of arms, a series of movements in which the gun is shifted to different positions. I had watched a video on these moves but hadn't memorized everything. Also, my biceps weren't prepared to move the ten-pound gun around as if it were a stick.

"Right shoulder shift!" Daniel shouted. At this command, I was supposed to raise the gun so the trigger would rest by my ear. My trigger dangled low. Daniel walked over to me in mock disgust.

"How long you been in this man's army, Bertram?"

"One day, sir."

"That's no excuse, Bertram," he reprimanded as he adjusted my gun.

"Shoulder arms!" I brought the gun down to where my right hand could grasp it firmly below the trigger.

"Order arms!" My left arm snapped across my chest, and lowered the gun to the ground, while my right arm secured it. I was getting the hang of the manual of arms, and it was fun.

We also learned how to "stack arms" by placing our rifles in a tepee formation, locked together using the bayonets or ramrods.

The 19th Indiana then practiced company drill. With ten soldiers, this only superficially resembled Darsie's experience—with one hundred men to a company. Yet the objectives were the same: to move as a unit and to be so disciplined that each soldier knows what to do, even as men are falling and dying within the company. Daniel instructed us in how to form a battle line. As we marched forward in two columns, he yelled, "By company, into line!" and we became two rows, still marching forward but now ready to fire upon the enemy. "Right wheel!" he shouted. This required the farthest right man to mark time (stand in one spot) while the rest of the line swung, like a pivoting ruler, to the right. A "left wheel" worked the opposite way.

After the School of the Soldier, we met at Daniel's house for additional company drill. Though we stumbled through mistakes, the soldiers of the 19th came together well. I liked the sharpness of our coordinated movements—like a knife so fine it can slice through a newspaper. Probably I wouldn't like marching so much if I had to do it all day, every day, for weeks as Darsie had. But initially, drill was my favorite part of being a "soldier."

———————

The Northwest Civil War Council, a nonprofit "living history" organization, sponsors four reenactments each summer. The events are all held in northwest Oregon state parks, from the coastal Fort Stevens to Willamette Mission, along Interstate 5. The battles are not recreations of specific events, but rather are generic engagements with skirmishing, cavalry, a few cannons, marching, and, of course, musket fire. Occasionally, charges set up in the grass detonate when a cannon goes off. In general, the North loses the first battle of each day, the South the second. The chosen year is always 1863 and the mock setting is always Virginia and Pennsylvania. Darsie Heath did not fight that far east, and though the real western and eastern Civil War armies were different in many ways—such as dress, speech, and behavior—for my purposes this would do. I would still learn about a soldier's life.

My first reenactment was at McIver State Park near Estacada, Oregon. The night before my first battles, I walked around the military and civilian camps and Sutler's Row, the street of nineteenth-century vendors. In military camp, men and boys erected canvas tents, which consisted of wall tents (structures with four upright sides), "A" tents (shaped like the letter), and dog tents ("pup" in modern language). Strings laid across the grassy field indicated each company's "street." Tent entrances, except for the commander's, which sat at the head of the street, would be placed precisely along these lines. The commander's wall tent had a rainfly in front and two flags on each side—the American Stars and Stripes and a regimental banner. Beneath the fly sat a portable writing desk, tables, stools, and water barrels.

In the civilian camps, women, children, and some men set up tents and cooking facilities for the wives and families of the soldiers. Elaborate scenes depicting nineteenth-century life erupted across the grassy field. I saw four-poster beds in the open doorways of a few tents. Trunks and rocking chairs and hutches with plates and pans reposed beneath rainflies. U-Hauls and trailers sat on the grass while people clad in varying combinations of nineteenth- and twenty-first-century clothing unloaded them. Fire pits had been dug carefully, so the sod could be replaced when our journey back to 1863 ended. Bluish smoke twisted through the park's field along the Clackamas River.

Walking around camp, masked by my beard and mustache, I thought about my Civil War "persona." At the School of the Soldier, the instructors taught us that we could each make our character's background and traits as detailed as those of a real person, from creating a fictional birth date to deciding upon intricate personal habits like picking one's teeth after eating. I decided to go for the simple model, based upon what I had read about the real women who served as soldiers during the war. Many were described as hardworking, quiet, and aloof. Obviously, a woman trying to live in a man's world in the 1860s would not want to draw attention to herself. These characteristics suited me well. Bertram would be strong, quiet, and polite—a writer and a loner. I would not like people looking at me too closely. After all, the spirit gum did not affix my beard and mustache seamlessly.

I considered my perceptions over the years of how men behave compared with women. It seemed that men generally smiled less, so I vowed to look more serious. In conversation, men often did not look directly at each other, nor would they coax information from each other as women often do. As a man, I would say what I thought whether or not anyone asked me; I would be bold and confident and not so sensitive. As Bertram, I would be less chatty than Betsy.

In terms of body language, I felt I knew that part well from my tomboy years. Without even thinking, I could walk with well-intentioned strides, stand tall with my feet apart, and sit with my legs spread. I would play with the hair on top of my head less and the hair on my face more.

Later that evening, the first sergeant of the 19th unveiled the regimental colors, a silk flag of ocean blue with a golden eagle in its center. Between the raptor's wings, the words "E Pluribus Unum" snaked upward, and below its talons read "19th Indiana." Three cheers went up for the flag as we toasted the banner of our bravery with wine and sparkling cider.

Saturday morning we gathered for the presentation of colors and dress parade. The 19th had been selected to present the colors in front of the entire battalion, which, for the Northwest Civil War Council, comprised ten companies and about a hundred soldiers. We donned white dress gloves. We practiced right and left wheels and moving with a flag flapping in the wind. Later, as the fife and drum corps played a tune called "Colors," the 19th took the field and presented the flag to our colonel. Officers saluted the Stars and Stripes with their swords; enlisted men did so with their rifles held in front of them. The band finished with "Duke of York" and "Dan Tucker."

Dress parade included standing at attention for the colonel's review, an inspection of arms and equipment, and attention to orders, which in the reenacting world often focused on making sure everyone knew not to bring their twenty-first-century vehicles into camp. The colonel then drilled us on the manual of arms. Finally, the adjutant—the assistant to the colonel—announced those chosen for guard duty. This weekend, the 19th Indiana would provide night guard for the Union camp.

By the time the long roll played, indicating battle, the April sun had climbed above the Douglas-fir trees and my wool uniform had grown hot. Sweat trickled down my back and beneath my beard. It itched. My nose ran from the spring-season pollen. I could do nothing about these discomforts, however, for fear of sending my facial hair askew.

"19th Indiana! Form up!" shouted the corporal. The privates arranged themselves by height—with the result that I became the last man. We joined the battalion and marched toward the battlefield. The crack of cavalry weapons broke the silence. Soon a cannon exploded. My heart raced, but not out of fear for my life; I just didn't want to do anything stupid. We reached the edge of the grassy field. Confederates poured out of the trees. Daniel shouted his first order while waving his sword.

"19th Indiana! Load!"

More sweat. My cheeks felt hot. Keep calm, I thought. Someone next to me "took a hit," reenacting parlance for appearing to be shot, and fell forward. Other 19th Indiana men pulled him back behind our line. The soldier on the other side inched closer to me, "filling the hole" left by our fallen comrade. I grabbed a black powder paper cartridge from the box on my belt, ripped the top off with my teeth, and dumped the fine grains into the gun's barrel. Then I reached for a blasting cap, which I placed over the gun's cone. By this time, men dressed in butternut-colored uniforms extended across the field with guns aimed at us. At me. Though I never forgot once that this was make-believe, the image of dozens of dark barrels pointed at me brought me closer to that ineffable experience my father and ancestor had only partially described. In another place and time, the guns had been filled with black powder and bullets.

"Is everyone loaded?" yelled the captain. I had forgotten to stick cotton in my ears, and the noise grew painful. At our affirmative replies, Daniel ordered, "Front rank, kneel!" Down I went on my right knee as a preordained charge went off nearby. Smoke, dirt, and bits of spring grass flew into the air.

"Ready!" Daniel screamed. I brought my Springfield musket up at a forty-five degree angle to the sky and pulled the hammer back to full cock. Running my tongue over my dry lips, I tasted the acrid black powder that had stuck to them when I'd opened up the cartridge.

"Aim!" I rested the gun's stock against my shoulder and pointed the weapon straight at the heart and flesh of one man standing seventy-five feet in front of me. Things were going well and I was certain no one could tell that I was a "fresh fish," as new recruits during the Civil War were called.

Smack! My gun exploded just one second before Daniel yelled, "Fire!" I winced, but had no time to obsess over my mistake as the captain hollered, "Load quickly, lads, load quickly!" Bertram would probably make a good soldier, but he would need to settle down.

—————

Guard duty required pairs of soldiers to work in one-hour shifts. Our responsibilities included patrolling the Union streets, monitoring campfires, and keeping watch for suspicious activity, as the Confederates had been known to make raids and steal flags. "Idaho Steve," a reenactor from Boise, and I would take the 1:00–2:00 a.m. shift.

A few soldiers still chatted beside the fires, but most had gone to bed by one o'clock. Steve smoked a pipe as we walked up and down the company streets. In front of one dog tent a soldier had stabbed his bayonet into the ground and placed a burning candle in the round part that attaches to the barrel of the gun. Two candles burned on the ground at either entrance of another dog tent. A member of the cavalry stayed awake to keep an eye on the horses. A screech owl trilled from across the Clackamas River, and clouds that had insulated the park and kept me warm the night before dissipated. Stars shone like pinpricks on a piece of black paper wrapped around a ceiling lamp.

The ambience of the 1860s camp enveloped me: horses stomping, wood popping, people whispering. It warmed me like the feel of the fireplace at my parents' home. The culture of camp, living outdoors, the smell of smoke, and the sound of violins and banjos reminded me of my childhood fantasies of wilderness survival. Reenacting wasn't exactly what I had envisioned back then, but the simpler time and a human world more closely connected to the earth made me feel as if I'd come home.

Civil War reenacting, because it is more theatrical than literal, is an imperfect method for understanding the war experience. Despite my best efforts, my life as Bertram Howell merely grazed the unique world that only belongs to combat veterans, like fingers grabbing at smoke. The smell lingered on my hands, the dirt and bruises stained my skin, but initially, at least, the feelings washed away a few days after an event. During my first few years of "playing soldier," however, I convinced myself that reenacting would illuminate the feelings and experiences that Darsie didn't write about in his journal and that my father wouldn't share. I hoped to sieve out the parts of them that lived within me. And as pieces dropped into my understanding, like a giant jigsaw puzzle, I believed that one day I would have a whole picture that would explain everything. About them and about me.

Though camp life appealed to me as a person, the battlefield provided the insight I wanted. For example, when the two sides closed in on each other, Daniel would give the command, "Aim high!" This was for safety. Even without a bullet, a blast of black powder in the face could do serious damage to a person. I learned that real Civil War soldiers, by contrast, were told, "Aim low!" Most of these individuals had been citizen soldiers, not professional military men. They naturally often aimed above heads, or they repeatedly stuffed bullets down their guns without firing. Many individuals wanted to serve their country. Most probably did not want to kill others who were only doing the same.

To make our battles look realistic, some soldiers had to "die." Reenactors often don't want to do this, because that means the fun of playing war is over. To alleviate this problem, Daniel would yell, "Take some hits, boys, then recycle!" "Recycling" involved falling as if wounded, limping back behind the main line, waiting a few seconds, and then rejoining the fight. In this way, we had many second chances, unlike true soldiers of war.

———•••———

An annual Fourth of July reenactment takes place at Willamette Mission State Park north of Salem, Oregon. It is a hot, long event, often stretching over four or five days. One year, the 19th Indiana grew in size with the addition of six reenactors from California. Frank, a soldier with a snow-white beard and mustache, complimented my own blond facial hair.

"It's great," he said. "No one can tell at all that you're a woman."

I felt pleased with my appearance as Bertram. People often couldn't tell my gender until I spoke. They said I looked good as a man. They said I soldiered well. Another man from our company, named Scott, had asked me where he could get a similar beard and mustache. I had looked at him, puzzled. Scott could easily grow his own.

"Yeah, but it itches terribly," he said. "I'd like to be able to take it off at night."

"Unfortunately, this itches too," I told him, "especially after I start sweating."

At the afternoon's battle, Chip, one of the California boys, showed up to formation without boots. The most authentic reenactor I had met so far, Chip seemed to have arrived via a time machine from 1863. His sack coat hung loosely on his scrawny frame, as if he had been living on half-rations for several weeks. His cheeks pulled in slightly on either side of his wiry mustache and goatee. Chip rarely smiled, spoke only in 1860s language, and spent most of his time off the battlefield frying salt pork in one half of an old canteen. When I'd sampled some, I'd expected the taste of bacon; what I got was more like the sensation of eating an old shoe. Chip had eaten salt pork for every meal.

"Where are your boots, Private?" the captain asked Chip.

"They give out, sir. I'm planning on getting a new pair off some dead Reb."

"Well, do it quickly. I don't wanna look at those fungus-infected feet again."

The 19th Indiana took it hard in this battle. I fell "dead" next to Frank, who was only "wounded."

"Die, you sons of bitches!" yelled Frank. The Rebels were supposed to lose this battle, but they weren't going down. I lay there listening to the screaming of the officers and the wounded. I wanted to feel the chaos, even though chaos reminded me of my nightmares with the tangled string. I wanted to feel the cannons shaking the ground, smell the gunpowder, hear the yelling soldiers.

> *Color bearer, you're with me!*
> *Battalion, form up! Dress the line!*
> *Sir, the wounded?*
> *If they can travel, move 'em. If not, leave 'em.*

Being "dead," I observed the battle inconspicuously so as to not give away my aliveness. With cotton in my ears, I felt strangely detached from the scene, as if maybe I was just eavesdropping on the fight. Is this what dying on a battlefield felt like? As their vision and hearing and other senses left them, did the mortally wounded perceive themselves to be part of the tragedy of war? Or was the experience something completely different? I could only imagine the answers to these questions. When the bugle sounded at the conclusion of our battle, I would stand up with only a uniform full of dry grass, a patch of horse poop, or maybe a sunburn to show for my suffering.

That night the 19th Indiana joined in a circle around the campfire. Frank pulled out a bottle of port wine from his knapsack.

"Now, we're going to start the 'Circle of Fools,'" he announced. "We'll pass the bottle around and each person makes a toast, and eventually the 'Circle of Fools' becomes the 'Circle of Friends.'" Frank started us off with a healthy swig. "Here's to the 19th for being such good hosts."

Sergeant Chris Scarano took the bottle. "And here's to the California boys for making the long trip up here."

When it came my turn, Bertram didn't drink the port, but he did make a toast.

"Here's to my parents, who have both passed away. And had they not, I probably never would have started reenacting."

"I'm sure they're looking down right now and smiling," said Frank.

"Yeah," added Rick, another California man. "I'll bet your dad is thinking, 'Cool beard.'"

"Oh, the son I always wanted," said someone else, and everyone laughed.

Before Frank and his comrades headed back to California the next day, Chip asked me about my future reenacting career.

"Do you think you'll do it awhile or just enough for your research?" he asked.

"That's a good question. I haven't really thought about it. Maybe just for awhile."

Chip considered this. "Kind of like the real Civil War boys, huh? They signed on thinking the war would be just a quick thing. And of course, it went on much longer."

Chapter 8

The Frying Pan

VISIT MADE HERE BY PARATROOPER

Lieut. James Howell Spends Leave Here
From Fort Benning, Georgia

Lieutenant James Howell, who recently completed his parachute infantry training at Fort Benning, Georgia, has been spending the past week here with his mother, Mrs. Blanche Howell and his grandmother, Mrs. Jas. McLaughlin. He is the first Geneseo youth to receive wings qualifying him as a paratrooper.

He received his wings upon successfully completing [five] required jumps from a plane which completed a four weeks' training period at the Georgia Paratroop school. Asked what feeling he experienced when making his first jump, he stated, "My stomach felt like it had a piece of ice in it and my knees were shaking like jello." He thought of the responsibility of setting a good example for the eleven boys ready to follow him when making that first thrilling jump into space.

The previous weeks of training for parachute jumping which Lieut. Howell completed included the physical toughening up of every parachuting warrior before the actual jumps. The course of learning how to pack the 'chute and a week-by-week process of tower training with every move at double time, is followed by free jumps and finally mass jumps. In a parachute jump, the paratrooper must guide himself to the ground, landing in a tumbling fashion so that he rolls over readily. He carries with him brass knuckles, trench knives,

*matches, sub-machine guns, hand grenades and almost any
other type of death-dealing device.*

*Lieut. Howell graduated from the Geneseo township high
school and attended Iowa State college at Ames. He entered
army service in September, 1941 and was first stationed at Camp
Wolters, Texas. After being stationed in [the] Panama canal
zone for about a year, he was transferred to Fort Benning, Georgia to which place he will report following his leave in Geneseo.*

—From the *Geneseo Republic,* Wednesday, July 9, 1943

Spring 1974, Tacoma, Washington

I was trapped by the rain. I read *Born Free* in the den, with Tiger on
my lap. Tiger was now five years old, but she hadn't settled down
much. She chased dogs around the cul-de-sac and had recently
started stealing food from outdoor grills, including my father's. I
once found her in the front yard eating a piece of barbecued chicken,
which must have come from the neighbor's evening meal since we'd
been eating hotdogs that night.

"Hey, Bets. How ya doing?" My dad walked into the room and
went to his desk.

"Fine. I'm sick of the rain."

"Rain! This ain't rain!" my father laughed. "If you want rain, go
to Panama. We had *deluges* when I was there!" After filing some
papers, he sat down on the couch with me and crossed one leg over
the other. Tiger left me for the new lap.

"Listen, the rain was so fierce in the jungle, we took our showers
outside."

"Really? Wasn't it cold?"

"No, it was a relief after the steamy jungle. And it poured at the
same time every day. We'd all get undressed, have our soap in hand,
and get ready for our fifteen-minute shower. The next day we'd do
it again."

I wasn't sure if Dad was pulling my leg. Rain the same time every
day? It seemed unlikely. But I didn't know, or care, much about the
tropics. I wanted to go to the African savanna and live in the bush

and see the lions, leopards, and cheetahs. Maybe I would befriend an orphaned lion cub like Joy Adamson had done in the 1950s.

"Did you like Panama, Dad?"

"Not really. It was a hard place to live. We all had malaria and dysentery, but we'd still have to go on patrols in the jungle. Once I saw an anaconda snake as big around as my thigh. It was sunning on the trail. We took a healthy detour around it. Another time I slipped and started sliding down a hill. I grabbed for something above me and got a handful of something with three-inch spines. My hand swelled up like a melon. No, the jungle is not a *nice* place."

I sensed that my father had decided the Puget Sound was a nice place. We did not have extreme cold like they did in Illinois. We did not have extreme heat like in Central America. What we had, though, was a lot of boring rain. Dad left the den and I returned to Joy Adamson's life on the African plains.

Apart from these few anecdotes and the string on the world map that stretched from Illinois to Texas, then Louisiana, and finally to Panama, I knew nothing about my father's beginnings as a soldier. Only years later, after obtaining his military papers from the National Personnel Records Center in St. Louis and reading accounts written by soldiers from his regiment, was I able to piece together a story never fully told to me.

At the time of the attack on Pearl Harbor, Hawaii, twenty-one-year-old Private James Howell was stationed in Panama with the 158th Infantry. At some point, the private, who garnered "excellent" marks for his character and efficiency rating as a soldier and had been promoted to corporal, was recommended for Officer Candidate School at Fort Benning, Georgia, which he began in February 1943. The previous year, Fort Benning, along the Chattahoochee River, had been selected as the centralized location for training infantry officers, as well as soldiers, for airborne warfare. The fort was named after Henry Lewis Benning, a Columbus, Georgia, native and Confederate major general who had served under Robert E. Lee.

Upon arriving at the fort, fondly known as the "Frying Pan," Corporal Howell would have gone through a three-day, if all went well (several weeks if it didn't), processing cycle. The first day he would have filled out forms, written an autobiography, and possibly been interviewed regarding school records. The second day was devoted to medical examinations, and the third day was the Academic Aptitude Test. This test measured the educational level and academic promise of an individual. Joining the military had become much more complicated between 1862—when nearly anyone could enlist, including women, because there were no background checks—and 1943.

Approximately two hundred young men were in my father's class. From a summary on the Infantry School I received from a librarian at Fort Benning, I learned that the officer candidate course back then included studies in three areas: weapons, tactics, and general subjects. In weapons classes they learned about Browning automatic rifles, machine guns, mortars, bayonets and grenades, and "technique of rifle fire." Tactics, which had by far the longest list of subjects, included such topics as combat training, "estimate of the situation," "rifle company attack in woods," "night advance and dawn attack," and "defense in rear areas." Map and aerial photo reading, hygiene and sanitation, leadership, automotive training, and, of course, physical training made up the general courses.

Each soldier became intimate with his M1 rifle: taking it apart, putting it back together, cleaning it. The training included sighting, position, and trigger-squeeze exercises. Kurt Gabel, a paratrooper with the 17th Airborne, 513th Parachute Infantry Regiment, wrote in his book, *The Making of a Paratrooper: Airborne Training and Combat in World War II*:

> *It was mandatory for each man to qualify as a marksman, expected of each man to make sharpshooter, unmistakably stressed as desirable for each man to make expert.*

No matter what level they attained, even the lowest-scoring man would be above average in his ability to sight and shoot at a target.

A company officer, with full responsibility for the discipline and development of the candidates, was assigned to each training class. The class was then divided into four platoons, and a tactical officer served as platoon leader. This often-avuncular man needed to know the potential officers intimately, and he observed them during classes and field exercises. Every ten days he held conferences with each man to discuss his work and grades. Additionally, each candidate also rated the fellow men in his group and listed their strong and weak points. The men's estimates of their comrades were particularly important. They reflected the ability of each candidate to garner respect and confidence from his fellow soldiers, a skill absolutely necessary when placing those same comrades' lives on the line.

On May 19, 1943, newly commissioned Second Lieutenant James W. Howell, with 148 others, graduated from the Infantry School. Several months after my mother's death, I discovered a brown leather scrapbook with worn corners and yellowed pages in the closet of my dad's den. In this book I found the program for the Officer Candidate Class, Sixth Company, Third Student Training Regiment. On the program's front cover, a seven-sided shield with a knife pointing toward the heavens had been emblazoned below the words, "Follow Me," and next to blue letters that read, "The Infantry School, Fort Benning, Georgia." In the program's center, a foldout photograph shows the proud class, most of the men standing, the ones in front kneeling down or sitting with their legs crossed. The pine trees of Georgia dot the landscape behind these young soldiers, dressed in their unadorned khaki uniforms. James Howell looks seriously at the camera, his soft, unlined face inscrutable. One month before becoming an officer, my father had turned twenty-three years old. Four decades later, he would tell me of the terrifying responsibility of giving orders as such a young man.

After Infantry School, my father attended four weeks of Jump School. The first week was devoted to an extreme physical-ondi-tioning program. Every morning, the new recruits were awakened at 4:00 a.m. to begin their day with a four- or five-mile run. The stakes ran high; dropping out just once expelled the candidate from jump school. They'd return to the barracks for breakfast, after which more physical fitness—including such activities as team rope climbing, tug-of-war, hand-to-hand combat, and running the obstacle course—awaited them until lunchtime. The obstacle course involved traversing terrain with steep banks, crossing gullies via a single-strand rope bridge, leaping over waterways with a hanging rope, and scaling high walls. Every training activity was executed at a dead run, and the candidates were timed. As the days passed, muscles solidified beneath T-shirts. Veins expanded to pump blood faster and harder. Now I understood how a body could keep marching even after a mind had fallen asleep.

The second week of Jump School was "ground training." Here, the men learned the jump commands, how to pack their parachutes, and how to exit from a mock-up of a C-47 aircraft. Each man mastered the art of manipulating his parachute while being suspended in a harness. I knew this training had saved my father's life as I remembered his story of the parachute that didn't open.

Being suspended in this harness was not comfortable. Gabel described the device:

> *Steel hoops suspended from wooden beams over an oblong*
> *sawdust pit had parachute harnesses attached by their*
> *four risers. The hoops were lowered by pulleys; the hapless*
> *trooper strapped himself into the harness, trying hard to*
> *place the leg straps flush against the insides of his thighs.*
> *Alas, when he was pulled off the ground and suspended*
> *over the sawdust pit, the leg straps closed on his scrotum*
> *like a vise.*

The would-be paratroopers learned how to execute the parachute landing fall, or PLF, which involved bending the knees, tucking the body into an arc, and keeping the chin on the chest and the neck tense. Fort Benning had a wind machine that would drag the men across the ground with their parachutes inflated, so they would know how to collapse the parachute under less-than-ideal conditions. They were taught that, while in the air, they would prepare to land when they came within fifty to one hundred feet above the ground. They practiced all these new skills from forty-foot towers with cables descending to the ground, similar to the jump tower I had "parachuted" from.

After ground training came real tower training. The men rode "buddy-seats" up the 250-foot towers. During the first two tower trips they descended to the ground in a controlled fashion. On the third trip, the men were attached to a thirty-eight-foot canopy, controlling their own descent, using every skill they had learned during the harness training. During tower training, in between being pulled up in the seat and descending, the men also learned how to defend themselves and kill others.

Gabel described his instructor during this third stage of training, Lieutenant Stanley A. Galicki, as a muscle-hardened man "with a dangerous feline quality about him." As the tower training was happening, Galicki gathered several recruits from Gabel's company around him to discuss hand-to-hand combat. This is what he told them:

> *The object of hand-to-hand combat is to render an opponent hors de combat. What does that mean? It means...kill him! In case you gentlemen have forgotten while engaged in the glamorous business of learning how to be a parachutist, you're being paid to be killers. That is your primary, your only function in life: to be killers!*

Lieutenant Galicki continued to emphasize his point: "The parachute is only a means of transportation by which you are delivered to the ground. And once you're there, you do what?"

Gabel and his comrades yelled, "Kill!"

Galicki asked them again.

"*Kill!*" they yelled louder, at which time he seemed satisfied. He then showed them how to accomplish this unarmed. They learned principles of jujitsu, pressure points, critical body areas, and attack techniques. Gabel writes:

> *Then came the demonstrations of defense against knife attack, bayonet attack, and pistol attack. After that it was "approach and dispatch" with the knife, the garrote, the rifle butt, and the hands as instruments to effect the*

silent, rapid, efficient rendering of the enemy permanently
hors de combat—a ballet of death, superbly performed.

By the end of the day, Gabel writes that they "were getting into the spirit and found it exhilarating."

I wondered if my father had heard similar words. Did he also yell back, "Kill!" with enthusiasm and get into the spirit of things? Did it seem like only a game at the time? He had told me once that one does what one must in a war; perhaps this early training had taught him that.

The fourth and final week of Jump School was devoted to jumping from a real aircraft in flight. During ground training, the recruits had learned how to exit from a simulated C-47 airplane. Now the men sat on benches along either side of a real plane in "stick" formation, facing each other (a "stick" referred to one group of parachutists exiting from the same door). The jumpmaster, the last man to exit and the one who made sure everybody left the plane, would begin with "Get ready!" At the command, "Stand up and hook up!" each soldier hooked the snap fasteners from the line attached to his main chute to the cable running along the top of the fuselage. These fasteners had to be secured with a cotter pin and a safety button so that they would not come off the cable. If a fastener failed, the jumper would be leaping into space without any mechanism to yank open his parachute.

When the jumpmaster yelled "Check equipment!" each man made sure the man in front of him was ready to go. They would look over backpacks and harnesses, static lines, risers, bellybands, and rip cords. If everything was OK, then at the next command, "Sound off for equipment check!" each person, beginning with the last man in the stick, would yell their designated number, "Twelve OK!" "Eleven OK!" and so on. Approximately three minutes from the drop zone, a red lightbulb to the right of the exit door would illuminate. During the following three minutes, the jump commands would be shouted. "Stand in the door!" got everyone prepared to exit. The first man in the stick would be ready with his left foot halfway out the door, hands straight out and head up. At the drop zone, the red light went out and a green one came on, and the men would hear the final command, "Go!" Each, in turn, would shuffle ahead as the entire stick jumped one by one.

After five successful jumps, including one at night, the soldier received his wings qualifying him as a paratrooper. In my father's scrapbooks, I found a certificate dated June 26, 1943, from the Parachute School, Airborne Command, United States Army. It read:

*This is to Certify That: 2nd Lieut. James W. Howell
has satisfactorily completed the prescribed course in
Parachute Packing, Ground Training, and Jumping from
a plane in flight. He is, therefore, entitled to be rated from
this date, June 26, 1943, as a qualified Parachutist.*

There is a picture of my father from July 1943, which I found in a mélange of family photos, taken during leave in Geneseo right after he became an officer and a paratrooper. He is dressed in his paratrooper uniform, with his sharply creased pants tucked into shiny black jump boots. "Blousing" their pants was a privilege for paratroopers; the regular infantry maintained "straight legs." My father's jump wings, his only decoration, are pinned above his left breast pocket. After seeing his family that summer, Dad returned to Fort Benning, Georgia, and began a rigorous routine of day-and-night training in preparation for the invasion of Hitler's Europe.

As I thought about my father's training and accomplishment, I remembered that Darsie, himself an enlisted man, had not seemed fond of officers. In April 1865 he wrote:

*I never complain though when I have enough to eat plenty
of Clothes. supplied by Uncle Sam & no fighting to do---
then I hate to hear the men curse The President—this is
often done—and to hear them blame our government with
evry thing—such as short rations no money, no tobacco.&c
when the fault his with Our officers.*

Yet, nearly eighty years later, his great-grandson would achieve something special in the military culture: the role of leader. To accomplish this, as well as to become a paratrooper, required boundless self-confidence. One could not hesitate when jumping out of a plane into nothingness. One could not hesitate when moving forward into the enemy's path or giving an order that might kill friends.

Chapter 9

Pleasant Duty

[Monday, September 8, 1862, Paducah, Kentucky]

The regiment did not stay here long. They received orders to go to Columbus and I was unable to go with them was left in the hospitle. I took the fever and it was four weeks before I was able to go about.

—From the journal of Private Darsie Heath,
72nd Illinois Infantry, Company A

The 72nd Illinois left Cairo in early September 1862, steaming up the Ohio River to Paducah, Kentucky. They traveled on *Fairplay*, a tinclad river transport that had been captured from the Confederacy that August. *Fairplay*, a side-wheeler with two smokestacks near the bow, must have resembled a giant beetle swimming upstream. It took twenty-four hours to navigate forty river miles. After disembarking, Private Darsie Heath was put on guard, and Captain Joseph Stockton made "officer of the day." Stockton wrote in his memoir:

> [I] *had to make the grand rounds, which means to visit all the pickets. I had to ride about fifteen miles in a drenching rain at 12 o'clock at night but I did not mind it as I was only too glad to have something to do. Men are all better satisfied at getting south of the Ohio River as they feel they are now in the enemy's country.*

Shortly after arriving in Paducah, Darsie became sick, and while the 72nd Illinois was sent back down the Ohio and Mississippi rivers toward Columbus, Kentucky (the regiment's garrison duty in Paducah apparently over), he remained in the camp hospital there. Left alone without his friends and brother, he wrote in his journal:

> *The Regiment was at columbus* [Kentucky] *doing*
> *guard duty. they had Battallion drill and Drefs parad*
> *evry day. they also took the camp Dihiarrea this*
> *became Chronic. the fever and ague also prevailed in*
> *camp more than the one half of the men were unfit*
> *for duty.* [My parents] *sent me a box from home with*
> *many nice things in* [it]. *this did me a great deal of*
> *good. I got acquainted with a Mr. McIntyre he was*
> *convalescent at the time he waited on me during my*
> *sicknefs like a brother I shall never forget his kindnefs*
> *The 2nd Battle of Corinth was fought at this time*
> *and they were trying to make room for the wounded. I*
> *was told that I would have to go to the regiment. I told*
> *the doctor I was unfit for duty he told me I did not*
> *want to go to the regiment this made me angry and I*
> *packed up my things and left. I was anxious to leave*
> *the hospitle but I knew I was unfit for duty.*

After returning to Cairo as he tried to catch up with the regiment, Darsie was examined by another doctor who asked him if he thought he was fit for duty. Darsie said no. The doctor then told him he could stay in Cairo to recuperate, an option that must not have set well, as he then wrote:

> *I was sorry then I told him what I had. I went to him and*
> *told him I thought that I could do duty and that the Doctor*
> *in the Hospitle at P. had advised me to go to my Regt. that*
> *I had a Brother there who would take care of me if I grew*
> *worse he then (verry reluctantly) agreed to let me go*
> [In Columbus, Kentucky, October 18th] *I was*
> *welcomed by the Capt. and the men I had walked up from*
> *the river to camp* [Captain Stockton] *was angry at me for*
> *that he said I should have sent him word and he should*

*have sent an ambulance I was well treated and also
received letters from home they were invaluable to me as
they kept up my spirits with the best of care. I grew some
better In lefs than a week the [regiment] started for New
Madrid [Missouri]. Then I was left alone hurt to take care
of myself.*

*this was the worst of my sicknefs. It snowed during the
week and there I was in the cold tent I was so week I could
hardly move and could eat nothing and was unable to
get wood for the fire in the tent A man of our [company]
waited on me then he was so slow he was as good as
no one. one evening I thought my last was come I was
downhearted for the first [time] since I was sick At night
I grew worse and I thought of all my past life. I told the
man to get me Ink and paper [I] moved my self to write
home. I do not remember who I wrote to yet I think it was
My Mother. I was awakened at noon next day I felt some
better In a few days the regiment came back they had
been in Missouri and took some prisoners they were in
high spirits I was some better when they came Jake wrote
home that I was well [Our parents] received the two letters
at the same time and an answer to the 1st came to me Jake
got to see it and blamed me for it severely he said I should
not let the folks know how bad I was——I kept growing
better and better evry day. I took walks every day. I tried
to get a furlough but could not. I sent home for money and
bought me anything that I thought was good for me.*

In 1862, the town of Columbus, Kentucky, rested along the eastern shores of the Mississippi River, approximately twenty miles
downstream from Cairo. Fort Halleck, where Darsie stayed sick and
downhearted until the end of November, when he was finally well
enough to travel farther south and rejoin the regiment, sat two hundred feet above the river. Early in the war, this location was recognized for its commanding view of the Mississippi. It had begun as
a Confederate fort, but was evacuated in March 1862 after Ulysses

S. Grant captured nearby Forts Henry and Donelson along the Tennessee and Cumberland rivers.

———•—

Summer 1999, Kentucky and Mississippi

Today's 156-acre Columbus-Belmont State Park is only one-tenth the size of the original earthworks and trenches of Fort Halleck. I had arrived here after leaving Cairo earlier that week. Beneath a lattice of maple and locust branches, I pitched my tent and then began hiking the serpentine ditches that once lay open to the sky and were occupied by soldiers from the North and the South. The earthworks have undoubtedly melted some over the decades, yet the prolific vegetation has largely held them together. Leaves crackled beneath my feet.

At the top of the precipitous bluffs, I found a white building with four windows facing front on the bottom floor and two dormers leaning out from the second. A sign next to the entrance read, "Civil War Hospital, Admission $.50." I wondered if this had been the hospital Darsie referred to when he wrote on November 22:

> *The Doctor procured a church for us in a Hospitle and we moved to it today. It was a cold place no stove in it and the glass all broken out of the windows. The Doctor gave me a cot and I fared well.*

Inside, the woman behind the cash register looked resigned to a day with few visitors.

"Was the hospital at this spot during the war?" I asked.

"No, I don't think anyone knows where it was originally. Recently, the park moved it back from the crumbling bluffs. This building is only a quarter of its original size."

I bought a book on the war years of Columbus and commented about the great view of the Mississippi.

"Yes," she agreed, "though the river has changed a lot over the years. It used to be more narrow and swift."

On a park bench, I read how the Mississippi River had repeatedly ravaged Columbus with its unpredictable flooding. Despite the

rt and need to constantly fight and cajole the river, Colum-
p.l, that is until 1927. That year, the worst flood of the twen-
..... cen....., sucked the town from beneath the bluffs that Darsie
had walked up and deposited her at the bottom of the Mississippi.
The riverside trenches and half of the earthwork forts vanished in the
ensuing years. What now remains of Columbus—a post office, fire
department, one convenience store/gas station, and one restaurant—
is located atop the disintegrating bluffs and volatile waters. I looked
out at the seemingly docile river and yet could see that it did what it
wanted whether we humans approved or not. It had added land to
Cairo, prodigal ground that still couldn't transform the town into a
success. It had taken the old Columbus to an early grave.

Sliding down a game trail from the park, I made my way to the
shore. Though steep, the hike didn't take long. Still, I'm sure it was a
challenging climb for someone who had been sick for six weeks.

Darsie survived. His body prevailed over the "ague," a Middle
English word for fever and/or chills. But what if he had not endured
illness or combat? One out of every sixty-five soldiers did not. In
the Federal forces, for every one soldier killed in battle, four died
of sickness, and more than twice as many soldiers died from disease as died from all other known causes. Additionally, the early
part of the war saw more incidents of disease, and newly formed
regiments suffered the most as hundreds of men began spending
twenty-four hours a day together. Bell Irvin Wiley writes in *The Life
of Billy Yank*:

> The peak of sickness each year usually came during July
> and August. In 1862 two peaks were experienced, the second
> coming in October, owing to a large influx of new troops.

Wiley also states that many soldiers stationed in Cairo drank
water out of the contaminated Ohio and Mississippi rivers. Perhaps
this had been the origin of Darsie's sickness. Whatever the cause,
my own existence owes itself to his tenacity.

By the time the 72nd Illinois left Columbus on November 20, its
ranks had been depleted nearly one-tenth by death and desertion.

glasses, "your ancestor was a Yankee?" I nodded.

"Well, ya come to the wrong place. None a them are buried here." She smiled and asked me to sit down. "My name is Mary Jane, these here are Nyleen and my cousin Sara. We're working on cataloging the names of everyone in the cemetery." Mary Jane's companions nodded politely while she continued talking.

"A Yankee ancestor, eh? Well, I've got a story to tell ya. My grandma used to live on the other side of the cemetery. Down the road, when the road was still here. She told me when she was eight years old the Yankees came through here. They came into her family's house, took out a barrel of sugar, threw it outside, then took out a barrel of flour, threw it out too. They cut them open. They were getting ready to run the horses through it all, see? One Union soldier saw my grandmother and asked her how old she was. She said, 'eight.' He said, 'I've got a little girl at home the same age. Put your apron out.' So, she did. He put some sugar in it and that was all they had for the rest of the winter."

I didn't say anything. Mary Jane's words didn't sound bitter, yet it was clear we carried very different legacies from the Civil War; my ancestor had been on the winning side.

Darsie wrote little about the College Hill/Oxford area, and Joseph Stockton not at all, but William Mohrmann related a story similar to Mary Jane's in his memoirs:

Oxford Miss. is quite an important looking place and we lay there for several days. On a foraging expedition from here I made a rapid march to get ahead and was first at a farm where the whole family was assembled on the porch, evidently in great fright at sight of the first Yankees. There were numbers of chicken and turkeys in evidence, but somehow I decided to go on to the next place, where I found nothing. On my return I found the slaughter of poultry in full blast and saw a cavalry man with drawn saber pursue a turkey in the bushes, but my shot settled my property rights in the gobbler, it also brought a shower of lefthanded blessings on my head from my spur wearing compatriot.

I asked Mary Jane if she knew where the Union troops had camped. "No, though some must have been in this churchyard. People estimate that maybe as many as 15,000 camped close to this building. The Union soldiers even stabled their horses inside the church. My great-great-grandfather, Goodloe Buford, wrote about the Yankee occupation. I'll send you a copy of what he had to say."

After returning to Oregon later that summer, I received Goodloe Buford's diary entry from Mary Jane. He hadn't minced words:

> *God in his wise but incrutable providence permitted the enemy to enter our quiet community with a force more than thirty thousand strong*
>
> *During the month they occupied College Church and its vacinity depriving the community the privilege long granted it of worshiping God in his own house*
>
> *No sooner were they in our midst than they exhibited the true characteristics of the Yankey. Many families when they left them were almost intirely destitute of necessary food raiment and bedding. They would enter dwellings at a late hour of the night, arouse the sleeping inmates and with the most profane blasphemous language demand money and search ladies trunks and private drawers and enraged at not finding nothing which they desired they would deface and destroy puncture with their sabers and bayonets. [T]hey not only robbed us of all property which they could appriate to their benefit but destroyed much which was of no use to themselves but which they knew was invaluable to us*

I realized then that up until meeting Mary Jane, my investigations had selectively ferreted out what I wanted to find: bravery, fortitude, selflessness. Those qualities, however, can be found in soldiers on both sides of a pointed weapon. So, too, can lawlessness, dishonesty, and greed. How much did I want to know? I had not expected to uncover evidence of a young farm boy from Illinois stealing and destroying. Darsie did not write about moral ambiguities. Or, he did so delicately. His January 13, 1863, entry read:

> *I was out foraging and stopped at a house 2 miles from*
> *camp—while there some of Co B came I got my chicken*
> *and left*

This abbreviated story reminded me of my father's fragmented anecdotes, and I thought once again about how war stories that lack details create falsehoods, making us believe that war is something it is not.

I wanted details *and* truth, a tricky combination when the people involved were gone and the writing only conveyed a part of the story. Maybe an eighteen-year-old farm boy from the Prairie Peninsula wouldn't ruin a family's supply of sugar and flour, or take their last chicken, but a soldier, after four months in the Union army, assimilated into a massive body of men that lived by other rules, probably would.

———

As the weeks went by, the men either survived the sickness, loneliness, and tediousness of becoming a soldier, or they didn't. What in Darsie's soul pushed him forward, I will never know. Pride, fear in being labeled a coward, belief in the cause, or perhaps a combination thereof. I could see, however, in his writing that as he began to feel better, he became more optimistic about his new life as a soldier. On January 16, in the snows of southwest Tennessee, Darsie wrote:

> *we were on guard and had to walk our beat to keep warm*
> *I had to walk and run the whole two hours to keep from*
> *freezing. Twas then I thought of home and its comforts but*
> *I was satisfied now since I was well we have to undergo*
> *many hardships but do not complain when our hour*
> *comes to stand we go at It as cheerfully as if it were a*
> *pleasant duty*

Then, on January 18, when the regiment arrived in Memphis he added:

We were marched to the navy yard and there releived the
17th Il. Co A was put on Guard immediately (as usual)
and it commenced raining and rained we had the best of
quarters there & we done like they do in Spain (let it rain)

As I walked in Darsie's footsteps, held his words in my hands, and looked for buildings and views that he might have seen, the chasm between us became clearer. Some sights were similar: the house in Geneseo where he had died; the streets of Annawan, which probably hadn't changed much; the earthworks at Columbus; and the church-yard at College Hill. Much, however, had been altered, or was gone: the tallgrass prairie, Darsie's home in Annawan, and the towns of Cairo and Columbus. I wondered if I would find anything along the trail that resonated Darsie's touch as much as his own words.

I also wondered what Darsie thought about the task that lay before him. He was a part of Ulysses Grant's Army of the Tennessee, which was trying in every possible way to capture Vicksburg, the last Confederate stronghold along the Mississippi River. Each day brought him closer to an enemy with real guns and bullets and a fierce desire to keep its own beliefs from disintegrating into dust. What did Darsie think about during the days he spent trying to catch up with the regiment? Or when he fell out of the ranks? Did he think, "I don't want to die. I don't want to kill anyone"? Or were these thoughts that only *I* had, based on my experience of watching cancer devour my father? Of knowing that I could be capable of my own darkness? Of feeling, at times, only a fragile connection to my own sanity? *You're holding on too tightly,* I had told myself many times, but I still clung—to what, though, I wasn't always sure.

One of Darsie's last entries from Memphis read:

Co A was clearing out whisky shops several of the soldiers
had been getting whisky of late notwith standing the order
of the Provost Marshal not to sell to Soldiers. we went and
found some whisky Shops and emptyed this Liquid out
and confiscated the Stoves

Had Darsie been a drinker? He never mentioned it in his diaries, but then he probably wouldn't. Anson Hemingway wrote in his diary in February that:

> *John Arlar [a Private in Company D] and several others were court martialed today for drunkenness and other disorderly acts.*

Joseph Stockton had described liquor and Memphis like this:

> *Memphis is at present a hard place, filled with soldiers. I regret to say many drunken officers are to be seen, while with the men it is almost too common to be mentioned. Orders came to destroy liquor wherever found and our regiment has destroyed a great many barrels. You might as well try to dam the Mississippi river as to keep the men from getting liquor.*

As I read about the whiskey in Memphis and the soldiers who couldn't resist its effect, I thought about my cousin's wedding in 1979, one of the many family events from my childhood where my father had humiliated me with his drunken behavior. Shortly after the ceremony concluded, the champagne bottles were uncorked and the drinking began. I didn't play bartender this time, but rather, sat in a corner, quiet. Two distant cousins, two and four years older than me, had come to Tacoma from Seattle. Daria and Stephanie intimidated me with their good looks, perfect clothes, and smooth demeanors. I felt gawky and uncertain next to them, wearing a dress I wasn't sure of and hair that I had curled and hair-sprayed myself. This really wasn't me, but since starting junior high I'd succumbed to the pressure of assimilation, and I didn't do it well. Being near those who did only increased my anxiety—and my father's drunkenness didn't help.

"Hey, I got to pee," Dad said at one point, weaving in between the guests, then crashing into a stereo speaker. Both fell over, my father with his arms and legs flailing. People sitting nearby tried to save their drinks in the scramble that followed. My face burned.

"Sorry, sorry ..." Dad slurred, trying to get up. I walked over and helped him. This wasn't an unusual occurrence and I wasn't surprised. My memory simply filed it away with the other times Dad had embarrassed or frightened me: driving drunk, flirting with waitresses, falling asleep during meals at restaurants. This was just the way things were.

As I now traveled farther south along the Mississippi River retracing Darsie's route, I thought about how each of us is made up of several personalities. We are by turns selfish individuals, animated storytellers, drunken fools, honest laborers, decorated citizens, and innocent casualties. My father was all of these people and more. But at the time I began my journey, only the drunk remained in my memory. The shadow from this one part of James Howell's life had intercepted all the others, leaving only images that were dark or vague. I couldn't remember the man I'd first known.

Chapter 10

River of Death

{United States Gunboat Marmora,
Coldwater River, Mr. S, Feb. 28, '63}

*The rubicon is crossed. Three and a half days of most
tedious, vexatious, bothersome, troublesome and dam-
aging steamboating has brought this expedition twenty
miles on its way, and disclosed to its view the end of the
now famous Yazoo Pass. A more execrable place was
never known. Should one propose to run a steamboat
to the moon, he would be considered equally sane by
those who had seen the Yazoo Pass before this expedition
forced a passage through it as the person who proposed
this movement.*

—From "The Yazoo Pass Expedition,"
Memphis Daily Bulletin, March 20, 1863

On February 3, 1863, Union Lieutenant Colonel James H. Wilson
set off a charge in the Mississippi levee downstream of Helena,
Arkansas. The levee here was one hundred feet wide and eighteen
feet high. The Mississippi River rose nine feet higher than the Yazoo
Pass, a short stretch of river outside the levee and flowing to the east.
Liberated liquid rushed through an eighty-foot breach in the levee
and Wilson reported, the "water [was] like nothing else I ever saw
except Niagara." The next day the breach had widened to 225 feet.
It took four days for the water to equalize such that the Union army
could begin the "Yazoo Pass expedition," Ulysses Grant's fifth attempt in two months to capture Vicksburg, Mississippi.

The Yazoo Pass connected the Mississippi to Moon Lake, a watery smile once part of the great river, and continued its course east until reaching the Coldwater River. The Coldwater then turned south, eventually becoming the Tallahatchie. At the town of Greenwood, the Yalobusha joined with the Tallahatchie to form the Yazoo River. The Yazoo River continued south for two hundred miles until returning to the Mississippi just above Vicksburg. Shaped like a magnolia leaf and an average of seventy miles wide, the land encompassed by the Mississippi on the west and the other rivers on the east formed the "Yazoo-Mississippi Delta," fertile earth consisting of a forty-foot layer of topsoil that would one day prove to be the richest in the country for growing cotton. In 1863, however, the Yazoo country was a formidable wilderness. Unpredictable flood-

THE SIEGE OF VICKSBURG, ITS APPROACHES
BY YAZOO PASS AND OTHER ROUTES
Courtesy of US Historical Archive

ing, labyrinthine waterways, disease, snakes, panthers, and wolves kept most humans from entering this dark land.

Lieutenant Commander Watson Smith led the first force, a ten-boat flotilla, from the Mississippi into the Yazoo Pass in mid-February 1863. It took two weeks to travel the distance of the pass—twelve miles from the Mississippi east to the Coldwater River. Overhanging cottonwood and sycamore trees grabbed at the ships. Branches ripped off smokestacks. Confederate soldiers and slaves had felled huge trees, some four feet thick and weighing forty tons, into the channel. On March 14, a second group, under Brigadier General Isaac F. Quinby, entered the pass, and on March 17 they reached the Coldwater River to begin the long journey south. Quinby's entourage included the transport ship *Empire City*, which carried the 72nd Illinois Infantry.

October 2000, northwest Mississippi

During a dry southern fall—a year after my first journey following Darsie's footsteps—I had made my way to Clarksdale, Mississippi, the birthplace of the blues and the nearest large city to the Yazoo Pass, an appellation that for me brought to mind a mountainous gap, not a slow-moving waterway. I was looking for John Ruskey, owner of Quapaw Canoe Company, who had agreed to help me reenact the 1863 Yazoo Pass expedition. In John's yard languished several aluminum canoes and one large, shiny wooden craft named *Ladybug*. A tunnel of vegetation led to the front door, where John, a man in his mid-thirties, met me wearing only a pair of shorts. He had wild, free-flowing hair that he tied back with a rubber band. He looked like a river himself, with a long, sinewy body punctuated by peaks and valleys of muscle.

Inside, away from the early-autumn heat, John brought out some Army Corps of Engineers maps of the Yazoo waters that he had purchased in Vicksburg. Not knowing anything about the rivers, I had told him only that I wanted to canoe from the Yazoo Pass to where Fort Pemberton, the Confederate stronghold where the Union fleet had been forced to turn back, had been.

"The Delta is in a drought," he said. "I looked at the Yazoo Pass from three road crossings and every one was dry. The only part that is accessible and floatable is a short distance out of Moon Lake. But it quickly dries up and stays dry until the confluence with the Coldwater. The Coldwater is flowing and entirely canoeable, but it's low, which means it's slow and will take some paddling and time."

My disappointment rose. I wanted to do the entire route. And the pass itself had captivated me the most. This segment had provided the greatest challenge to the Union forces. On Sunday, March 15, 1863, Darsie had written:

> We left Moon Lake at sunrise and entered the Pafs It was
> verry narrow and we had to go slow the pipes were let
> down on the deck and we had to keep low to escape the
> limbs that brushed we only went ten meter It was tedious

Along this waterway only a twilight world had existed beneath a dense canopy of intertwined branches. Here the river bent so sharply that hundreds of men had to haul the ships around with hawsers, which slowed the flotilla. This long-ago landscape was the wilderness of my childhood imagination. It was the "backwoods" where my friends and I played war, times a thousand. It was a landscape that I desperately wanted to see.

"My suggestion," continued John, "is to do two day trips: one from Helena to the mouth of the pass, and the second from Moon Lake east as far as there's water. Then we'll put in at the confluence of the pass and the Coldwater. From there it will be possible to canoe to Fort Pemberton."

This sounded good to me; I would just have to live with the reality of drought conditions. The next day we loaded up John's 1956 two-ton Chevy Apache truck with river gear for the float from Helena, Arkansas, downstream to the mouth of the Yazoo Pass. John wore shorts and a wide-brimmed hat. Around his neck dangled a piece of rope with a compass and lighter attached. As we drove to Helena, I read passages aloud from Darsie's journal.

"On March 9, 1863, he wrote: *reached Helena at 5 in the evening landed and got our supper on an Island.* The next day they moved downriver: *We are on a sand bar, 3 miles before Helena waiting for smaller transports to carry us through the Zoo Zoo Pass—we are in a poor place to camp no wood to cook with.*"

John looked thoughtful. "Does he write anything else about the sandbar?"

"No. The next entry is March 14, when the 72nd boarded the *Empire City* and turned into the mouth of the Yazoo Pass."

The sign on the levee wall at the Helena harbor read, "Long ago is not so far away." Before taking off, we sat in the canoe and discussed the 1863 expedition.

"I'm pretty sure this is where the Union ships were docking," John said. "It was the only harbor between Memphis and Vicksburg." He had cut out the pertinent sections of the Army Corps maps and set them in plastic sleeves in a three-ring binder. He pointed to a place on the map. "About four miles south of here is the Montezuma Bar, which I think is the sandbar your granddaddy camped on before traveling into the pass."

Water Pony, John's seventeen-foot aluminum canoe, sliced into the waves as we paddled into the center of the river. Though I knew the Mississippi could be dangerously unpredictable, I trusted John and his canoeing skills. I assumed he must have grown up in the Delta.

"No, actually I'm from New Mexico," he said. "But I've always wanted to travel the Mississippi. In the early '80s, a buddy and I built a raft in Minnesota and floated for five months. We learned all about the river, read lots of books, played music. We built a huge chessboard, four feet square, as the cover for our box of supplies, and played chess as we meandered downstream. It was in the middle of an involved chess game that we collided with a TVA [Tennessee Valley Authority] tower and had to make our way to shore. That was my first introduction to the state of Mississippi."

Hazy air on either side of the river obscured the land. October is the time of year for chopping cotton and burning fields. Cormorants and gulls flew over us and tugboats passed by toward destinations north and south. John said that grains and crops generally went downstream to New Orleans for global destinations. Oil went north to various places along the Mississippi and Ohio rivers. Workers waved to us cheerily from the tugboat *Grandma Girt*. Another tug, *Crimson Tide*, pushed thirty-six barges past us, creating hefty swells.

Four miles south of Helena, we landed on the sandbar. The glare of white sand blinded me when I took off my sunglasses. It was large—one-quarter mile wide and one mile long—partially due to the drought. It would have been a prime spot, in terms of size, for several regiments to camp, and as it was upriver from where James Wilson blew the dike, it would not have been flooded. John spread out a blanket, arranged our lunch, and then jumped into the water for a swim. Though I am fond of swimming in lakes and rivers, the muddy Mississippi did not appeal to me. I ate some fruit and crackers and then began exploring.

The nearest vegetation, shoreline strips of black and sandbar willows, waved quiet greetings. There were no large trees. Darsie had written that there wasn't any wood to cook with on the sandbar, and probably my view wasn't much different than his had been. From what I had seen in Cairo and Columbus, I knew the great river's energy and inclination toward change in the form of flooding, sucking land away on some shores and depositing it on others, allowed little time for trees to grow. I looked across the bar and imagined hundreds of dog tents, campfires smoking from the green wood of willows, and men moving about. Thanks to my reenacting experiences, begun that spring, I knew how to envision the camp down to the smallest detail.

John had his watercolors out and was painting the Helena Bridge when I returned to the canoe. I sat on the sand and thought about my father.

While transcribing Darsie's journals, I had opened up several U-Haul boxes in which I had packed away my father's possessions. Buried beneath baseball caps, scrapbooks, and the American flag that had draped his casket, I found four small notebooks. They were not journals of prose, but rather notes and ideas, including jokes, lists of books to read, and "Trips I would like to make."

On the "Trips" page, Dad had written, "Going down the Mississippi River by raft." He had made a table of necessary equipment, including a twelve-foot rowboat, a five-horsepower outboard motor, water cans, and fishing gear. Another entry in the little notebooks was, "Projects for year ending 21 July '56," one of which was, "Type up Grandpa's diary," which I assumed referred to Darsie's journals. While transcribing them I had wondered if my father had ever read them. If he had, then perhaps his desire to raft the Mississippi was a mission, much like my own, to know Darsie better.

The notebooks also told me my father had wanted to be a writer. He listed sixty-five ideas for brief articles, including "Mosquitoes: History and Geography," and "Prospecting in the Yukon." There were ideas for short historical essays on the Civil War, including one on "Lesser known battles and leaders." His fictional story ideas ranged from someone finding a time bomb on a pleasure yacht, to a soldier, captured by the Chinese, devising an escape route. Some of his topics were clearly autobiographical: "Older people having children," "Time I forgot to buckle my leg harness—first jump in five years," and "Answer of a father to his son when son says to father that he (father) hasn't ever done anything."

Reading these notebooks had provided me a glimmer of my father's complexity. He hadn't been just a man who drank too much and shouted, "Sieg Heil! In case we lose!" or a middle-aged father, or a person who liked animals. He had been a man of many layers. However, for each clue I found, several questions surfaced that would never be answered. What *were* his thoughts about having a third child at age forty-five? What *did* the father say to his son? Like searching the landscape for Darsie, I strove for completeness in putting together a narrative of my father's life. Not only did I want details, I wanted *all* the details. Only an entire story, it seemed, could ameliorate the effects of physical separation.

John and I packed up *Water Pony* and continued downstream to the mouth of the Yazoo Pass. He estimated the entrance to be east of Montezuma Island, approximately another four miles south of the sandbar. It is no longer possible to enter the pass from the Mississippi. Following the 1927 flood, the levee was built up to colossal proportions. We landed in a narrow channel and watched the hazy sun dropping for the night. The world had turned silver, where only that afternoon it had been a brilliant gold flecked with airborne soil. The memory of my father took me into a familiar melancholy as the Mississippi rolled by. I told John that the river, because of dams and levees and the efforts of humans to squeeze it into a predictable existence, seemed sad to me. He didn't agree.

"I don't think it feels bad. No matter what we humans do, it just keeps on being its river self. It creates its own levees anyway. It does great curves and bends and then cuts the bend off abruptly, causing its isolation. It destroys and renews itself all the time."

The next morning we drove to Moon Lake, five miles east of the river. On March 14, 1863, Darsie wrote in his journal:

> at 4 PM we went on board the Empire City and moved
> slowly in the direction of the Yazoo Pafs we entered it
> at dark and In ½ an hour we were in the quiet waters of
> Moon Lake.

John and I carried *Water Pony* down to the pass, east of Moon Lake. Sycamore and pecan trees leaned together over the channel. The pass's banks dropped sharply and I stepped carefully while carrying the canoe. John, barefoot, walked up and down the rocky, slippery surface as if without a care. In three days I had seen him wear shoes only once, when he had taken me to the opening of a cotton museum in Louisiana on my first night in Clarksdale.

We headed east. For the Union troops, entering the Yazoo Pass marked the beginning of a dreaded journey into an unknown, dark wilderness. Joseph Stockton, recently promoted now to major of the regiment, wrote:

> *The Yazoo is considered one of the most sickly regions in*
> *the South. Its name* [in Choctaw] *signifies 'River of Death,'*
> *but I trust the high state of water may relieve it of its*
> *unhealthy propensities and spare us our men.*

It was no longer a pristine stretch of river; oil and diesel gas floated on the water's surface, trash could be seen along the banks and in the water, and the vegetation in many places had been trampled. The water moved like cold syrup, and it wasn't long before we encountered our first set of "Confederate logs," as John called the trees that had fallen into the waterway. Though not the same tangled configurations that Darsie saw, they had a similar effect. We got out of *Water Pony* and John began hauling her over the mess. After beginning again, John and I let the canoe drift as we watched an American woodcock probe the Delta mud, its dark chocolate browns and lighter tans blending perfectly with the Yazoo vegetation.

"Of course, after they blew the hole in the Mississippi levee," John said, dipping his paddle noiselessly into the water, "this entire area was flooded. The pass was much wider."

Even so, the river tortured the Union fleet as it moved forward. Overhanging bald cypress and cottonwood trees swept smokestacks and men off the decks. Raccoons and snakes fell from the trees and had to be escorted off the boat into the murky water of the pass. After three long days, the *Empire City* and the rest of the entourage emerged into the north-south flowing Coldwater River.

Too quickly we ran out of water. John and I returned to Moon Lake and ate lunch on Texas Island, a piece of land shaped like the lake itself and ringed by "bald cypress people," a term I had ascribed to the bald cypress trees' "knees." My guidebook of eastern trees called these tubular projections "peculiar root growths," but I imagined faces and arms and expressions tucked into the wood's ridges. While we ate, John talked about rivers.

"In general, a river makes a turn for every seven lengths of its width. Rivers want to change course; it's just their way, otherwise they get agitated. They need a lot of room. A river like the Mississippi needs a huge amount of room. This is why the levee is built so far back from the river channel, anywhere from one to ten miles, to give it space to change course."

"Does the Mississippi flood often?"

"It doesn't flood here in the Delta unless the Ohio and Mississippi are at flood stage when they come together at Cairo, Illinois.

"When your granddaddy came through here," John continued, "the Delta was a wilderness. A few people lived here and there, but nobody had yet tapped its richness for growing cotton. Even up until 1910, about 75 percent of the region was still forested. The largest hardwood forest in North America, ten million acres, existed in the floodplain of the lower Mississippi. There are no native remnants left, only stands of second growth."

I had found the wilderness of my childhood dreams! Only I was a century too late.

———•——

The next day, on a cool but sunny October morning, John and I began the ten-day, 112-mile trip down the Coldwater River to Fort Pemberton. We had loaded *Water Pony* with three Rubbermaid tubs, a cooler, a Coleman stove, two coffeepots, a cast-iron Dutch oven, and four dry bags. Additionally, we had packed one milk crate with miscellaneous items, including a cut-open gallon milk jug with a candle inside, two pairs of rubber boots, and several gallon milk jugs filled with water. I felt like a member of the Corps of Discovery.

"We can go up the pass on this end as far as there's water if you'd like," said John. He pointed to a flat area on the north side of the pass. We paddled over and tied up the canoe. On March 17, 1863, Darsie had written:

> started at daylight and reache cold water. we stopped at
> the mouth of the Pafs there to take the horses off the boat
> they needed exercise

"This seems like a possibility for where the troops camped before traveling down the Coldwater," John mused. We walked around in the tangled Delta vegetation before climbing back in *Water Pony* and pointing her bow south.

The Coldwater, with a riverbed twice as wide, looked very different from the tight world of the Yazoo Pass. Gone were the numerous bald cypress trees, which prefer stagnant or very slow waters. The shoreline vegetation now consisted of two distinct levels: a midcanopy layer of species such as Osage orange and willow and an upper layer of sycamores and pecans. Yellow and green grasses bordered the water's edge. John and I stroked the vitreous surface with our paddles and began the "2000 Yazoo Pass Expedition."

That evening, as we paddled around a sharp turn, looking for a suitable sandbar for the night, a young white-tailed buck showed itself briefly, then dashed through the forest heading downstream. We kept on and found the deer waiting for us. Again it ran. Again it waited until we caught up. It looked at us and woofed.

"I think it must be playing with us," John said quietly. "It's clearly not trying to get away or even hide itself." Our first camp, discovered just downstream of this encounter, became "Buck Snort Bend."

After getting set up and exploring the hardwood forest around our camp, I examined the Coldwater, which had a thin layer of vegetative scum covering the muddy water. John had already jumped in and was swimming about like an otter.

"How is it?" I yelled.

"Great! It's a little tough to get any purchase, the bottom is so muddy, but the water is perfect." Stuffing my desire for a crystal clear river, I took off my clothes and jumped in. He was right. Perfect.

Later, John built a fire and made a meal of fried potatoes and onions, corn baked in the coals, and green salad. We listened to a barred owl's "who-cooks-for-you" hoot and two groups of coyotes barking. Darsie, too, had most likely heard owls from the river, but probably not coyotes. These small canids would not have been as numerous in 1863 as in 2000. There was less open space then, and resident panthers and wolves would have kept the coyotes' numbers in check.

The next day we swam again in the Coldwater. With the slow current, I could stand in one place and witness the riverine world, almost as if I didn't exist. My feet settled into the silky Delta mud and released air bubbles entangled in the river bottom. They darted up my legs and stomach until finding freedom, and destruction, at the water's surface. I closed my eyes and, upon opening them, saw a painted turtle's head above the surface five feet from me. A few seconds passed and a second turtle emerged between us. We shared the cool water and warm sun for a couple of minutes, then the turtles vanished.

Just before sundown John and I hit the Pompey Ditch, a diversion that siphoned off much of the Coldwater's volume at its headwaters. Here we experienced our first strongly flowing water. The ecosystem changed abruptly. Gone were the sandbars, thus our convenient camp spots, and the river now looked very channelized—with steep, uniform banks. Neither one of us wanted to haul the gear up the bank so we paddled on in the twilight, looking for some anomaly in the homogenous shoreline. Eventually we arrived at a narrow strip of level land next to the water that had most likely resulted from the bank giving way to gravity.

In the ensuing days, John and I began making better time, though we were still traveling slower than the 1863 expedition. While I had come on the river to decelerate my perception of time, the Union army, by contrast, had been working against the clock. John and I lingered and explored the bayous or whatever happened to catch our eye; the Union boys had had no interest in exploration. We were on the water for the journey; they, to reach a destination.

The Coldwater widened. Sycamores slanted at forty-five-degree angles or more into the channel. Limbs resembling trees grew straight up from these. Some of the bigger trees had let go of the bank, and in the water provided a catchment for everything from plastic containers, tires, and basketballs to branches, logs, and one dead deer. One turtle lay atop a pile of garbage and a young raccoon walked across a log, the upstream side of which had caught a cooler, a five-gallon plastic bucket, pieces of fishing line and rope, and cans and bottles. The ugliness of the present tainted my fantasy of the past. It seemed no matter where I went, geographically or mentally, the landscape was an amalgamation of the pristine and the polluted, the mysterious and the understandable, the perfect and the twisted.

One evening John suggested we do some night paddling. I leaned back against a dry bag with my feet up on the bow and let him worry about navigating us through the twilight. The Coldwater slipped away below. Crickets chirped, and birds, chipmunks, and squirrels scurried in the forest, making so much racket that I often thought they were deer. A group of wood ducks and a great blue heron accompanied us, ever moving downstream in relation to our position. The yellows of a dusky sky gave way to a pink, then purple, then blue-black, and finally a black sky. Stars appeared and, as the light vanished, I wondered how we would avoid logs and debris jams above and below the water's surface.

"Smooth water will look different from water surrounding protrusions and pileups," John told me. "It will appear lighter, whereas water around obstacles will look darker and more textured." He also pulled out a large Maglite to occasionally scan the river ahead. Just east of the town of Lambert, Mississippi, we came to a stretch of river devoid of vegetation on its west bank. There in the occidental sky hung a sliver of the new moon and the planet Venus.

After we traveled thirty-five miles, the Coldwater became the Tallahatchie River. It widened and deepened as we went farther south. These factors slowed our progress, but they had been a joy to the 1863 expedition. William Mohrmann had written in his memoirs:

> *The progress of the steamers was very slow, the branches of the trees destroyed bit by bit the flimsy upper works and until we came into the more capacious Tallahatchie, it was all very tedious.*

That night we arrived at the confluence where the Panola Quitman Floodway and Tillatoba Creek enter the Tallahatchie. With only the sliver of moon, we could see little, but heard clearly the sound of agitated water. We maneuvered carefully into the current, avoiding the churning water, and on the far side found a wide-open sandbar. Unfortunately, it was collapsing—though hopefully, we thought, not fast enough to wash us away in one night. We tied the canoe parallel with the bank to give it some protection and John poked four willow branches into the sand perpendicular to *Water Pony*.

"At least we'll know by morning just how concerned we should be," he said.

John started a fire and lit a candle inside the plastic milk jug for our kitchen light. Tonight's dinner would be a salad of lettuce, tomato, cucumber, onion, carrot, and celery, with olive oil, cumin, oregano, and lemon juice. My body felt good—inside from the healthy food, and outside from living in the open air.

As we chopped vegetables, I asked John if he ever wished he were part of an earlier time.

"Not really, though I wouldn't mind having been in America before the Europeans came, but I like things the way they are. There are a lot of beautiful places in the world to see. And, it might not happen in our lifetime, but I think the world is on the verge of some new era. Something, somewhere has to give. It's true humans have precipitated a lot of it, but we're a part of the environment too, and a new time is coming on, just like the ice age or other eras. I think that's pretty exciting."

The next morning I got up and examined the willow branches. One had sailed down the river and a second was poised to go. I looked north of camp where we had crossed the river. Three linear bodies of water joined forces and, downstream in the middle of their combined current, was a small tangle of river wood, the cause of the rippling noise. Darsie had seen only two waterways when he came through—the Tallahatchie River, the farthest west and the one we both had traveled down, and Tillatoba Creek, flowing from the east. The Panola Quitman Floodway in the middle had not existed in 1863.

As we packed up and left "Disappearing Sandbar" camp, I thought of John's positive outlook. He saw what was *there*. I usually saw what was *missing*. Could this change? What did I still have? Darsie's journals, of course. Dad's notebooks. In cleaning out my parents' home, I had also found cassette tape recordings of parties my parents had given and "voice letters" we'd sent each other over the years. Photos and old video reels documented our life in the 1970s. I had paid little attention to most of this ephemera because I'd not wanted to fan my guilt over not being able to save my father's life, nor my regret at what was left unsaid during the three months when cancer was taking him away from me.

Yet, not remembering began to feel like the time I woke up hunched over in a corner of a dark room after blacking out from drinking too much. For those first few seconds, I had no idea who, or where, I was. Living in a present without a past seemed just as untethered.

As we floated past Glendora, Mississippi, and began a stretch of the Tallahatchie that flowed east, the sky darkened. Chipmunks quit scuffling, the wood ducks and blue herons took cover, and the minutes began moving slowly, like a small child carrying an egg on a spoon. We saw only four turtles; there was not much sense in basking in this weather. One beaver popped its head up beside the canoe, like a harbor seal, and a coot stood on a log as if waiting for a water taxi.

Below Phillips' Cutoff, a straightaway built in 1964 that substituted two miles of uniform river travel for almost twelve on the serpentine channel of old, we landed at "Sycamore Camp." We could find no sandbars, and so, for the first time, had to pull all of our gear up the steep banks to relatively flat ground beneath a huge sycamore. I set up my tent, which fit snugly within the tight world of the Delta forest. John built a fire under the motherly tree. Its enormous leaves, five-lobed with large teeth along the edges, resembled dinner plates.

That night a storm hit. Rain battered the tent. The wind couldn't seem to make up its mind which way to go, so it went in every direction at once. Through the tumult, I heard the thud of a large branch or tree striking the ground not far away. Only then did I begin to worry about dead branches or leaning trees, and I tried not to think about what Joseph Stockton had written on March 29, 1863, from the 72nd's camp near Fort Pemberton:

> Last night we had a fearful storm of wind, which played
> havoc with the old trees and branches. They were blown
> about in every direction and our lives were in constant
> danger from falling branches and trunks of trees. In Ross's
> Division, just adjoining ours, there were five men killed
> by trees falling on them. I have never passed through a
> more trying or frightful scene. There was no chance of
> getting away, for one place was as bad as another. The rain
> poured in torrents, so we were in a bad plight.

The wind still blew in the morning, but a shaft of sunlight had penetrated the cloudy sky, illuminating the river in front of our camp, and the rain had stopped. I stepped out of my tent, dry as a tumbleweed, and looked up. Sure enough, not twenty feet above me hung a dead branch, four or five inches in diameter and about ten feet long.

After breakfast we shoved off in *Water Pony*. Soon the first in a series of downpours arrived. Raindrops left elongated streaks down my face and neck, around my eyes, nose, and mouth. The wind blew dried and curled leaves off of tree branches. Each species had a different trajectory. Long, thin ones looked missile-like, spinning fast and zooming toward the water at high speed. Others, like those from oak trees, rocked back and forth like swings, descending with grace. The giant sycamore leaves formed a cup shape, gyrating downward like a funnel.

Six miles upstream of Fort Pemberton we settled in at "Willow Camp." An herbaceous layer of grass and sapling willows covered most of the sand on this bar. John took the canoe across the river to collect firewood and I watched the sun drop in the sky behind him. The rain had stopped late in the afternoon. My towel lay sprawled on the willows to dry, along with a wet T-shirt and a soaked pair of jeans.

I swam in the Tallahatchie, the chocolate water no longer bothering me. The river closed around my body, spilling through the strands of my hair and between my toes and fingers, and as I dove down, water of a thousand ages filled my ears and nose. I opened my eyes in the murkiness, but could see nothing.

As I dried off and watched the Tallahatchie continuing its journey south, I decided that if a river could think, it would ponder not where it had been, but only where it was going. I remembered the entry Darsie had made toward the end of his second journal, on April 8, 1865. It was the day before the Civil War officially ended, and perhaps he was thinking about the arbitrary nature of experience and where he had been and where he was going. He wrote:

Now why am I keeping a journal? I skarcly know why.
not for myself I'm sure: for God knows if I am ever spared
to return home I shall only be to glad to forget all of the

scenes and hardships of The Three yrs is it for anyone else?
is there any one who would spend time in looking over it?
A Glance at it would show him or her it is not interesting
enough to peruse.

As John and I made dinner in silence, my head overflowed with
thoughts of my father, my great-great-grandfather, and myself, and of
everything that linked us to each other. *My* life, as I uncovered the war
experiences of these men in my family, began to fall into context.

Our last night on the river we camped one mile downstream of
Fort Pemberton. The day before, John and I had walked the grounds
where the Confederate army had stopped the Union flotilla. Several
hundred yards upstream from where the Tallahatchie and the Yazoo
rivers converge, the Tallahatchie, flowing east, bypasses the Yazoo,
flowing west, forming a narrow neck of land. In 1863, this "island"
was only approachable by water. Confederate Major General William W. Loring directed his troops to construct fortifications here
made of sandbags and cotton bales. They installed thirteen cannons
atop the earthworks. Loring christened the site Fort Pemberton, after his commanding officer.

For eleven days, after Isaac Quinby's brigade came within sight
of Fort Pemberton, the 72nd Illinois and other regiments skirmished
with the Confederate defenders. The Southerners had scuttled a
captured Union steamer, *Star of the West*, to the bottom of the Tallahatchie, and the Northern troops could not get around it. Additionally, they could not take the fort on foot because of the flooded
landscape. Eventually orders arrived to withdraw back to Helena,
Arkansas. Darsie wrote on April 6, 1863:

on Board at daylight and off up the river I was Detailed to
load the Boats last night worked all night Co A went on the
Ada Hines-we go up the Pafs much faster than we went down.

After nearly 140 years, Fort Pemberton had melted into the
earth, the only evidence of its existence being a rise near the riverbanks where the cotton bales had been stacked. A soft breeze sent

ocher needles from the bald cypress trees cascading to the ground. I could sense tendrils of the past all around me, but no matter how hard I tried to see them, they remained invisible.

———•——

The next morning, the sky still rained as we paddled *Water Pony* to the take-out point.

"Look at the bare ground on the river banks," said John. "You don't see any water runoff at all. The soil is so absorbent it takes a huge amount of rainfall before you see the effects of a rainstorm."

The land indeed seemed unaffected by the pounding action of the water. "The Mississippi doesn't flood here in the Delta unless the Ohio and Mississippi are at flood stage when they come together at Cairo, Illinois," John had told me. Perhaps humans weren't so different from the Delta soil or the lower waters of a river, I thought. Events and memories could gather on the landscape of a life, and much could be absorbed before the effects were noticeable. Grief could also accumulate for years, through several individuals' lives, before flooding the narrow confines of one person's existence.

———•——

April 9 [1863]. *The Yazoo Pass expedition has ended and boats all back. Our return was monotonous, as we all felt dispirited at our failure. There was great rejoicing as we once more entered the Mississippi River, the men cheering, and a salute from the battery on board our boat. During the trip we buried two of our regiment who died from sickness. Poor fellows, no headstones left to mark their last resting place. The transports are complete wrecks and it is wonderful how they got back.*

April 10. Disembarked at our old camping ground below Helena on the sand ridge.

—*Major Joseph Stockton*

———•——

cover of the hill waiting
for the signal from the
Colonel of the 4th M. we were
then ordered to move to the
PART II: me in sight
of the rebel works they poured
in a ___ musketry in
our ___ A was killed
in the first fire, here Sept.
Harding was shot he never
spoke after he was hit he

Battles

battle, *noun*
1. armed fighting; combat or war
2. any fight or fighting; conflict;
   struggle

lived for an hour perhaps
but ___ ___ ___ we
any at ___ we were then order
-ed to move off to the right
left and there we were in
range of our own and the
enemies Batteries here we lost
the most men. Co B had 5
men killed by a shell
we were ordered to charge
the 95th would not move

Second Lieutenant James Howell and Everett Snodgrass,
Geneseo, Illinois, 1943

Private Bertram Howell
Willamette Mission, Oregon, 2002

Chapter 11

The Vicksburg Charges

[Monday, May 18, 1863, Big Black River, Mississippi]

*we marched on towards Vicksburgh. we reach there
on outside at dark. we had hard marching the dust was
flying so thick we could not see each other, and the day
was verry warm we had no water either we form a line
and lay on our arms we had nothing to eat and could
kindle no fire to get our supper*

—From the journal of Private Darsie Heath,
72nd Illinois Infantry, Company A

Taking Vicksburg from the north, either overland or by the river system, wasn't working for Ulysses Grant. Confederate cannons, placed in and around the city, gazed down on the Mississippi River like vultures. Earthworks with men and guns guarded against attacks from the east. Vicksburg seemed impenetrable. Two more plans after the Yazoo Pass expedition also failed, but Grant never gave up. On April 12, 1863, the 72nd Illinois left the sandbar below Helena, Arkansas, and headed south on the Mississippi River to Milliken's Bend, a Union camp fifteen air miles north of Vicksburg. Grant's latest idea was to get his troops south of Vicksburg on the Louisiana shore, run a flotilla of gunboats and transport ships through the gauntlet of Confederate firepower on the hill city, and, presuming the ships survived, ferry his men, artillery, and provisions across the Mississippi. The Union army would proceed northeast toward Jackson, Mississippi, and then west to Vicksburg. Few on Grant's staff believed that such an undertaking would be successful. They were wrong.

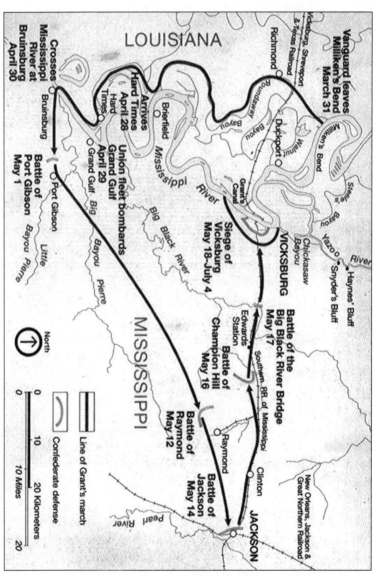

THE VICKSBURG CAMPAIGN

Courtesy of Vicksburg National Military Park

On April 27, Darsie's regiment was assigned to Brigadier General Thomas Ransom's brigade of the 17th Army Corps. They were placed at the rear of the column and, for this reason, arrived late to the ensuing battles.

Of the five major battles of the Vicksburg campaign, the Battle of Champion Hill, twenty-five miles east of Vicksburg, was the most crucial, involving 29,000 Union soldiers and 20,000 Confederates. After one long day of bloodshed, the Southern troops fell back toward Vicksburg with 3,800 casualties. Grant's army lost 2,400. The 72nd Illinois did not arrive at Champion Hill until sometime late in the afternoon when the last of the Confederates were pulling out. Darsie wrote in his journal on May 16:

> [We] *reach champion hill at dark We are to late to be in the fight our troops had whipped the rebs and took 2000 prisoners. We pass the Battle field and encamp for the night this was the first battle field I had ever seen the Hill was covered with dead horses and mules were lying all alon the road the wounded were crying for help. the ambulances were busy but could not get them away fast enough.*

Other men in the regiment were also impressed. Anson Hemingway wrote, "It was a hard fight. There is a great many wounded and killed on both sides." John Avey, of Company C, told his son in a letter, "I saw hundreds of the rebels laying shot through the head on the field."

Many of the soldiers of the 72nd seemed to remember their experience at Champion Hill differently. Darsie wrote that they passed the battlefield before setting up camp. By contrast, Joseph Stockton remembered, "We were pushed forward to the front and slept on the field of battle. Dead rebels and Union soldiers were lying all around us."

According to Anson Hemingway, "We went about 2 miles beyond the battlefield and camped for the night." William Mohrmann wrote that the 72nd followed the Confederates until late into the night and then bedded down somewhere.

As I read these different versions of the same event, it struck me how deceptive memory can be. Not only do we each view an occurrence differently as it transpires, but in retrospect, that same experience can warp and bubble to where certain aspects are dropped or enhanced based upon our own attitudes. We see what we want to see. We forget what we want to forget.

Wherever the 72nd stayed that night, the dead and the living began to mingle. William Mohrmann described "a peculiar experience" had by Company A's First Sergeant Oliver Rice. Apparently, Rice had not kept up with the regiment and was forced to bed down along the road without his unit. He noticed another man asleep and lay next to him, sharing his blanket. In the morning, Rice found he had slept next to a dead Confederate.

Two days later on May 18, after a final engagement at the Big Black River, Ransom's brigade came to the eastern outskirts of Vicksburg. It was a miserable march. With wagons, horses, and men stirring up the ground in front of them, the 72nd slogged through ankle-deep dust in scorching temperatures, with little to eat or drink. When they finally came within a mile of Vicksburg's defenses, it was dusk. The 72nd, ordered out as advance guard, formed a line of battle and lay on their arms all night. Fortunately, their part of the offensive line extended near a residence, owned by the Shirley family. There some of the boys found water, bacon, and cornmeal. Darsie, however, wrote that he had nothing to eat and there was no wood with which to make a fire.

It must have been a very long night.

⎯⎯•⎯⎯

The next morning, skirmishing with the enemy began early. The land between the opposing armies was steep, undulating ground, abundant with ravines and deep gullies. Though it was only a mile or less line-of-sight distance to the Confederate works, the 72nd and the other regiments of Ransom's brigade would have to descend into the North Fork of Glass Bayou, then come up the other side. The hillsides around Glass Bayou had been cleared for cultivation long before. Walking the hillsides would have been a simple, albeit

dangerous, matter. The bayou itself, however, was a tangled nightmare of river cane and trees the Confederates had felled. Major Joseph Stockton was ordered to reconnoiter a path to the brigade to
the north. In *War Diary*, he wrote:

> *I never had such work in all my life, climbing up and down
> ravines, my horse at one time getting so tangled that I was
> afraid I would have to leave him—through cane, over and
> under fallen trees.*

Apparently, Stockton had no luck finding a connection, though
he did locate two batteries of the Chicago Light Artillery. On the
morning of May 19, Ransom's brigade, including the 11th, 72nd, and
95th Illinois, and the 14th and 17th Wisconsin, stood alone on a ridge
between the forks of the bayou.

By 2:00 p.m. the brigade had left the ridge and positioned itself
at the base of the hill leading up to where the Confederate 37th and
38th Mississippi regiments sat waiting for their attackers. The Union
men advanced up the steep, open hill. That morning Ulysses Grant
had been propelled forward by two thoughts. One, he felt the Confederates were too demoralized by their succession of recent defeats
to offer much resistance. And two, he believed his men were so high
on success that they would never settle into siege operations without a good, strong fight, which is precisely what they got.

Darsie wrote that as they moved up the hill and across the open
ground, they drew the fire of the entire enemy line, including a
battery on their left that shot railroad iron at them. Perhaps Ransom's brigade got hit so hard because they had jumped the gun, so
to speak. According to Warren E. Grabau in *Ninety-Eight Days: A
Geographer's View of the Vicksburg Campaign*, two of the regiments
(he doesn't say which) mistook deployment orders for orders to attack. Joseph Stockton wrote that twenty men from the 72nd were
killed or wounded in the first five minutes. Four regiments got just
beyond the North Fork of Glass Bayou before taking cover in ravines. The 95th Illinois made it to within one hundred yards of the
Rebel works. The 72nd made it out of the ravine and partway up the

other side, stopped by Confederate abatis, a fortification of sharp-ened branches and trees pointing outward. They could not move forward. They could not go back. Darsie and his comrades waited until dark, then returned to the Union ridgetop. Nobody from his company died on May 19.

After this assault, which failed at every location along the Union line, Grant was ready to settle in for a siege—however, his staff felt otherwise. They contended that May 19 had been poorly organized. They said that many regiments had not been fully engaged in the attack. If these details were attended to, they claimed, then victory could be had. Grant eventually agreed.

Where Ransom's brigade had stood alone on May 19, by May 22 it was tied into Sherman's corps to the north. There was still a gap to the south where the north and south forks of Glass Bayou came together, but Major General John Logan's division had deployed just south of the bayou near the Jackson Road. At least now there were more men to throw at the Confederates. At least now the Confederates' fire would be more diffuse.

For three days, the Union army prepared. Officers strategized by day and organized regiments into position. At night, the men dug rifle pits on the ground that had been a slaughter field. Both sides skirmished during the sweltering May days, and every Union soldier knew that they would soon attack the same formidable Confederate defenses.

I think experiencing battle for the first time must be one chal-lenge, and returning to it another challenge altogether. Stephen Ambrose writes about the difference between green and veteran soldiers in his best-selling book *D-Day, June 6, 1944: The Climactic Battle of World War II*:

> *For a direct frontal assault on a prepared enemy position,*
> *men who have not seen what a bullet or a land mine or*
> *an exploding mortar round can do to a human body*
> *are preferable to men who have seen the carnage. Men*
> *in their late teens or early twenties have a feeling of*
> *invulnerability.*

A man may return to combat, but he will never again feel the safety of conjured immortality. As my father had told me weeks before his death, "A soldier is always ready to die."

At least one man in the 72nd was afraid *before* the first battle. William Mohrmann wrote before the May 19 charge:

> *A cold ague shook me, my teeth chattered and I began to*
> *be seriously afraid, that I would be afraid.*

For many, only the fear of being called a coward kept them moving forward.

At dusk on May 21, several officers of the 72nd Illinois sat around a campfire eating their hardtack ration—a biscuit made from flour, water, and salt—and drinking coffee. Private David Temple, a bugler from Company K, ate his supper nearby. As he raised his spoon to his mouth, he suddenly fell over dead. A bullet had pierced Temple's heart and killed him instantly. Nobody could determine the direction of the sharpshooter. The men buried Temple that night, performing a soldier's service and singing a hymn. Joseph Stockton wrote, "Who knows who may be living tomorrow night."

On May 22, the 72nd Illinois numbered four hundred, less than half their original number nine months previously. In Darsie's company, the original ninety-three had dropped to sixty-nine. And of the four remaining boys from Toulon, only two—Darsie and his friend Scepter T. Harding—were now poised for the second Vicksburg charge. Jake Galley had stayed behind sick just after the 72nd crossed the Mississippi in early May. Robert Holmes had also been left, perhaps for the same reason.

Darsie and Scepter had known each other for only four years when they fought together at Vicksburg. On May 22, Darsie's nineteenth birthday was less than a month away. Scepter was twenty-two.

At 10:00 a.m., the 72nd Illinois marched in two ranks down to the North Fork and then began climbing up the other side, with Darsie's company in the advance. Grant's plan was to throw everything he had at John Pemberton's Confederate forces. He knew his troops couldn't move quickly over the rough terrain, so his plan was to execute relentless pressure. On the 72nd's right walked the men of the 95th Illinois, and on their left, the 1st Minnesota Light Artillery. The men slithered over, under, between, and around the felled trees. The sun soaked the soldiers in their wool uniforms. According to Joseph Stockton, when they came within thirty yards of the Confederate works, creeping on hands and knees, the Rebels filled the air with musket fire. Four men in Company A were hit. Two of them, including Private Scepter T. Harding, were killed instantly. The other two died that night. They were, as Joseph Stockton wrote, "four as good men as ever drew breath."

After some time, the order to resume the advance came. The Confederates met them with a roar from their guns. The soldiers in blue dropped like stacked dominoes touched off by the flick of a finger. Within twenty minutes, the 72nd lost between 110 and 130 men according to various accounts, one-quarter of the regiment. But they had almost made it to the Confederate works. Joseph Stockton wrote:

> *Our colors were planted about fifteen feet from the ditch* [in front of the earthworks], *but we could not go forward, the fire was too severe, men could not live; we laid down and only the wounded fell back.*

Both Stockton and Darsie said that shots from their own batteries hailed down upon them as well. General Ransom tried to rally his men to keep on. No one moved. At last, he ordered them to fall back to the ravine in good order under the protective fire of the reserve regiments. The survivors carried the wounded out. They left the dead, including Scepter, a man with three younger siblings and middle-aged parents who worked the family farm back in Toulon. For the next three days these dead men lay where they had fallen, bloating and turning black with the gases of decomposition. Grant would not initiate a cease-fire to bury his men, but Pemberton finally did.

At midnight on the twenty-third, the 72nd was ordered back to its camp. There would be no more direct attacks after this; the Union forces would now settle in for a siege of the city. I have imagined Darsie that night writing by the campfire, or perhaps by the light of a candle stuck into the round part of his bayonet, stabbed into the earth. Darsie's face is like obsidian from the black powder, his hair matted against his head from sweat, his mind filled with the cacophony of all that he'd witnessed. Whatever his true thoughts and feelings, he wrote only briefly of the day's events:

> *we then came in sight of the rebel works they poured in a*
> *storm of musketry in our ranks. four of Co A was killed in*
> *the first fire. here Septer Harding was shot he never spoke*
> *after he was hit he lived for an hour perhaps but I think*
> *he did not suffer any at all We were then ordered to move*
> *off to the left and there we were in range of our own and*
> *the enemies Batteries. here we lost the most men. Co B*
> *had 5 men killid by a shell we were ordered to charge.*

Darsie didn't write about the dead bodies, the blood, the loss, the futility, or the adrenaline. He didn't write about his fear and that which was most difficult for him. Fortunately for me, however, someone else did.

Sometime during the May 22 attack, Corporal William Mohrmann had helped carry Corporal Thomas Russell, shot through the bowels, back down the hill to where the stretcher bearers awaited. Later Mohrmann would write:

> *When I resumed my place as file-closer Private Heath,*
> *being badly demoralized commenced to crawfish down*
> *hill and after a warning order I crawled on top of him and*
> *boxed his ears soundly and he got over his nervousness.*

Some days later, during the Union army's ensuing siege of Vicksburg, a shakeup in the officers of Company A occurred, including Corporal Mohrmann being promoted to second lieutenant. After explaining these changes in his memoirs, Mohrmann wrote:

> *The funny feature in the whole business to me was that the*
> *man whose ears I cuffed during the charge voted for me to*
> *be his officer.*

November 2000, Vicksburg, Mississippi

The 1,858-acre Vicksburg National Military Park, established in 1899, is shaped like a thick number seven. Union Avenue winds down the seven's eastern and northern outside edges; Confederate Avenue snakes along the inner, western boundary. The avenues follow the placement of the defenders and attackers of the city. The North Fork of Glass Bayou flows south in approximately the center of the seven.

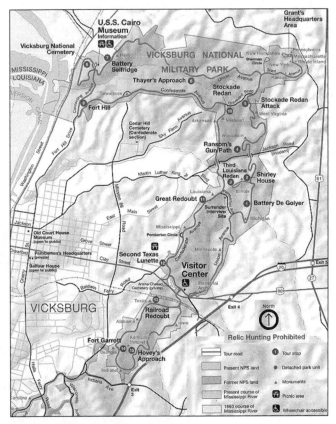

VICKSBURG NATIONAL MILITARY PARK

Courtesy of Vicksburg National Military Park

Standing on what had been the Union-held ridge above the North Fork, I faced a tangled jungle of trees and shrubs. In 1863, the men could see across to the opposite slope. Now, vines hung like snakes from one-hundred-foot magnolias and maples. A faint path stretched into the forest before me, and I would use it to guide me along the 72nd's route. It was only a mile straight across the drainage to where the Confederate infantry, the 37th and 38th Mississippi regiments, had waited for the Union attack.

In my backpack, I carried copies of Darsie's journals, a quart of water, food, and a map of the park. I found the going much easier than anticipated, as animal trails and openings in the lush southern forest made for a quick hike to the bottom. I skidded upon the soft, loess soil, through the ferns and over the summer's leavings. Low water in the North Fork made the crossing simple, but the stream snaked back on itself. A small "island" had been formed between these meanderings, and I stopped for lunch on this teardrop of earth.

A cool breeze blew along the creek. Star-shaped sweet gum leaves above me caused the autumn sunlight to filter down to the earth in a kaleidoscope of colors and shapes. Carolina chickadees and red-breasted nuthatches called from the trees. A winter wren scuffled in the dried leaves next to me. I thought of the nightmare of human carnage the land had witnessed. Another 72nd Illinois descendent had recently shared with me a story that his great-grandfather had told him about the first charge.

"My great-grandfather looked over to his buddy, whose head had just been decapitated," Dick Peterson told me. "He claimed he watched the head bouncing back down into the bottom of the ravine. I was ten years old when I heard this story and my grandmother—his daughter—used to scream at him for telling us these horror stories. During that charge, he received a bullet in his shin. When he heard the surgeons wanted to amputate, he got up from the hospital table and left. Nobody was going to take his leg."

Dick's great-grandfather was William Metzger, a private and drummer boy from Company E who lived until 1940, when he died at the age of ninety-four. Surprisingly, gangrene never set in from the wound and Billie Metzger often showed his great-grandchildren the lump in his shin where the bullet remained the rest of his life. While the birds called around me, I took out Darsie's journal and read again about the events of May 1863. On the twenty-third, the day after Scepter and so many others had been killed, he wrote:

> *our skirmishers are still firing and the Batteries are*
> *playing away*

And on May 24:

> *at ten AM we move to a ravine further to the left there*
> *is large detailes to dig rifle pitts and build forts. we*
> *are making roads through all the ravines and planting*
> *batteries evry day Jake Galley and R Holmes came to the*
> *regiment today*

I walked upstream along the North Fork. A well-worn Boy Scout trail followed the water's edge. River cane towered above me. Suddenly, a rusted blue marker, disappearing into the fabric of the forest, came into view. Pushing back the branches of long, narrow leaves obscuring the sign, I read:

U.S.

RANSOM'S APPROACH

BEGINNING OF RANSOM'S APPROACH

TO THE CONFEDERATE WORK IN HIS

FRONT. WORK ON IT COMMENCED

ABOUT JUNE 15, 1863

Markers such as this one cover the ground of the national military park. They help guide people like me traveling over 140-year-old footsteps. It seemed likely, however, given its location, that few had ever read this one.

A narrow, dry drainage led me up the other side of the North Fork of Glass Bayou. Somewhere on this slope, Darsie's courage had failed him. His fear had overwhelmed him and he had panicked.

As I crawled under vegetation, thick in this draw, I wondered about that fear. It's easy to understand being afraid of dying, but maybe Darsie's agitation wasn't only about a fear of death. Maybe it was about a fear of killing. I remembered what I'd learned about Civil War soldiers shooting above heads and ramming bullet after bullet down their barrels, but never firing. We learn from a young age not to hurt others. Even weeks of training, the noblest cause, or saving one's own life probably can't easily undo that early lesson.

South of Glass Bayou, along Union Avenue, is the Illinois State Memorial, one of thirty such monuments dedicated to the Northern and Southern states with regiments that fought at Vicksburg. Modeled after the Roman Pantheon, with forty-seven steps leading up to it—one for each day of the siege—the structure's entrance is decorated with six pillars, which support a portico and bronze eagle. Inside the domed building there are sixty bronze tablets that list the 36,000 Illinois men who fought at Vicksburg. Each tablet corresponds to an individual regiment. The backgrounds of the plaques have worn black; the only bronze color remaining belongs to the names of the men who served. "Heath, James D." is listed at the top of the third column of privates of "Company A, 72d Infantry." Ironically, during World War II, many of the larger cast-iron tablets and markers dedicated to the service of the Vicksburg soldiers were removed. The metal was needed for military supplies for a new generation of soldiers.

As I stood inside the domed building, people entered the memorial without speaking. They held papers in their hands and scanned the walls for names. Some stayed for several minutes, connected to a person from another time, while others came and went quickly, having no one to look for.

My last stop in the park was the Vicksburg National Cemetery. Established in 1866, this landscape is the final resting place for seventeen thousand Union soldiers, only five thousand of whom are known. Several 72nd Illinois men were listed in the cemetery's database, and I set off to find their headstones.

On May 25, 1863, after Confederate General John Pemberton's

request for a cease-fire, the fallen of the two unsuccessful Union attacks were hastily buried. Joseph Stockton wrote:

> *The stench from the bodies lying unburied on the*
> *battlefield becoming so great a flag of truce from the*
> *enemy made its appearance and permission given to bury*
> *our dead. I did not go on the field, having no relish for*
> *such sights.*

To identify the men, names were etched on whatever material was available—in many cases, a board. It wasn't until after the park was established in 1899 that a concerted effort was made to locate these men and reinter them in the cemetery. By this time, many of the markers had rotted.

Some names on headstones were vanishing beneath an onslaught of yellow, orange, and black molds. In Section G, a boomerang-shaped area in the middle of the cemetery, I found Thomas Russell of Company A, the man whom William Mohrmann had helped carry down the hill before disciplining Darsie for "crawfishing" to safety. Nearby lay David Temple, the bugler who, while eating, had fallen dead from the mysterious bullet that came out of nowhere. For the remainder, I had no stories, yet I still felt like I knew them.

I never found Scepter Harding, however. He wasn't listed in the database. Did he rest in one of the twelve thousand "unknown" graves? Maybe Scepter still reposed beneath the sweet gum trees on the hillside above Glass Bayou. What happened to Darsie's friend may always be a question without an answer.

On July 4, 1863, Confederate General John C. Pemberton surrendered his Army of Mississippi to Union General Ulysses S. Grant. The 72nd Illinois was one of the regiments chosen to enter the city and take possession of the courthouse. The heat and dust swirled around the men as they marched along Jackson Road into the citadel. They passed Confederate soldiers standing on both sides of the dirt road. The vanquished had stacked their arms. Joseph Stockton wrote:

> *There were no cheers as we passed through these men*
> *but the salutations were "How are you Yank?" "How*
> *are you Reb?" "Give us something to eat Yank," when*
> *our boys would throw them hard tack, coffee and what*
> *else they could spare. The march was a terrible one and*
> *notwithstanding that it was marching into Vicksburg.*
> *I never saw so many men affected by the heat. When*
> *we reached the Court House I saw our glorious banner*
> *floating from its dome where only in the morning the*
> *rebel flag had been waving to the breeze. Our men could*
> *restrain themselves no longer and gave one long, loud*
> *cheer. We marched around the Court House, which is a*
> *fine large building, and then halted, stacked arms while*
> *waiting for further orders.*

The structure today—with its cupola, four porticos, and thirty-foot columns—is the Old Court House Museum, which officially opened in 1948. Plans to tear down the abandoned structure were thwarted when a woman named Eva Whitaker Davis convinced the Vicksburg citizenry to maintain the past with a museum. She organized workers, raised the money required, and wrote this to the *Vicksburg Evening Post*:

> *It is hallowed ground; not just one or two have trod this*
> *doorstep but throngs have crowded into its halls and on its*
> *lawn. It is a monument we erect to our memory while we*
> *yet live.*

Eva Davis's tireless work paid off. On June 3, 1948, she raised both the Confederate and United States flags atop the building and opened the doors to the public. More than fifty years later, I walked into the museum looking for more pieces of my past.

"Welcome to the Old Court House Museum," a man greeted me. He was in his thirties with round glasses and dark, wavy hair that was trimmed above his ears and curly below his neck. His soft voice broke the quiet of an early morning with as yet no visitors. His name was Jeff Giambrone, and he was a historian for the museum.

I told him that I had come looking for information about the 72nd Illinois.

"You are welcome to use our research room," Jeff offered. "And, of course, you know about the stone here that someone etched '7-2-I-L-L' on?"

"No, I don't," I said excitedly. "What's that?"

"Come on, I'll show you."

Behind the building, near the museum's rear entrance, stood six stone columns. At the base of one, on a slab of roseate-colored slate, an array of graffiti had been carved. I read names such as "Merrill," "Cook," and "J.W. Smith," but the etching that stood out the most contained two-inch letters and numbers that spelled "72 ILL."

"I imagine one of the soldiers did this on the morning they entered the city," Jeff said. Nothing I had read from Darsie, Joseph Stockton, William Mohrmann, Anson Hemingway, or the other 72nd men had mentioned this inscription. It could have been the work of any of the three hundred or so surviving soldiers.

I asked Jeff if he had ancestors who fought in the war. He nodded.

"My great-great-great grandfather was in the 6th Mississippi Infantry and two great-great-uncles were in the 38th Mississippi. I wrote a regimental history of the 38th. It's not a regiment you would have heard about, as they never left the state, but they did fight at Vicksburg." Jeff looked thoughtful. "In fact, I think the 38th was fighting across from the 72nd." He left to get his book, *Beneath Torn And Tattered Flags: A History of the 38th Mississippi Infantry C.S.A.*

"Here it is," Jeff said, after flipping through pages. "Page 73: I quoted this from Edwin Bearss's book, *The Vicksburg Campaign*":

> *In front of the 38th, Ransom's Brigade advanced in four columns and were met by a withering fire from the Mississippians.*

"The 38th was impressed with the Northern soldiers' bravery," he continued. "I also quote Captain James Jones, who wrote years later":

They [the Federals] *came on as rapidly as the fallen timber would permit, and in perfect order. We waited in silence until the first line had advanced within easy rifle range, when a murderous fire was opened from the breastworks. We had a few pieces of artillery which ploughed their ranks with destructive effect. Still they never faltered, but came bravely on. It was indeed a gallant sight though an awful one. As they came down the hill one could see them plunging headlong to the front, and as they rushed up the slope to our works they invariably fell backwards, as the death shot greeted them. And yet the survivors never wavered. Some of them fell within a few yards of our works...Surely no more desperate courage than this could be displayed by mortal men.*

"So," I said, "our ancestors were shooting at each other."

"Yeah. Quite the coincidence."

When I left the museum, I bought Jeff's book and asked him to sign it. Outside, in the crackling, autumn air, as the season's leaves glided around me, I read his note:

To Betsy—

I am glad my g-g-[uncles] *missed your g-g-grandpa.*

Jeff

Chapter 12

Backwoods Tactical

If only there were evil people somewhere insidiously committing evil deeds and it were necessary only to separate them from the rest of us and destroy them. But the line dividing good and evil cuts through the heart of every human being. And who is willing to destroy a piece of his own heart?

—Alexandr Solzhenitsyn, novelist, Nobel laureate (1918–)

THE FIRST TIME I felt connected to my ancestry in a more fundamental way than family reunions and holiday obligations happened right after my mother's death in 1996. I was looking at a collage I'd made of her life for the funeral and I realized that she reminded me of a book written in a foreign language; I recognized many words, but the overall meaning couldn't be translated. That night, however, I thought about something she had once told me about her oldest brother. "Paul got all the talent out of us five kids. He could paint, write, sing, and play the piano, whereas the rest of us were lucky if we could tie our shoes."

I didn't remember Uncle Paul well. He had died of heart failure when I was thirteen. We used to visit him at Mount Angel Abbey north of Salem, Oregon, where he'd become a brother with the Catholic Church in 1966, and we made frequent trips during the summer from Tacoma to the monastic butte. I usually found the visits painfully boring; my parents and uncle just sat around and talked, enjoying the view of the Willamette Valley. The rose gardens and goldfish ponds provided some diversion for me, but the hushed grounds and robed monks made me nervous, while the quiet made me think too much, and thinking too much often led me to thoughts of death.

As I had combed through my parents' home in autumn 1996 looking for what I wanted to keep, I found a stack of my uncle's half-finished oil canvases. A portrait of an unfamiliar dark-haired woman gazed back at me from one. Another showed an idyllic church perched beneath a deep blue sky and surrounded by bright green grounds. Though the work didn't appeal to me as art I would hang on my wall, I recognized and appreciated the skill, as I had attempted to draw many times over the years and always failed miserably, my sketches never resembling anything recognizable.

Yet, the same genes to create visual art lived in my body as had lived in my uncle's. For the first time in my life, I knew something about myself that I based upon fact, not intuition. I *could* draw. The talent was *inside* of me. I took out some pencils I'd purchased recently and began.

That night, alone in my parents' home, I focused my whole attention on capturing the eclipsed face and upper body of Stephen Gordon, the lesbian protagonist in Radclyffe Hall's 1928 novel, *The Well of Loneliness*. I drew her portrait from the book's cover, a publisher's frozen vision of Stephen, a woman with hidden eyes, wearing a fedora that dips below her forehead and to the right. Stephen stands with her arms folded, the men's suit jacket she wears creasing just below the shoulders.

I examined how parts of the picture related to other parts. How far did the fedora extend over Stephen's shoulder? How wide was the gap between the teardrop nostril and closed lips? How long was the face compared to the fedora's height? I now understood details and proportion that I had never addressed in my previous drawing attempts. I used a heavy, softer lead to depict shadows streaming across one side of her neck, left cheek, and the bridge of her nose. I drew dark without boundary where the hat and hair blended, and light and thin where a whisper of a line indicated the right side of Stephen's face. After two hours, I was done.

I'd been right. I *could* draw. In that moment, I knew that, whether they were alive or dead, a tapestry of people, with all their experiences, thoughts, and characteristics, lived on inside of me. The ability to draw was a gift. Other legacies, as I uncovered them, both scared and elated me—especially the ones connected to my father—but it would be several more years before I would really begin to understand them.

———•◦•———

April 2002, western Oregon

As the spring days stretched longer and the grass turned greener, my reenacting unit, the 19th Indiana Infantry, made plans to attend a "backwoods tactical" in Oregon's Willamette Valley. This event, not open to the public, was to include one Union company, the 19th, and several Confederate companies and cavalry. We packed for a "hardcore" experience, bringing only what we could carry. I stuffed my knapsack (an uncomfortable version of the modern backpack) with a wool hat, long underwear, extra undergarments and socks, wool gloves, a sweater I bought at a thrift store that looked somewhat "nineteenth century," and a skillet. I rolled up my two wool blankets, one half of a dog tent, two metal stakes, and a rubber poncho, and strapped this to the top of the knapsack. Slung over my shoulder, I had my haversack, a bag sometimes known as the soldier's "purse," which contained apples, jerky, dried fruit, trail mix, bags of soup, my journal, and a camera.

We drove to "Fort Perry," eighty acres of grass and oak woodlands outside of Albany, Oregon. Gene Perry, the owner and a modern-day cowboy, welcomed us and explained the lay of the land.

"Crabtree Creek flows just inside those woods beyond the grassy field," he pointed past the barn. "Straight in from here is an old settler's cabin that the 'Confederates' sometimes camp around. However, if you follow the line of trees upstream, and then head in where there's a break in the forest, there's also a nice open area for a camp. It's about a half mile, but you're welcome to go wherever you want."

In the parking lot, I strapped on my packs and my leather belt with the cartridge box, cap box, and bayonet scabbard attached.

The knapsack cut into my shoulders like a rope, pulling the contents back and down. The short fifty-foot walk to the barn, where we would sleep the first night, proved challenging. At the reenactments, we always unloaded our gear straight from the cars into canvas tents. Nobody had ever actually *packed* it anywhere. My face burned with exertion and shame as I thought about Darsie walking fifteen to twenty miles a day with just such a load, and of my father jumping out of an airplane on D-Day with 150 pounds of weaponry and supplies strapped to his body.

"Okay, boys, this is what we'll do," said Chris Scarano, who had become captain after Daniel had resigned and was now facing us with sweat trickling down the sides of his face. "We'll sleep in the barn tonight, go out in the morning for the day with just haversacks, leathers, and guns, find a good campsite, then send runners back for the knapsacks and bedrolls."

"Three cheers for the captain!" someone shouted.

The next morning we marched across the field to the cabin. We loaded our guns and kept watch. This tactical was a very different experience from the other reenactments. Instead of a generic event, we were following a specific outline. This weekend, the 19th Indiana had been sent out ahead of the main Union army to scout for Confederates, who we knew were showing up sometime soon. The first sergeant sent a private to scout the trail along Crabtree Creek. He reported back that no Rebs had been spotted.

As we headed toward the second campsite that Gene had mentioned, the crack of muskets heralded the arrival of the Rebel contingent. They were hiding out in an island of trees in the grassy meadow farther upstream from the barn. The 19th Indiana spread out along the edge of the woods by Crabtree Creek. Explosions of black powder ringed the meadow all day. A small group of Rebs tried to surround us, but we captured them after a close exchange of gunfire. The Union boys hollered epithets at the soldiers in gray.

"You're done, Reb! Do you hear me? Done! D-U-N!"

"What are you doin', Johnny? Sending out children?" someone yelled after we captured a particularly young-looking boy.

"They usually do!" replied another.

"Die you bastards!"

"Somebody better write his mother!"

Private Bertram Howell kept quiet. I have no voice for yelling, and when I do, it sounds like a small animal that has been separated from its mother. I kept to my task, loading and shooting. In between firing, I ran back and forth between the captain and first sergeant with messages, jumping over slash brought down by the wind or Gene's chain saw.

The protocol for this event was that if a Reb shot us, and we could tell when a gun was pointed our way, then we would indicate our demise by placing our hats atop the barrels of our guns and raising the guns high. We'd then sit in the "life zone," an area designated by the captain and out of sight of the Rebel soldiers, count to sixty, and then recycle back into the ranks.

By late afternoon, all of the Confederates had boldly left their island of trees and come to the edge of the woods where we were spread out. We had held them off for several hours, but the 19th Indiana was outnumbered, and the Rebs knew this. I stood behind the thick trunk of a fir tree that leaned toward the meadow, firing round after round. A short "Johnny" with a long reddish beard moved in so close to me that I could see the three sergeant's stripes on his sleeve. He wore brown pants, a gray coat, and a wide-brimmed tan hat. A silver buckle, engraved with the letters "CS," on his light brown belt, gleamed like a mirror in the sun.

This man never saw me. I loaded my gun, pulling a round of black powder from my cartridge box, ripping off the top, and pouring the fine grains down the barrel. He kept looking to my right where the other Indiana boys were having a hot fight with his comrades. I pulled out a gold-colored cap and put it on the cone of my gun. Raising the Springfield, I tucked it securely into my shoulder and aimed down the sight at the chest of the man with the red beard. Then I yelled.

"Hey, Reb!"

He turned and looked at me, as surprised as if his mother had just tapped him on the shoulder. I pulled the trigger. His chest disappeared in the billows of smoke that poured out of my gun. The man's face fell. He slowly put his hat atop his gun and moved away to the Confederate life zone, and for the first time since I'd started reenacting, I knew exactly whom I'd shot.

———•◦•———

That night we camped next to Crabtree Creek, beneath maple trees dressed in licorice fern bloomers. The duffy ground of many seasons of fallen leaves and needles felt as soft as a feather bed, and we all looked forward to better sleep than we'd experienced on the hard floor of the barn the previous night. Crabtree Creek rippled. Springtime blossoms melted on the wind. The yellow-green growth of trees and shrubs poked out of buds that had held tightly and protected the new shoots all winter.

We cut poles of maple and fir and got our five tents set up. Each of us pulled out one half of a dog tent and joined it with that of our sleeping buddy. My buddy was Jeff Baker, a tall man whose feet and/or head would hang out of the open-ended tents, replicas of those designed for men whose average height was much shorter than ours. I laid out my rubber poncho and two wool blankets.

Assigned to fire detail, I made several trips to the creek for rocks to make a cooking area. Narrow and shallow, Crabtree Creek barely covered the smooth stones of its bed. Branches laden with moss hung uneasily above the water. I grabbed a big, flat rock, useful for resting a skillet. Then another. The stream compensated for the vacuum I'd create. A bubble would erupt where each rock had been, sediment flecking the otherwise transparent liquid. Then it would clear. I looked down and the red-haired Confederate replaced my own reflection. What if the situation had been different? What if I'd really killed him? Would I still just gather stones, the next task on my list, a few hours later? Bob was his name. Bob had shaken my hand after the tactical ended.

"I surprised you," I'd said.

"Yeah," he grinned, "you did."

That night we built a big fire and boiled water for soup and tea. Jeff fried Spam in his skillet. The first sergeant made biscuits. Everyone talked of the daylong skirmish with the enemy. Like at the reenactments, I was amazed at the details the boys remembered about the fighting. My experience felt insular; I was too busy loading the gun, finding someone to shoot before he shot me, and running messages back and forth. I had no time to see what else was going on. I vaguely mentioned hitting a few Johnnies.

The fire died down, and we headed for our tents, the cold air tracing down my back like a dropped ice cube. It would be a long night. I wrapped myself up in my blankets and tried to move close to Jeff without him noticing. I wanted just to think about the day's fun, but instead another nearly forgotten childhood memory intruded: of a boy—faceless now— a gun, and me.

My dad's gun rack, the one he built in the 1970s, had hung in my parents' bedroom closet. Three slots, cushioned with brown felt, held a .22 rifle, a double-barrel shotgun, and a .30-30 rifle. A shelf below stored bullets and cleaning equipment.

I never had much interest in the guns except when we drove to a gravel pit outside of Tacoma and shot them for target practice. Dad would set up a piece of cardboard with black concentric circles drawn around a red core, while empty beer cans or clay pigeons provided other targets. I fired the shotgun once, but it was not snug against my shoulder when I did so, and I ended up with a big bruise and a pain that took my breath away. My father, however—the postal service employee who wore leisure suits and had a beer belly—was a good shot. He made the beer cans dance like heated atoms and turned the red heart-shaped bullseye into shredded fiber. I knew that my father had jumped out of planes and killed the German woman and marched so long he fell asleep while walking. I didn't know he could shoot so well.

In those years, a fourth gun rested in the corner of our dining room near the sliding glass door to the backyard. It was a BB gun. Boxes of BBs sat on Dad's workbench in the garage. After fishing old beer cans out of the garbage and setting them up in a pyramid formation on a mound in the yard, I'd start shooting. I was also a pretty good shot.

One day, when I was about ten, I left the backyard with the BB gun and hid in the shrubs on the side of our house. After awhile, a kid walked by on Oxalis Street. I raised the gun and shot him, hitting him just behind the ear. I felt pleased and only vaguely guilty. The boy wasn't hurt badly, though I'm sure the speeding copper BB stung a lot. He ran toward my hideout. I ran away.

This memory is a fragment now without a larger story, like driving in a fog where you can't see the road's edge. I don't remember my motives, the boy's face or name, or my ensuing punishment, but the raised gun, his head in my sight, and pulling the trigger couldn't be clearer. Later my father found me, and all I remember is him—big and very angry—quickly coming toward me. I am sure of one thing, however: I didn't shoot the BB gun again for a long time.

Chapter 13

I Company

*To forget is to fail the duty of honoring the fallen. And
to forget is to ignore the duty of warning those who in the
future may dream of war without knowing war.*

—Charles U. Daly, from the foreword
to *Parachute Soldier* by William H. Tucker

IN FEBRUARY 1944, eight months after graduating from paratrooper training, Second Lieutenant James Howell arrived in Scotland,
and in March he traveled to England. He was assigned as a replace-
ment officer for the 505th Parachute Infantry Regiment of the 82nd
Airborne. The 505th had left the United States in April 1943, bound
for North Africa. It had participated in the invasions of Sicily and
Italy, and when it arrived at Camp Quorn in Quorndon, Leicester-
shire, England, in February 1944, the 505th settled into a routine of
training the men who had been out of action since the previous October and of assimilating the replacements.

For an officer with no combat experience, the 505th was a tough
outfit to join. These soldiers had lived for months in the brutal heat
and dust of French Morocco, survived two combat jumps, and had
spent a total of more than three months fighting, resulting in the
combat deaths of ninety men and injuries to half of the regiment.
They were cocky and tough. They were rightfully proud of having
survived the Sicilian and Italian campaigns and of having liberated
both areas from German occupation. Into their hubris and invinci-
bility came my father, a green officer from the Midwest.

My education into my father's experiences began with reading

Allen Langdon's regimental history of the 505th, *"Ready": The History of the 505th Parachute Infantry Regiment, 82nd Airborne Division, World War II.* I focused on the actions of the Third Battalion, specifically I Company, in which my father had served as an assistant platoon leader. The details overwhelmed me. In a section titled, "The Third Battalion On D-Day," Langdon wrote:

> *Following the counterattack,* [Lieutenant Colonel] *Krause ordered "I" Company to attack "Hill 20," the high ground at Fauville from whence the attack had come and from where the mortar and artillery fire was now being directed at Ste. Mere Eglise. He apparently ordered Captain Swingler to first swing west and hit it in the flank, but for reasons unknown, when "I" Company first hit the highway it was not much farther south than the "G" Company roadblock. In any event, they continued on in attack formation on both sides of the highway, but got no farther than the first small hill, about one mile south of town, where they walked into an ambush that the repulsed German force had laid for them. Somewhere in the ensuing fight and the confused withdrawal, Captain Swingler was killed and several men wounded. With the loss of the Captain, and some indecision on what to do on the part of the officer who took over, the company retraced its steps back to Ste. Mere Eglise.*

With Darsie's experiences, I had been able to match his writing with my own visuals as I'd retraced his steps. It would be unlikely I'd be going to France or Germany anytime soon, and this information was too remote, dense, and broad; I wanted to know what happened to *my father.* I wanted *his* story, not a textbook version of the entire regiment, so I began looking for writings focusing on my father's company.

In his book *Put On Your Boots and Parachutes!* author Deryk Wills, a photographer with the Royal Air Force during World War II, compiled hundreds of stories from the soldiers of the 82nd Airborne. He had quoted William H. Tucker from his book *Parachute Soldier:*

"The new Lieutenant, James How[e]ll, had really proved himself." Elated at finding my father's name in print, I obtained Deryk's phone number in England and called to ask him what this meant.

"When these battle-hardened paratroopers were assigned to new officers," he told me, "they were always worried, as many did not match up to the task ahead. They had usually come out of officer's school and had been to jump school at Fort Benning, and they were as green as hell. It usually came down to the platoon sergeants to lick them into shape. If the officer was no good, the sergeant would have a quiet word with the commanding officer and he would be drafted out quickly. By all accounts, your father was made of sterner stuff, and once he had shown that he knew his stuff, his men would follow him everywhere."

Remembering the writer Stephen Ambrose's words about the difference between new and experienced soldiers, I wondered if my father's "greenness" was initially a benefit; he didn't know what a bullet or a land mine would do to a human body.

I began calling the surviving soldiers of I Company. Several of the men remembered the "new lieutenant." William Tucker, who had been a private in the Second Platoon, told me, "I remember seeing him in England and thinking, 'Geez, who is that guy? He looks pretty good to me. Can we get him into our platoon?' Y'see, I didn't much like our officers. Lieutenant Howell was a very handsome man. Looked like he shoulda been a general."

Parachute Soldier, which Tucker published in 1994, was based on a diary he had kept from 1942 to 1945. The only other mention of my father came in the chapter on the fighting in Holland, where Tucker wrote, "Lieutenant Howell led the attack from the company command post down the road and tried to outflank the Germans." It wasn't much information, but it made me feel less alone with my father's war stories, since others obviously knew them too.

During these readings and phone calls, my alcoholic father took on new dimensions that finally seemed to resonate with me. He became braver and smarter than the man I thought I had known. Still, I craved more. I wanted to know what Lieutenant Howell had encountered during the war, what had tested him, and how he had "proved himself." I wanted to understand how he had survived, not just physically, but emotionally as well. Unfortunately, when I questioned William Tucker if he knew of any specific events involving my father, he said no.

"We were in different platoons. In combat, you often didn't see people from other platoons." Then he asked, "Do you have any of your father's letters?"

"No."

"That doesn't surprise me," he said. "He always seemed like a quiet guy."

Next I contacted men in the Third Platoon. George Clark, now a winter resident of the Florida Keys, was the platoon leader whom my dad served under as assistant during the Normandy jump. He also commented on Dad's looks.

"We all admired him for being so handsome, and we were all so ugly. He was a quiet, fine man. Top-quality officer and gentleman, highly respected by all."

"Do you remember anything about him after the jump into Normandy?" I asked.

"We were thirty-eight straight days on the attack in France, but nothing stands out in my mind about where Jim was or what he did. I didn't get to know him personally."

Strange, I thought, *how could the platoon leader not know his assistant? How could he not remember what the assistant did?* Even as I felt frustration, though, I knew. Memory is selective, especially when many actions are happening at once. Only a sliver of each battle's events had lodged in my mind at the reenactments and the backwoods tactical. The enemy in front. My comrades beside. And even sometimes those images became smeared as the events piled on top of each other.

"A lot of the officers bunked together," George continued, "but I never bunked with Jim." He paused. "I really hate to discuss the situation, because I'd rather forget the whole thing." Suddenly, George seemed to be somewhere else. "You'd turn them over and they'd look fine, but they weren't." *The dead friends*, I thought. "That's what I want to forget. I don't want to remember." Another pause. "I still have nightmares. I kick my wife in bed, screaming."

George's pain raced through the telephone wires at me, from three thousand miles away, from sixty years in the past. Guilt suddenly flooded me as I realized I was asking men like George and William to return to their nightmares for my sake. For so long, *I* had wanted to forget my own past. Now, I wanted to connect with my father's experience during those trying years to know him better, but I also had another, more selfish reason. I wanted to find out if I had the same kind of resiliency to endure my own memories and the pain of feeling like the lone survivor.

Even worse, George had been an officer, a decision-maker. His burden, like my father's, encompassed an additional sphere. Kurt Gabel had written in *The Making of a Paratrooper: Airborne Training and Combat in World War II*:

> And only the man who gave the order—if he lives—must
> live with the consequences. Though the squad shares
> equally in his grief and may reach out to him to comfort
> him when he has erred, the leader remains weighted with
> the responsibility. Doubt remains to deepen the grief.
> Had he done all that should have been done, asked all the
> questions that should have been asked?

I thanked George and told him I hoped my call hadn't been too upsetting.

"It just wasn't worth it. All those men dying," he said.

Despite my misgivings, however, I kept making phone calls.

Jack Hillman, an enlisted man in the Third Platoon, said of my father, "He was very affable, a gentleman. He knew men and the needs of the men, how to guide and lead them quietly. Lieutenant Howell would help you out with instructions. But, I didn't get to know him well. The enlisted men didn't get to know the officers very well."

"Do you remember seeing him during the fighting in Normandy?"

"On the ground, I met up with George Clark, but in the heat of battle, you don't know who you're seeing. It was a confusing time, very upsetting, but we got through it."

The jump into Normandy, the airborne part of Operation Overlord, was to occur in darkness, and even if every paratrooper hit the drop zone exactly, they would still need to find each other before the Germans did. To this end, each man was given a "cricket," a small metal device that could be clicked—a sound that imitated the insect. One click to initiate the exchange, two clicks in response. The men were also assigned passwords. In Normandy, "Flash" was the password to hail someone and "Thunder" the answer. In this way, hopefully, they would be able to locate and identify each other during the early hours of June 6, when the dark sky was lit up by the full moon and shadowy figures could be either Allied or Nazi.

At 10:00 p.m. on June 5, 1944, several hundred C-47 transport planes left England carrying the approximately two thousand soldiers of the 505th, including my father, as well as the rest of the American 82nd and 101st Airborne Divisions and the British 6th Airborne Division, across the English Channel to the drop zones in France. The men had been given airsickness pills, which caused most of them to fall asleep during the two-hour flight. Each trooper carried 150 pounds of gear on his body, which included an M1 assault rifle, hand grenades, main and reserve parachutes, and food rations. Some of the weight was distributed in supplies tied to their legs, which they were to release as soon as their parachutes opened.

Leaving the English Channel behind, the multiple-V formation of C-47s ran into a cloud bank. The pilots veered left or right and descended to three hundred feet or climbed to two thousand feet to avoid midair collisions. Consequently, when they left the clouds, the formation was lost and very few troops landed at their drop zones. As the Allied aircraft became visible, the Germans opened up their antiaircraft guns. Outside the doors of the C-47s, the darkness became illuminated like a New Year's fireworks display. The paratroopers were thrown around inside the aircrafts as bullets tore into the planes and came up through the floors. Through the open doors the men saw nearby C-47s exploding or screaming to the ground on fire. Accelerating to provide less of a target, the pilots had the remaining planes moving at 150 mph. The troopers were supposed to jump at 90 mph.

The men I have spoken with and read about said they couldn't wait to get out of the C-47s. Many planes dropped low to avoid the enemy's radar. Consequently, these paratroopers jumped from between 300 and 400 feet rather than from the expected 750. Paratroopers in other planes that had stayed high jumped with planes flying below them. Stephen Ambrose writes in *D-Day, June 6, 1944: The Climactic Battle of World War II* that one pilot called out over the radio, "I've got a paratrooper hung up on my wing." The advice came back for him to slow down and the man would slide off. As soon as their chutes opened, the paratroopers were on the ground. For some, there wasn't enough time and the chutes never opened.

If their parachutes opened properly, and they didn't get hung up in trees, and they didn't break any legs, and they didn't get hit by bullets flying through the air, and they didn't drown after landing in countryside that had been flooded by the Germans, then their first task on the ground was to find their comrades. At this point in my research, I remembered my father's "cow story," which happened just after he landed in the countryside of northwest France.

"I was all alone, and, except for the sound of planes overhead, it was quiet," Dad had recalled. "Then I heard footsteps. They were walking slowly and deliberately toward me." He laughed. "It was just a cow, come to see what all the commotion was."

Unfortunately, crickets, if knocked loose upon landing, and passwords, if forgotten in the excitement, did not always help determine friend or foe on the ground. Additionally, the men were instructed not to fire on anyone in the dark, as the noise would attract attention. Cam Anderson, a paratrooper in the 101st Airborne whom I met in Tennessee during my second trip retracing Darsie's Civil War experiences, told me the jumpers were supposed to only use knives to defend themselves that night, but that at some point he set his gun sights on a figure walking down a hedgerow. (Hedgerows were vegetative fences separating properties in France, thick and tall enough to pose problems even for tanks.) The approaching man, a major with the 82nd Airborne, never responded to Cam's cricket. Cam almost killed him, but fortunately recognized him before pulling the trigger.

I continued my interviews.

Stanley Kulikowski, a sergeant in the Second Platoon and now a resident of Long Island with a thick New York accent, said Lieutenant Howell's name was familiar, but that he couldn't quite place him. Then Pete, Stanley's son, got on the line. Pete keeps up on the doings of the World War II 505th men and couldn't remember my father ever being mentioned.

"A lot of the men didn't want to get to know anyone new after they'd seen friends die. That's how they would have felt arriving in England after the invasions of Sicily and Italy. The officers might remember your dad more than the enlisted men."

I asked Pete what he knew of his father's stories.

"They're anecdotes mostly. He told me about killing chickens for food around a farmhouse in Holland. In another, he came around the building and found a German with his hands raised, saying, 'Don't shoot me, it's Christmas.'

"I never asked my father if he killed someone," he continued. "I know he did, but I couldn't ask him. That's just not something I could do. He never told me anything really hard about killing people."

After several more phone calls, I sent out a blanket e-mail to the 505th mailing list. Quickly I received a reply from Joseph Schwan, who had been an enlisted man in the Third Platoon. He wrote:

> Your dad and I were very close, and we knew each other only a short time. But, you must know that a leader is a leader only when a leader's men follow him through hell and hot water, and your dad was one of only a couple officers that I would follow through hell with. He was only a little older than I, but was that type of individual that was quiet, quietly assertive, and no one questioned his orders. Jim was the epitome of a leader. I loved that man and had the highest respect for him.

After more than a month of combat in Normandy, the 505th was relieved and returned to England. Of the 144 men of I Company to fly out of Camp Quorn on June 5, only 44 walked back through the gates of the army camp the next month. Training began immediately for the next assault.

Chapter 14

A Tennessee Winter

[Saturday, October 29, 1864, Mississippi River]

The 72nd Ill. left Vicksburg Mifs on the 29th day of October aboard the Steamer Continental for Cairo Ill. Nothing worthy of note occurred on the way until we passed Columbus Ky—about 10 miles above Columbus we came to where the Steamer James White had struck a snag and went down we took all the Passengers on our boat also some Cattle which were on the boat and left it there.

—From the journal of Private Darsie Heath,
72nd Illinois Infantry, Company A

FOR SIXTEEN MONTHS after the victory at Vicksburg, the 72nd Illinois was assigned provost guard duty in and around Vicksburg. They made two expeditions during the spring and summer of 1864 to Benton and Grand Gulf, Mississippi. The orders Joseph Stockton received on May 3 for the mission to Benton, a village northeast of Vicksburg, read, "March 5 o'clock in the morning, two days' rations in haversacks, eight days' rations in wagons, no tents or extra clothing." A brigade of three regiments would monitor and check enemy movements. Union command wanted to prevent the Confederates from reinforcing their army north of Vicksburg. Four days later, outside of Benton, Stockton ordered Companies A and F out as skirmishers. A fragment of an exploding Confederate shell struck Lieutenant Richard Pomeroy of Company F in the leg. The men, possibly including Darsie, carried him back to the hospital where he died that evening.

The blazing summer of 1864 crawled by. According to the *Vicksburg Daily Herald*, the 72nd Illinois kept busy chasing thieves and smugglers and attending presentations of swords to various officers of distinction. I wonder if, given the monotony of guard duty day after day, the 72nd men felt relieved when Special Orders No. 222 arrived in October, which directed them to East Point, Georgia, via Cairo, Illinois, and Nashville, Tennessee. The regiment was to join Major General William Sherman in his soon-to-be-famous "March to the Sea."

On November 6, after being paid four months' pay, Darsie spent the day in Cairo. At 5:00 p.m. he started for camp, a half mile up the Ohio River in a muddy wood. He wrote:

> *when I got there the regiment were going on the Boat.*
> *we were expecting to go home to vote when we came to*
> *Cairo but were disappointed. We had all our baggage on*
> *the Boat by 9.Oc. and then the Boat Started up the river.*
> *Paducah is supposed to be our destination*

They reached Nashville on November 13; Sherman's army left Atlanta on November 15. Their late arrival, a seemingly small twist of fate, would cost the 72nd Illinois dearly. Instead of meeting up with Sherman, Darsie and his comrades were sent south to Columbia, Tennessee, to prepare for Confederate General John Bell Hood's advancing Army of Tennessee. Hood had left Atlanta heading northwest for Nashville and the Ohio River, trying to draw Sherman away from his coastal rendezvous. It didn't work. Sherman went to the sea, encountering little resistance. Hood went to Tennessee and collided with a destiny that would virtually destroy his army.

Orders came to be ready to march light the following morning. Darsie wrote that the men either threw away clothes they could not carry or mailed them home. On November 14:

> *we struck tents and in High Spirits left for Columbia*
> *distant 42 miles. a good many of the Boys were slightly*
> *inebriated when we left for this reason we had to march*
> *to Columbia. we were offered Transportation-by-Rail But*

our Colonel said he wanted to take some of the Whisky
out of the men this was the first marching I had done for
more than 1 year and it mad my feet quite sore besides we
marched on the Pike [road] *and the soles of my shoes were*
thin and the stones Hurt my feet.

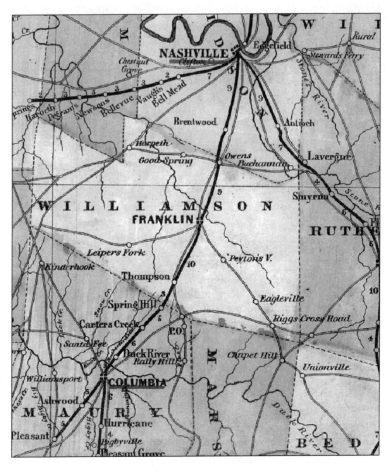

NASHVILLE, FRANKLIN, AND COLUMBIA TENNESSE
Courtesy of US Historical Archive

In 1864, Columbia, Tennessee, was a town of fifteen hundred people, situated along the Duck River, a sinewy waterway flowing into the Tennessee River fifty miles as the crow flies to the west. Columbia had first been occupied by the Union army in March 1862. By 1864, it looked as ragged and worn as the people who still eked out an existence there. With the local men off fighting, the crops went untended. Livestock had either been stolen or had wandered away, and homes, barns, and buildings had been burned. A teetering chimney might be the only remnant of a once prosperous household. Slaves still occupied the landscape, but their owners had little control over them, and the Union commanders didn't want the responsibility of dealing with them. Columbia existed in the haze of war, not dead but not alive either.

The Duck River, a crooked devil of meanderings, flowed for 106 miles to its mouth, more than twice the straight-line distance from Columbia. Hollows and bluffs enclosed the waterway beneath hills that rolled across the land like a sea of cotton. Oak and hickory trees stood bare in the autumn air, providing little cover for the armies that moved among them.

For two weeks, the 72nd Illinois stayed in and around Columbia building fortifications and crossing and recrossing the Duck River to fight Confederates. It rained "most of the time," according to now–Lieutenant Colonel Joseph Stockton, commanding officer of the 72nd. The river rose. The soft soil slipped into the Duck and made a mud soup that came up to the men's knees. The temperature hovered in the forties.

The Union army knew that Hood was headed north. The Confederate leader hadn't beat the Federals to Columbia, but he did intend to arrive first at Franklin, a town in between Columbia and Nashville. It would become a footrace over the pikes and through the hills.

Approximately twelve miles west of Columbia lay the village of Williamsport, a small community built around one of the few ferry crossings over the Duck River. In November 1864, Union General Joseph Cooper was stationed at Williamsport with a brigade of the 23rd Corps. Since little was happening in Williamsport, Cooper's men needed to move north to Franklin.

Lieutenant Colonel Stockton gathered his line officers together on November 29. The 72nd Illinois now counted 325 men, just one-third the number that had left Chicago two years previous. The present total included sixteen officers; in August 1862 there had been thirty-seven. Company A counted forty-five; originally they had numbered one hundred. Captain James Sexton of Company D wrote that Stockton explained the latest order in a "short, but foreboding address." He quoted Stockton:

> *An officer and twenty men are needed to volunteer to*
> *undertake a perilous and laborious expedition through*
> *the lines of the enemy. They must bear dispatches to*
> *General Cooper at Williamsport, twenty miles* [sic] *away.*

Stockton does not mention this incident in his memoir. I wondered about his feelings when addressing less than half the officers who had signed on in Chicago. Does a commander see who is not there as well as who is? Kurt Gabel wrote about the military decision-maker's responsibility in *The Making of a Paratrooper*:

> *A corps commander may make a wrong decision and lose*
> *divisions and regiments, and perhaps he could still go to*
> *bed that night and sleep. But a squad leader who makes*
> *a wrong decision would lose men, men who trusted him*
> *implicitly and obeyed without question. There would be no*
> *sleep for the squad leader.*

Sexton wrote that Stockton described the mission as such:

> *There will be many dangers and privations. The land west*
> *of Columbia is infested with guerillas. Cavalry sent on this*
> *mission have been captured and likely hanged. The party*
> *will need to exercise courage and discretion. And even if*
> *successful in delivering the messages, the chances are great*
> *the soldiers will be captured and made prisoners of war.*

Captain Roswell Mason of Company A volunteered to lead the expedition. He then formed his forty-five men in a line and said:

> *I am authorized to accept volunteers—twenty men—from the regiment to go with me on detached service. There will be plenty of hard work and danger, and no glory. If any men from this Company wish to go, let them step two paces to the front.*

In his 1895 book, *Chevrons and Shoulder Straps*, Adjutant George Heafford wrote, "Without a moment's hesitation the entire company stepped forward as one man." Darsie Heath and his friend Robert Holmes were two of the twenty selected.

June 1999, Columbia, Tennessee

Bob Duncan's real estate office on Seventh Street in Columbia is only a few blocks from a small, gray building called the Athanaeum, which had served as the Union headquarters in November 1864. I'd been told Bob was *the* expert on the Civil War around Columbia, and I had many questions about this assignment down the Duck River that had resulted in Darsie missing the Battle of Franklin, a fight that killed or wounded 9 of the 16 remaining officers and 150 of the 325 men.

Bob—a pudgy, mustached man who wore large, square glasses and a ball cap—ushered me into his office. One part of the large room was filled with notebooks, maps, and filing cabinets, all used for the business of buying and selling land. On the other side, a ten-by-fifteen-feet sheet of plywood lay on supports. Atop the plywood existed the most elaborate miniature world of forts, soldiers, and landscape I had ever seen. Two-inch pewter figures, all hand-painted with details such as beards, eyebrows, scars, shirts, and hats, stood motionless across the plywood. They held muskets, loaded cannons, fired weapons. Farmhouses, rock walls, forests, and fences divided the battlefield.

"What's all this?" I asked, thinking of my toothpick fort from the third grade.

"Ah, this," said Bob, in that relaxed, Southern drawl that makes even one-syllable words sound long and melodic, "is my hobby. I'm a gamer."

"A gamer?"

"Yeah. War games. I get together with other gamers and we enact scenarios from different battles. This is set up right now for the Crimean War in Russia. See the turbaned soldiers and rocky outcrops?" Bob spoke as if I knew what he was talking about.

"War games?" I asked. He smiled.

"Yeah, it's what us old, fat men do when we can't run around anymore." Bob looked to be in his late forties. He lit a cigarette and sat down at his desk. "Now, you said over the phone your ancestor was with the 72nd Illinois?"

I nodded and told him what I knew about the Williamsport expedition based on Darsie's journals, as well as the writings of William Mohrmann, James Sexton, and George Heafford. "The mission obviously made a great impression on several men," I finished, "but I can find nothing about it in the official records."

"It wouldn't have been written about officially," Bob said, "because it was so routine as to warrant little lasting interest. It was, however, unusual in that the cavalry typically executed such work."

Bob then explained how Nathan Bedford Forrest, the famous (or infamous, depending on which side you were on) Southern cavalry commander, had routed the Northern horsemen out of the Columbia countryside and back into town. This conflicted slightly with James Sexton's account that the Union cavalry had been captured and probably hanged. In any case, Darsie's foot journey resulted from the cavalry not being available.

The Santa Fe Pike, also now known as State Highway 7, snakes west of Columbia, slithering in and around the hills north of the Duck River. Bob said the Illinois men would have traveled this route to Williamsport since the south side of the river was even more steep and impassable. "After reaching Williamsport," Bob continued, "Company A would have headed to Franklin via the Leiper's Creek Road. They would have been hotfooting it on this trip. Nobody wanted to run into Nathan Bedford Forrest and his gang. I can take you on a driving tour tomorrow if you like."

I met Bob at his office the next morning at eight, and soon we were heading west in his pickup. On the way out of town, he asked me if he could tape-record our conversation. "I write a history column for the local paper," Bob explained, smiling, "and they criticize me because I don't write enough about Yankees."

The forests of the Duck River watershed closed in over us. Hickory, maple, and poplar trees, all exuding various shades of green, leaned into the narrow roads creating a speckled tunnel. I read Bob passages of Darsie's journal while he drove.

"On November 29, he wrote:

> *We have orders to march this morning. There were two regiments 15 miles down the river at Williamsport some one was wanted to carry a dispatch to them to retreat to Franklin immediately Our Lieut Volunteered his services and chose 20 of Co "A" to acompany him I was among the Number the Colonel came and bid us goodbye told us we were going on a rather hazardous undertaking and he might not see all of us again I would have went then and bid goodbye with my brother who was in the Color Guard but had no idea of anything happening to me and never thought the regiment would get into a fight. we left camp at 10 Oc went to brigade HdQtrs. There we awaited orders about 1 Oc P.M. we started we kept close to the river marching fast where the roads were good*

Bob nodded. "This whole area was a lot more open in the 1860s than it is now. The settlers had already been here awhile and had cleared much of the forests for building materials and fuel. There wouldn't have been many hiding places."

Darsie next wrote:

> *towards Evening we met some Skouts of ours they had two Prisoners with them who said they belonged to Wheelers Cavelry. the Skouts told us to be careful and we would get*

throug all right We lightened our knapsacks all we could
I threw my blanket as I could not carry it.

"Why would he throw out such a crucial item?" I asked Bob.
"Probably on that journey the boys felt like, 'Well, if I'm going to die, what does it matter?' Also, they counted on the quartermasters to resupply them. Obviously, this didn't always happen."
I continued reading from the journal:

we had to wade creeks cross fences climb hills and tramp
throug mud all the way about 9. Oc at night we came
to a creek wide and deep we thought we were out of our
way. we saw a light on the other side R. Holmes and I
crossed and inquired the way we were only one mile from
Williamsport

Williamsport, now a town of approximately eighty people, is not on the way to anywhere and could probably vanish with few in the surrounding countryside taking notice. This indistinct existence, however, was not always the case. As early as 1807, Edward Williams, for whom the town is named, began operating a ferry here—one of the few safe places to cross the river in those days. In 1855 a bridge was constructed that connected Williamsport to the north for seven years, before it was burned by Confederate cavalry as a "military necessity" (rebuilt in 1871). The town, like a sleeping cat on a hot afternoon, didn't stir as Bob and I approached it.

One market/deli, three churches, a grange hall, and an old barn broke up the neighborhood of homes resting in the middle of spacious lawns. Additionally, a pallid, flat-topped structure had two pillars out front supporting a drive-through area that resembled an old gas station. Bob pointed to it.

"There used to be a tannery business next to that old store. The tannery may have been where the Union headquarters was."

———

Leiper's Creek, one mile east of Williamsport, flows north-south for fifteen miles before pouring into the Duck River. The stream ambled around my feet as I waded in the vicinity where I thought

Darsie might have crossed, in between the Santa Fe Pike and the river's mouth. Water as clear as a mirror flowed over riffles with stones colored in deep blues, reds, and browns. The pools, by contrast, deepened to an opaque black. I moved into the dark water, soaking my pants to the thigh.

The west bank's limestone wall rose straight up fifteen feet, then leveled and disappeared beneath a canopy of jungle. Northern cardinals sang and flew around like balls of fire. The winter waters of 1864 would have made crossing Leiper's Creek a much greater challenge than I now faced. Additionally, November 29 was the night of the new moon, so the twenty men moved in complete darkness, good for avoiding Forrest's cavalry, but bad for maneuvering around an unfamiliar landscape. According to Darsie, at approximately ten o'clock that night, all of Company A arrived at Williamsport and delivered the message to General Cooper. He wrote:

> *we were all tired and hungry. I was invited into the*
> *Colonels tent and had a nice supper of Ham Eggs & Coffee*
> *after this I felt better the Regts were ready to march in an*
> *hour and we left quietly*

I sat on a log in Leiper's Creek and thought about Darsie, two years in the Union army when he had made his way to Williamsport. Perhaps his fear during the Vicksburg charges had settled into a sharpened sense of awareness and fortitude. Perhaps he had developed the discipline to keep his nerves in check when death or injury awaited just out of sight. Thinking of Darsie, I remembered my father demonstrating the art of avoiding enemies.

In 1975, my parents bought a patch of woodland near Lake Cushman, a reservoir on the Olympic Peninsula, an hour's drive from Tacoma. The property, less than one-quarter of an acre, faced a newly constructed cul-de-sac named Coho Court, similar to Snowberry Circle, only wilder and with fewer homes. The second-growth forest hosted a snarl of spindly trees on our land and the back boundary melded into a common greenbelt that made our ownership seem bigger than it was. Looking back now, I remember it was not a beautiful stand of trees but, for my wilderness craving, it more than sufficed.

During one of our first visits to the property, Dad and I explored while Mom hung back near the graveled cul-de-sac smoking a cigarette. I ran around the woods like my cat Tiger chasing after a dog. Sharp sticks and hidden stumps lay beneath a thick mat of salal while the dead, decurved branches of the fir trees pawed at us like skeletal wooden fingers.

"This is like the Yukon!" I shouted. My father laughed.

"Yeah, I guess it is."

"Do you think there are any mountain lions living here, Dad?"

"Well, maybe not right here on our property, but certainly around Lake Cushman." I smiled, pleased.

We arrived at the boundary. I felt quite lost, but Dad seemed to know the way back. However, he wanted to return a different way.

"Why?" I asked.

"You always go back a different way than you came, kid. Otherwise, you might run into someone waiting for you."

"Like an ambush?"

"Exactly like an ambush."

Bob and I drove northeast along Leiper's Creek Road toward Franklin. At the village of Leiper's Fork, also referred to as Hillsboro during Darsie's time, Bob pulled off the road where water poured out of the embankment.

"This is 'Fly's Spring,'" he said. "The soldiers would have certainly stopped here for water."

Five miles farther we stopped again, this time at a grassy flat on the banks of the Big Harpeth River. I read to Bob what Darsie had written about their experience after leaving Williamsport:

> We marched all night and all next day. about 4 Oc we
> came to HillsBorough 8 miles from Franklin. Here we
> heard firing in the direction of F. and the Col thought we
> had best not go there so we started for the Nashville Pike.
> We procured a conveyance to carry our knapsacks.

Bob laughed. "Ya know what 'procured a conveyance' means, don't ya?" I shook my head.

"It means they stole a wagon!"

On the night of November 30, 1864, Darsie and Robert and the others from Company A listened to the battle at Franklin. They once passed so close to the fight that they could hear the cheering of the men who charged. They camped at the Big Harpeth River and the next morning waded waist-deep in the water to begin the final thirteen miles to Nashville. The survivors of the Franklin battle were relieved, and impressed, to see the return of all twenty of their comrades. Adjutant George Heafford wrote:

> [Brigadier General Thomas] *Ruger publicly tendered* [his thanks] *at Nashville a few days later. Forced marches against Forrest's Cavalry were as play to these foot soldiers.*

Likewise, William Mohrmann felt relief at the men's return:

> *To our greatest satisfaction Capt. Mason with the other half of Co A turned up all right in the afternoon. They had performed their errand by following the course of Duck river in the dark, wading through it several times and reached their destination after midnight. In an hour the detached brigade left for Franklin but found it necessary to take a wide circuit around it to avoid falling into rebel hands. They heard the infernal din of the battle and were quite willing not to be in it, but they had to practice pedestrianism to their utmost capacity, estimated they had marched 60 miles.*

It is possible that by volunteering for the hazardous duty, a task coupled with the very real possibility of being captured, Darsie may have saved his own life. This is what I had postulated one evening around the campfire to Chip, the Californian I'd met at the Willamette Mission reenactment. To my utter surprise, Chip chastised my ancestor.

"He should have been there! When they heard the fighting, they should have gotten to the battlefield as quickly as possible."

"But it was night! They had no idea what was going on, or where anyone was."

"Doesn't matter. They were needed. They should have been there."

When I mentioned this comment to Bob Duncan a few years after we'd first met, he scoffed.

"Hell, if they had headed for the fighting, they would have walked right into the Rebel line and been captured immediately."

Upon arriving at Nashville, Darsie was met with the worst kind of news. On December 1, 1864, he wrote:

> We saw some of our Officers in Town they told us that the regiment had been in the fight at Franklin and had lost 167 men killed wounded and prisoners My Brother was reported killed he was shot while planting the Banner on the works this was a sad strike for me as he was the only friend I had

Chapter 15

The Movie Shoot

It is well that war is so terrible; else we should grow too fond of it.

—General Robert E. Lee (1807-1870)

Autumn 2002, Ferndale, Washington

I STOOD IN A ROW of unfamiliar reenactors. Four of us from the 19th Indiana had come from Oregon to this small town south of Bellingham, Washington, along the I-5 corridor. Becoming a Civil War soldier had taken me into battle at reenactments, a backwoods tactical, and now the set of a movie. Today we would shoot the trailer for *Chapel Hill*, a local production of a fictional love story woven around the single bloodiest battle of the Civil War: Antietam. My comrades had all vanished into the waves of blue and I nodded curtly to a few soldiers next to me. They nodded back. Mist enveloped us, and despite my wool clothing, I felt chilled.

The assistant director, a young woman with long, wavy red hair and a radio microphone clipped to her back pocket, walked down our line handing each soldier a pair of "Hollywood gaiters." Unlike real gaiters, which have buckle snaps and leather bands, these fit loosely around our calves with Velcro. Just before the battle in Maryland on September 17, 1862, Confederate General John B. Gordon had noted, "So far as I could see, every soldier wore white gaiters around his ankles."

We continued to wait. My beard, mustache, and hat helped to keep my head warm, but my fingers and toes became numb. Brogan boots, I'd discovered, were not the least bit waterproof. I could look forward to a day of wet, cold feet.

"Okay, you're dead, you're dead, you're wounded, you're dead," Brian Young, the director, said as he walked along our line informing each of us in the front two rows of our predetermined fate. Our "Bloody Lane," as the Sunken Road came to be known after the battle at Antietam, consisted of an eight-foot-wide swath through the grass that had been carved out the day before by a bulldozer. This "road" sat three feet lower than a buck-and-rail fence extending along its length. Once filming began, we'd march one hundred feet toward the fence, dying, falling wounded, falling into the ditch, or soldiering on, as deemed by Brian.

"You're wounded," he said to the man next to me. "And you're dead," to me. Brian, in his thirties, wore a ball cap and what looked like an army surplus coat. Apart from a five-o'clock shadow, he seemed like a big, congenial kid. He smiled, laughed, and thanked us repeatedly for volunteering for his project. Brian carried a bull-horn and always seemed to be doing about five things at once.

The first thing we did that morning was march. With guns at shoulder arms (carried vertically at our sides), we stared straight ahead and took large strides for the camera. Brian wanted to capture hundreds of legs, dressed in gaiters, moving forward into a sealed destiny. The crew set up sheets of plywood along the direction we marched. Then the man with the camera sat on a wheeled board and was pushed along the plywood by a person with a two-by-four. I stared at this operation, fascinated to learn how moving people are filmed without the camera bouncing.

"Don't look at the camera!" Brian suddenly yelled through the megaphone. "That's called 'spiking,' and if it happens we have to cut the whole scene!" I looked away toward the fence and ditch.

"Settle!" he yelled next. Everyone stopped talking.

"Lock down! Quiet for sound! Position! Action!"

We marched for ten seconds with the cameras trained on our legs. Then Brian shouted, "Okay, back to one!"

The morning unfolded as Brian directed us on how to march across the field. A special-effects camera hovered above the fence on a boom truck. Brian explained how the camera could make our group of two hundred look like ten thousand.

"We're going to set sticks next to the farthest right men. We'll film you marching about fifteen paces, then move you all to the right of the sticks. Men in the back, I'll want you to move forward so it looks like different people. Take your hats off if you're wearing them. Move your haversacks to the other shoulder. Then we film you again doing the same thing. The camera splices the clips together to make the scene look like hundreds of soldiers marching together. Everyone understand?"

We nodded. Though still fascinated, after the tenth time of shuffling around the sticks and marching fifteen paces, I felt antsy to get to the fighting. Finally, we arrived at the fence.

"Okay, gentlemen, I want you to fix bayonets," Brian directed through the megaphone. We looked at each other, surprised. We *never* fixed bayonets during reenactments except during flag presentations and inspection of arms. Having a sharp blade firmly attached to our guns during battle was too dangerous, and the rules of the Northwest Civil War Council didn't allow for use of the bayonet.

"We have to have bayonets," Brian explained, and then added, "just be really careful. The two stunt men we'll focus the cameras on will have rubber bayonets. But, even if you don't think the camera is filming you, pretend it is! Stay in character until I say 'Cut!'"

By now, we'd eaten lunch and the autumn day was rapidly fading. Black and white umbrellas, pitched above cameras, kept the equipment dry, but the operators frequently had to wipe the square, black lenses with dry cloths. I shivered, my breath exploding in puffs in front of my face.

Before filming, a man trotted along the line blowing smoke from a machine that doused us in a bluish haze. As the Union soldiers arrived at the fence, I fell "dead" and got really cold lying on the muddy ground. For the next sequence, I ignored my death sentence and raced up to the fence, climbed over it, and picked a Confederate to fight. So many of us crowded into the trench that, during this first attempt at the scene, we jostled wildly about, like bumper cars at a state fair. A man near me started to laugh and soon everyone was giggling.

"Cut! CUT!!" Brian yelled. He stomped over to us, flecks of mud flying up onto his black pants.

"You're all smiling! What the hell are you doing *smiling*? This is not funny. You're killing each other, for God's sake! Now, let's do this again and if *one* person smiles, the entire scene ends up on the cutting room floor!"

Brian's words sobered us. I returned to my position near the fence on the other side of the trench.

"Action!"

I ran forward and jumped the fence. The top rail fell and a few men collapsed over the wood. A young boy on the enemy's side rushed toward me. We met on the slope, tussling and dropping down into the trench. He wore a gray jacket that fit his slim body snugly and a brown hat with the brim pushed back. I actually had more hair on my face than he did, but his youth or good looks didn't concern me. I thrust my bayonet near his side and withdrew it as he reeled back. Then I brought the butt of my gun up toward his head, which he quickly snapped back. Our choreography couldn't have been better. If the camera was on us, it had seen me "kill" him.

After this exchange, I slipped on the muddy incline at the same time several large men fell around and on top of me. *The bayonet!* My gun stuck straight up in the air, the silver blade waiting to skewer someone. I pushed against the heavy bodies for a space in which to stand.

"Jesus, move!" I panted, but no one paid any attention. "Goddamn it, I said, *move!*" I shoved a paunchy soldier with sweat and rain running down his face and finally got to my feet. Just as I pulled the gun close to my body where it couldn't hurt anyone, I saw two soldiers fighting next to me. One brought his musket up too high. The bayonet narrowly missed the other man's eye. My legs started shaking from excitement and nerves. The scene was becoming more realistic than I'd expected; after more shoving and near-stabbing, I felt immense relief when Brian yelled "Cut!" and no one had been hurt.

The last scene was a shot of the battle's end, where Union and Confederate soldiers lay dead and dying along the Bloody Lane.

Every muscle in my body ached from the cold and falls I'd taken throughout the day. I eased gently into an open patch of mud as others did the same. A man's leg flopped across mine, while another's arm landed on my stomach. A woman with a long ponytail walked around us pouring "blood" from a bucket onto the ground and using a turkey baster to squirt the red liquid onto people's faces and clothes. A light rain cooled my face, which was windburned and hot from the adrenaline rushes. We had little to do in this scene except provide the backdrop for an exchange between the two main actors in the story. Even just being dead, however, wasn't easy.

"It looks too contrived!" Brian shouted. "Your bodies have to be piled haphazardly, mangled!"

We shifted position. Some men stood up, then fell over limp. Too tired to get up, I simply crooked my neck as far as possible to make it look broken. After Brian shot the scene, no one moved.

"You can all get up now," he shouted into the bullhorn.

I stood up slowly and looked around at the dirty, bloody, smelly soldiers I'd just spent twelve hours with. Some spoke quietly. Some said nothing. Suddenly tears began pouring out of me. I didn't want the men to see me crying, so I hurried off to the tent of Mr. BBQ, a caterer Brian had hired to feed us. Standing in the drizzle alone, I ate a plate of barbecued pork, salad, and beans. *I got into the spirit of things*, I thought. I'd pretended to be a killer and to be killed and though I'd done this many times before, something had changed. The game did not feel like a game any longer, and I wondered if, in another life with another career and other choices made, I would have been able to do my duty. Many times throughout this long, cold, wet day I'd felt exhilarated. Now, however, I had to cope with other emotions I hadn't expected.

Chapter 16

Making a Good Death

When you are dying, the doctor says you're dying. You assemble your family around you and sing hymns and you are brave and stalwart and tell the little woman that she has been good to you and not to cry. And you tell the children to be good and mind their mother, Daddy's fixing to go away. That was called making a good death, and it was very important.

> —Shelby Foote, Civil War historian, on nineteenth-century deathbed rituals, as quoted by Tony Horwitz in *Confederates in the Attic: Dispatches from the Unfinished Civil War*

Early 1991, Tacoma, Washington

ON JANUARY 17, 1991, a coalition of forces from around the world, including the United States, began an air war against Iraq's military as Saddam Hussein's armies occupied the country of Kuwait. The American nightly news seemed to drop every domestic and international story that didn't have to do with the war. The television lit up with images of fighter jets taking off from aircraft carriers, people wearing gas masks in Israel (where they feared retaliation from Hussein), and journalists reporting the war for those of us who couldn't be there in person. I didn't remember much about Vietnam. Now I had a second chance to watch an age-old human drama, which should never be considered a spectator sport, but often is in this age of visual media. By February 24, when the ground war began, Hussein's forces were all but defeated. Within ten days, Iraq would surrender and shortly thereafter, U.S. forces would begin returning home. The brief conflict, a seemingly undeniable victory, would have far-reaching consequences. At the time, however, for me, the Gulf War provided only a nerve-racking background for a more immediate catastrophe: my father's terminal illness.

Though the doctors had determined his cancer was inoperable on December 31, 1990, they hadn't known for several weeks where it had begun. By February 1991 they knew: the upper reaches of the colon.

"We can do chemotherapy," the young doctor with the impassive face had told me, "but it won't do any good."

I hate you, I thought, but said, "Maybe it would buy some time?"

"Maybe, but probably not."

In January, Dad chose to undergo treatment despite the doctor's assessment. I think he did so to give my mother and me false hope. After a few weeks, however, he would stop the useless depletion of his limited energy and would go to the hospital only to have his stomach cavity drained, a consequence of blood and waste accumulating outside of the colon, and to receive blood transfusions. Though these procedures wouldn't prolong his life, they made him feel better.

One weekend in February I drove to Tacoma; night had fallen by the time I pulled into Snowberry Circle. The cul-de-sac had changed dramatically in the twenty-two years since we'd first moved there. Seedlings in yards had grown into trees. Lawns had become old, tired, and brown. Neighbors had changed. The rocks my dad and I had sat upon in 1969 were now hidden by parked cars and fir trees.

I turned off the car engine and breathed deeply. The nightmares of my childhood permeated my every waking hour now: confusion, helplessness, a tangle of circumstances that I couldn't undo. I felt like I walked on ice floes, fragments that shifted with each step. The drama now unfolding with my father had begun in November with his simple declaration that he "didn't feel well." Each month since then had brought new situations, new pain. I didn't know what awaited me this weekend.

I walked up the drive and onto the cement path leading to the front door. The Big Dipper and North Star still twinkled from the garage door, and the four arborvitae shrubs Dad planted two decades before had grown into a wall of greenery four feet tall and three feet thick. Some things changed. Some stayed the same. With the living room drapes open, I could see Dad sitting on the couch watching TV. *The war*, I thought. He smiled when he saw me and got up quickly to unlock the door. For a moment, it seemed like the good old days.

My father wore blue sweatpants and a snow-white sweatshirt broken up by blues, golds, and reds, with the words, "We Support Our Troops" printed at the bottom. We hugged and I felt his expanded abdomen. Pulling away, I saw his eyes, sparkling with my arrival, suddenly go gray. He looked over my shoulder, then sank toward the floor. I snaked my arms around him, catching him and thinking he had died. My mother saw what was happening from the kitchen and hurried in with a chair. Dad sat down. He wasn't dead, just dizzy and out of breath.

"Guess I got up too fast," he panted. I looked at Mom, who had tears in her eyes. My insides felt like they were leaking out of me.

"I'm okay," my father said, as bombs exploded on the television. He stood up carefully and returned to the couch. Mom took the chair back and I sat beside him.

"How are you doing, Pop?"

"Fine."

Dad's eyes told me what he would not. He was exhausted and he'd given up. I went to the bathroom and sobbed into a towel. After a few minutes, my mother knocked on the door.

"Betsy, dinner is ready."

"Okay."

Mom and I sat at the dining room table beneath Dad's map with the colored strings. She had made one of my favorite dishes from childhood, creamed cod over boiled potatoes. We picked at the food while Dad continued watching TV. I felt hot, and sweat trickled down my sides.

"Why's it so hot in here?"

"Because Dad's so cold."

"Oh." Several minutes passed.

"How's work?" Mom finally asked.

"Fine. I'm going to an amphibian workshop next week." My job as a wildlife biologist with the Forest Service in Oregon involved classes on many topics during the winter months.

"Oh. What do you do there?"

"There will be speakers talking about their research on frogs and salamanders. They'll discuss populations that are declining and also how to survey for certain species. We want to start our own inventories on the district."

"Huh," Mom smiled thinly. "That's great, honey."

"Yeah." *This is a stupid conversation,* I thought, *when Dad is dying in the other room. Everything is stupid. Life is stupid if this is what it comes down to.*

Silence set in and after a few minutes my father teetered in and sat by the fireplace.

"Hi, Dad!" Mom said cheerily, as if everything were just fine. I hated her bravado. I hated all of us for pretending.

"Hi. Just thought I'd join you girls."

"We're glad you did. Aren't we, Bets?"

"Of course," I said, looking at my father. He seemed smaller, except for his stomach. He sat with his legs together, hands clasped on his lap. Opus, my cat that had moved in with my parents after I began a nomadic life with the Forest Service and had become "Dad's cat," brushed against his leg. He pushed her away.

"I can't stand the cats rubbing on my anymore," he said quietly. I wanted to cry. Everything about my father seemed to be vanishing. Opus looked bewildered as well and headed for the back door, deciding perhaps that it was better to be outside than to be rebuffed. I let her out as Dad stood up.

"This isn't going to work," he said. "The smell of food is making me sick." He left for the living room.

Mom and I cried silently over our creamed cod. She looked at me with tears falling down her face.

"I look at him," she whispered, "and all I can think of is Doris. I just can't do this again, Betsy." Doris was my mom's older sister who had died in 1977 after battling lung cancer for a year. Mom had taken care of her for part of that time.

"I guess we have to, Mom," I said with courage I did not feel.

"Yeah, I guess we do."

———

Dad's silence roared through our little home. He didn't want to dictate his war stories. He didn't want to talk about anything, it seemed. Initially, after his diagnosis, there had been a flurry of activity and discussion about wills, living wills, and other legal matters. Now, the paperwork was done. Dad's only remaining task was to wait, and he did so laconically.

My father now slept in his den on my old bed because the motion of my parents' water bed made him sick. Mom put an egg-crate foam pad on top of the twin mattress to cushion his increasingly bony frame. A saucepan from our camping days sat at the head of the bed. Dad threw up into this two or three times a day.

My father's silence represented a personality shift so severe that I felt, in effect, he had died the day he heard his diagnosis. It only took his body two and a half months to catch up with the news. A seed of anger sprouted within me as Dad's obsession with his own pain seemed to grow. It didn't seem to matter whether I was there or not. *He*, in either case, was not with me. His disregard for what I was going through and his deflection of my attempts to connect with him called forth a long dormant episode from my past, a time of abandonment and personality change that I'd hoped never to experience again. It had happened almost exactly seventeen years before and had driven a wedge between my mother and me that would forever define our relationship.

———

One day in late February 1974, Mom and I were walking to Chambers Elementary School, where I attended third grade. The year before, my mother had started volunteering for my second-grade teacher two days a week. We laughed that now she was still in second grade, but I had moved on. I liked third grade. We were learning to read silently, everyone had been quite impressed when I had brought my microscope in to show-and-tell, and I had just received a good grade for my toothpick fort.

Chambers was two blocks from Snowberry Circle, built against the cemetery woods. It took about ten minutes to walk there, a little more if I had to bring Tiger, who often followed me, back home.

On this Friday morning, Mom and I walked through the mist of a late winter chill. We had just arrived at the entrance to Madrone Circle when a white three-quarter-ton truck pulled up to the stop sign. The driver, a young man with a vacuous face and sandy hair, motioned for us to cross. We hesitated. My mother waved him on. He insisted again, smiling in a gritty, impatient way. This game of politeness led to frustration, and finally we all moved at once. The driver hit the accelerator just as my mother stepped into the truck's path. Her body contorted into a backward "C" on the grill, traveled several feet, then fell abruptly to the asphalt as the screeching of brakes rose above the howling engine.

The world from where I stood suddenly changed from clear, sharp proportions to the muddled opaqueness of a dream. My mind froze, my limbs also went numb, and my ears filled with a sound like raging water. Fortunately, my legs still worked and they transported me over to the driver, who was getting out of his truck.

"Are you all right?" he asked.

"Yes." I looked down at my mother. Her eyes were closed and half of her body lay under the engine. *She's dead*, I thought, and ran for help.

Mom stayed at the military hospital for four days. Her absence seemed longer. Up until the year 2000, when I received her medical file on this incident, I thought that she had been there for two weeks. I don't remember anything after the accident, except explaining what had happened to a police officer and visiting Mom once in the hospital. She had a black eye and scrapes on her face. She moved slowly toward us in the waiting room, dragging what looked like a coatrack on wheels behind her. My knees shook and I fought hard not to cry.

When my mother returned home, she wore a scarf over her head to cover where they had shaved her hair. Besides being knocked unconscious for several minutes by the truck, she had suffered a basilar skull fracture and some broken ribs, but apart from the black eye and shaved head, she seemed the same. *My* biggest concern was a new terror I'd developed of moving vehicles.

One day after school, she told me she wanted to buy me a gift.

"Why?"

"For saving my life, of course."

We drove to the local Fred Meyer store, where I selected a View-Master camera and two discs with images of wild animals.

"Thank you, honey," she said again as we walked toward the car. I grabbed her arm to hurry us through the parking lot.

"Sure, Mom. I love you."

"I love you, too."

Despite appearances, however, it soon became apparent that my mother wasn't the same person. In the medical report I later obtained, I discovered she had returned to the hospital four days after being released for "severe occipital headaches." I don't remember this. The report also stated that she suffered dizzy spells while changing sleeping positions at night. I don't remember this either. These episodes apparently were short-lived, and by morning she was able to "return to essentially normal function." What never changed, however, was the loss of her senses of taste and smell.

Though my mother seemed grateful I had "saved her life," as she put it, the months after the accident saw a fraying of our relationship. A growing anger inside of her seemed to erupt easily, like the striking of a match. One evening, I remember finding her in the dining room looking through the sliding glass door into the darkness. I asked her what she was doing.

"I'm thinking about going for a walk," she said coldly.

"But Mom, you can't, it's night."

"I can do whatever I want!"

My mother knew how afraid I'd become of walking where there might be moving vehicles. I begged her not to go out. These many years later, I don't remember what happened next. I don't think she went walking, and she may have just shut herself in her bedroom to calm down.

I never knew what might trigger these strange episodes, and I don't remember this volatility before the accident. Once she slipped into this mood, it was like she was driving down a narrow street, focused and not turning back. Another time, when I sensed she was angry with me, I went to my room and wrote her a letter apologizing for whatever I had done. I snuck to the kitchen and placed it on the table. Later, I heard her tearing up the paper. This, then, became our relationship. I begged her for contact; she wielded power by ignoring me. Nothing I could say or do appeased her, and only the passage of time—sometimes hours, more often days—softened the hardness of her rage.

In this environment, with my father on swing shift at the post office, the evenings were long and lonely. I spent a lot of time in my room, playing with Tiger and her kittens and trying to stay out of my mother's way. I'd set up my microscope and perform physicals on the cats. I cleaned their claws and brushed them. When they wearied of these ministrations and went outside, my room took on a great expanse as I imagined living in the wilderness. In my fantasies, I always lived alone, far from people, who could be too unpredictable.

Eventually, my mother's dark moods diminished in frequency, but never in intensity. Her new personality—with its unpredictable, unfair nature—caused me to withdraw from her. Now I understand that her head injury, as well as sensory loss, probably affected her in ways over which she had no control, but at the time I hated her for making me afraid. Though we struck a balance of sorts in the years to come, we never completely came to terms with our fraught connection.

Additionally—because I didn't remember this behavior occurring before the accident—I assumed *it* was the sole cause of my mother's pain. Now, I'm not entirely sure. The sensory loss she suffered certainly was a part of it. However, after beginning my research into the combat lives of Darsie and my father, I realized that my mother's behavior seemed more like that of a haunted war victim, while my father, apart from his withdrawal through alcohol, seemed the happy-go-lucky guy. I think, as with many aspects of life, the situation was very complicated: parts of each of us may have oozed into the others, causing my parents and me to become a blend of one another's personalities and experiences. Perhaps, we carried each other's burdens as well, and the past, because we left it buried, continually affected our present in ways we couldn't begin to define.

———•••———

There wasn't much I could do at home apart from driving my father to chemotherapy sessions and, when these ended, wandering aimlessly from room to room. One evening, when the constant silence threatened to suffocate me, I went to my cousin's house. He and I got drunk, and I passed out on his couch. The next morning, when I returned home, Dad was on the couch in his sweatshirt and sweatpants.

"Hi," I said, trying to act normal. My dad had seen a lot of hungover people in his day; I'm sure I didn't fool him.

"Hi."

"Whatcha watching?"

"*The Price Is Right.*"

I steadied myself by sitting down on the love seat. It felt like the ringing bells and screaming contestants would burst my eardrums. Nausea threatened to overwhelm me. I peered at Dad out of the corner of my eye. His mane of white hair looked as regal as ever.

"Well, Pop, at least your hair isn't falling out," I said, encouragingly. He looked at me angrily.

"The hell it ain't."

"Huh?"

"It's falling out all over."

But I hadn't noticed. I had seen only what I wanted to see. My father stared at the television, but I sensed he wasn't really with me in the living room watching this American drivel. Perhaps he was back on the farm in Geneseo, with his brother and Big Grandpa and Little Grandpa. Maybe he was thinking about his grandmother's words—"We were put on the earth to suffer"—but now didn't think they were so funny. Maybe he was making his first parachute jump, with a feeling of ice in his stomach, or maybe he was leaving the plane in Normandy, into a dark sky lit up like the Fourth of July. Maybe he thought of the old German woman; or the one hundred men of I Company that didn't return to Camp Quorn, England, in

July 1944; or the North Korean that he'd blown up with a hand grenade. Maybe he reflected on the nightmares he'd suffered all of his adult life, or maybe he thought about none of these awful things and instead focused on everything he had loved and would miss about being alive.

With my mind a maelstrom of emotion and thought, I slipped without any warning into a void of the unthinkable. *I could kill him*, came the idea—so abrupt that the words were like jolts of electricity. *I could end his suffering.* No longer able to stand watching the pain of this man whom, apart from all our troubles, I loved more than anyone, some part of me lit upon a possible solution. But it wasn't a solution I welcomed. My bowels suddenly felt like they were about to release, my heart sped up, and the blood in my veins seemed to turn to glacier water. *No!* I shouted inside my head. *No! I would never hurt my father.*

I stood up, desperate to get away from Dad's lifeless presence. Staggering into the backyard, the damp Northwest air descended around me. Everything looked dead: our fruit trees, Mom's garden, the grass. Death and the process of dying were suffocating me. I saw a shovel leaning against the fence.

I could take that shovel and hit Dad over the head, I thought. *No!* another part of me screamed. Falling on the cold ground, I was certain I was losing my mind. In the end, of course, I would not kill my father, but for weeks after this incident I walked on eggshells, afraid my mind would snap at any minute and I would do something terrible.

One evening, several days later, as my parents and I sat on the couch, my father cleared his throat.

"While you're both here, I want to say something." Then he looked at me. "Bets, I want you to take my guns back with you to Oregon." When I looked puzzled, he moved his gaze to his folded hands. "They're too much of a temptation."

I nodded, my stomach convulsing into a tight knot, and my mother and I, without speaking, wrapped the two rifles and shotgun in an old blue blanket and put them in the back of my Honda Civic. Later, I returned to the couch where my father sat.

"Thanks," he said.

"Please keep trying, Pop."

"I will." But I wasn't sure if he would.

———◦———

On March 6, my father nearly died in his den. He couldn't breathe and he couldn't move. My mother called the ambulance, which transported him to the hospital. The doctors stabilized him, but it was clear that his life had only a matter of days remaining, and they told him he could leave. He declined.

"I think you better come home, Bets," my mother said over the phone. "This is your last chance."

I hung up, thinking of all the moments that pile up in life, how time seems to stretch on and on forever and never change. I thought of all the years my dad had been there, but I had barely noticed him. Time had rippled by and I'd foolishly assumed he always would be there. *That* life, however, was not to be.

Two days later, I walked into Dad's hospital room. He was asleep, his head hanging down and his mouth open. His hair was flattened in back, and what remained on top stood up like a bird's crest. His limbs resembled stick figures I had drawn as a child. Only the over-sized stomach seemed to have any energy.

Dad was groggy after waking. His eyes, large like a salamander's, did not at first seem to see my mother and me. A jet flew by and the windows rattled.

"Sounds like an F-14," he said.

"You can tell that just by the sound?"

"Hey, kid, you learn a few things as a soldier."

For the next five days, my mother and I spent several hours each morning and afternoon at the hospital. I felt paralyzed by what I saw, smelled, and heard. One day, my father wet the bed. On another he spit up sickly sweet, bloody bile into a kidney-shaped bowl I held in front of him. When I could no longer stand being in the room, I roamed the halls of the spidery, one-story hospital and prayed for a miracle.

In the years to come, I would see these last weeks of my father's life as wasted. I would hate myself and my mother for not helping him make a good death. I would hate him for his withdrawal. I would hate all of us for what we never said. Maybe it's a selfish matter for the healthy to want so much from the dying, since I cannot appreciate my father's physical or emotional suffering, but I do understand the pain associated with helplessness—the paralysis I felt watching him die and being unable to do anything about it.

Chapter 17

Iuka

[Wednesday, January 18, 1865, road
between Iuka and Corinth, Mississippi]

*we encamped 12 miles from Iuka making in all 20
miles we had traveled that day we were tired and were
glad to rest when night overtook us after gathering me
some grass that grew in abundance near a swamp close
to our camp I and Charles Stambaugh laid us down
to rest soon we were awaked by the Shouts of our comrades crying fire on looking up we saw our bed on fire
it came near burning us up would if It had not been
arrested by some watchful comrade we then lay without
"Straw" the rest of the night*

—From the journal of Private Darsie Heath,
72nd Illinois Infantry, Company A

FOLLOWING THE BATTLE AT FRANKLIN, and another at Nashville
in mid-December, the Army of the Tennessee, including the 72nd
Illinois, chased General John Bell Hood's Confederate army south to
Pulaski, Tennessee, where they were then diverted west to Clifton, a
small village on the Tennessee River. On January 8, they boarded a
ship and traveled upriver seventy-five miles to Eastport, Mississippi,
where they would go into winter quarters. Darsie wrote:

*we are on a miserable tub of a boat it is loaded with cattle
on the Boiler deck. we can have but little room I and my
partner (Charles Stambaugh) were procured a good place*

on a coil of Cable here we remained during the voyage. we
were near the Boiler and put up our tents to keep out the
wind-we were very comfortable except at night our bones
ached with lying on the uneven bed.

For the next month, the regiment remained in the Eastport-Iuka
vicinity. They provided security to surrounding homes and made
an expedition to Corinth, a town twenty miles to the west and built
around the crossroads of two vital railroads, the Memphis-Charles-
ton and the Mobile-Ohio. According to William Mohrmann, on
their return, Company A was selected to provide "a sort of provost
guard" for the area's residents.

It was during this time that Darsie wrote about a two-day episode in which he became trapped in the home of a Southern doctor
in a landscape teeming with soldiers from both sides and no clear
lines of occupation. It's the only place in either journal where my
great-great-grandfather elaborated on his experiences as a soldier,
and, though choppy and at times confusing, the narrative filled in
some of Darsie's personality that, for me, had been lacking. However, despite the detail, the event wouldn't be without its lingering
mysteries.

Autumn 2000, northeast Mississippi

Iuka, named after a Chickasaw Indian chief, began as a small Native American village along a tributary of the Tennessee River in
northeast Mississippi. According to legend, Iuka, who lived during
the late-eighteenth and early-nineteenth centuries, had been in-
formed of healing waters located near the river. Sick and helpless
at the time, Iuka had his followers carry him to the spot. He drank
the water and was reportedly cured. The news spread like wildfire
and made such an impression that the town of Iuka, officially established in 1857, became a place of pilgrimage for the ill and dying.
In 1904, Iuka water won a medal for purity at the St. Louis World's
Fair. However, during the difficult years of the 1930s and '40s, the
town's fame evaporated, and the spas and hotels that had been built

during the 1880s closed.

In the nearly deserted city park just off the main square, I found the gurgling waters, now flowing out of pipes extending from round brick cisterns, and a sign that read:

WORLD FAMOUS MINERAL SPRINGS PARK

DRINK TO YOUR HEALTH

A few parents played with their children nearby and some people walked their dogs, but no one rushed to drink the special water. I took several gulps for good measure.

A few blocks north of the park, across the railroad, is Iuka's center. Stone walls and newly planted magnolias, sugar maples, and Eastern redbuds dotted the open landscape around a central gazebo. Even in October the heat kept people off the streets in this town of three thousand. I sat in the shade of "Jay Bird Park" and reread Darsie's Iuka story:

> our Company was sent into the town in advance of the regt
> and one man was Stationed in each house to protect the
> property of the owners I chose a house on the outskirts of
> the Town as there seemed to be plenty there. I was soon
> at "home" there when I told the woman I had been sent
> to guard the property she invited me in the House Later
> in the evening the Doctor came he also treated me very
> kindly I was however a little uneasy when I found that
> I was on the outside of the Pickets The Doctor told me
> however that there was no danger. at least he thought so.
> he laid with me by the fire that night he said he was not
> used to lying there and would wake when the least noise
> was made I soon forgot my danger and went to sleep we
> were not disturbed during the night.
>
> Early the next mor[ning] while we were at breakfast
> a rebel soldier came to the Spring and asked one of the
> servants who was there if any "yankees" were in the house
> she replied "there was one" he went away after we had

eaten I went to the door and saw three of them in the
wood not 200 yards distant I then went over in town to
see if our Boy's had gone Saw the Sergeant he told me
to go back to the house. I told him of the Soldiers I had
seen he then said t'were better to remain where I was I
replied I was not afraid to go I said this because one of my
company hearing our conversation said "Heath did the
Gurrillas drive you away" "not Bad says I" I then returned
to the house and remained there the whole day

Company A left Iuka that morning without Darsie, who ended up hiding in the doctor's office, an outbuilding, the rest of the day and night after the Rebel soldiers began looking around the house for Yankees. In the afternoon sometime, the doctor and Darsie began to think about how he could escape. Darsie writes that the doctor

was for taking the wagon and going to Eastport. I was to
ly in the bottom of it concealed under a pile of blankets
this I thought would not work if the rebels were like us for
I have stood picket myself and I always liked to search
wagons not for men but something good to eat; and as we
were obliged to go throug the town and also through the
enemies pickets it was not very safe several other plans
were proposed none suited me except the one which came
in my mind first to wait until dark then steal away I was
finally agreed that this was the safest plan and I was to
make the attempt as soon as it was dark enough

That afternoon, the office grew cold from the winter air and the lack of a fire, which had not been built because the doctor told Darsie he rarely built fires in the office—and smoke coming from the building might arouse suspicion. About two o'clock, the doctor went to the office. Darsie wrote:

he had brought with him ink and pen he said I should
write to some one of my comrades telling him how I was
placed as this would clear him if any suspicion were

*attached to him if I did not succeed in making my escape
now for the first time a suspicion seized me that the man
intended to betray me however a look at him satisfied me
I then wrote to Lieut Wm. Mohrman then in command of
Co "A" telling him the truth of the whole matter. and also
acquitting the Doctor in a way that seemed to please him
"muchly" I also told the Lieut to write to my parents if I
did not return*

The day crept by, people came and went, and Darsie listened to
their conversations:

*two women were at the Dr all day they were talking of the
"Yanks" one was Blood thirsty she said her husband had
been knocked down bycause he tried to save his property
when the soldiers were destroying it. I was afraid one of
the servants might tell them and then I would have in for
it. the long wished for hour at last arrived—the Doc came
and told me it was dark enough for me to venture out. I
was glad to leave the Old Shop.*

Finally, night arrived and Darsie left with the doctor and his
twelve-year-old son, both of whom were to help guide the way. After
finding them to be slow traveling companions, Darsie thanked the
doctor for his kindness, told him he would see him the next day in
town, and set off on his own for Eastport. He eventually found the
right road, and

*was soon splashing through the mud I had forgot to
mention that It had been rainy for a day and night and
hence the mudy roads—in which Mifs can excel all other
States if in nothing else.*

In the early hours of that morning, Darsie ran into Union pickets:

*I was wet tired and awful mudy and when I heard the
"halt" of the sentry hardly knew whether to run or stand*

the "click" of a lock soon made me make up my mind and
in answer to his "Wo yu cum fromm" I told him that I was
a friend I knew then that I was inside our lines as few
Germans are found in the rebel army

Darsie stayed until daylight with his "German friends," soldiers
from the 198th New York Infantry, then started for camp. His comrades were relieved at his reappearance and congratulated him on a
narrow escape. Soon the doctor showed up:

> *The Doctor came as he promised and brought the letter I*
> *had written I of course secured this as I did not want the*
> *Lieut to see it under the circumstances The Dr wished to*
> *see the General and I went with him to see Genl Thomas*
> *he sent us to General AJ Smith and we found him on the*
> *Boat General Smith did not like the Doctor at first as*
> *he told him he was a neutral man Smith said he had no*
> *simpathy for such men. he said he would rather he was*
> *the G---d d-- -- dest rebel in the south. he said also he*
> *intended to "drive evrything in Mississippi to hell that*
> *wore Breeches" when I put in a word for the doctor it done*
> *some good for he was told to come in in a few day's and he*
> *could have all he wanted—*

A few days later Company A was put on guard again and Darsie
returned to the doctor's house.

East Port Inn, a bed-and-breakfast one block from Jay Bird Park,
reminded me of a Valentine's Day card. Soft white with pink shutters,
it sat quietly beneath southern hardwoods that were just beginning
to lose their leaves. I'd had enough of sleeping on the ground and
knocked on the door. No one answered. Eventually I found Betty
Watson, the proprietor, in the kitchen. Looking to be in her midfif-
ties, Betty wore a pink turtleneck and red lipstick, and resembled
the outside of her home.

"A room?" she said to my inquiry. "Oh yes, the downstairs is available." She showed me the spacious accommodation, which included a sitting area. Large windows let in copious amounts of light and potted jungle plants seemed to have taken over the space.

"Well, I'll let you get settled," Betty said. "By the way, do you want to join us for dinner tonight? My boyfriend is cooking, and he's French, so it'll be good."

I accepted and spent much of the day sprawled out in the sunny sitting room. Just before dinner, I walked back to Iuka's plaza. Across from Jay Bird Park was Moore's Jewelry, one of several businesses lined up along Front Street. Darsie had written that the doctor who had helped him was named More. It seemed a long shot but it couldn't hurt to inquire.

The young woman and older man working the counter listened to my story, which I ended by asking if the Moore of this business had an ancestor during the Civil War who had been a doctor. Though they thought the adventure interesting, they regrettably had no idea if the owner was related to the person in Darsie's tale.

During the ensuing days, I would talk with local historians and dig through census and plat records from 1865 at the Iuka library looking for information about a Dr. More and where he resided, but I never found anything conclusive. Though I felt like this part of the journal gave me more of Darsie's personality, I still had questions. I didn't understand exactly how much danger he had been in, given the seemingly fluid movements of both Union and Confederate soldiers, and I didn't really understand how he was talking with his comrades one minute then trapped in the doctor's house the next. However, memory could be selective, I knew that, and what's written down in one person's journal doesn't always capture the whole story. To add to the mystery, William Mohrmann had written this in his memoirs regarding Company A's stay in Iuka:

> I was detailed with my company as a sort of provost
> guard for the night that we stayed in Iuka and we
> quartered ourselves in a church. The destitution of the
> few inhabitants in these parts was pitiful and as there
> was nothing left worth stealing our duties as guards were

*nominal. When we were back in our camp our orderly
reported that private Heath was missing. It developed
that this man not satisfied with the hard benches in the
church had quartered himself in one of the houses in Iuka
for the night and not rejoined the company next morning.
However, he turned up at daylight the next day and told
how he'd "found" when he awoke that the rebel cavalry was
in town and his host hid him in a stable loft and guided
him at night past the pickets.*

Darsie's experience, mottled as it was for me, had obviously
made a great impression on him. He devoted fourteen pages in his
journal to its telling.

When I returned to Betty's place, her French-chef boyfriend
Bernard had saturated the house with the smells of baked chicken,
potato pie, and homemade bread. The other dinner guests included
three men from Utah, who boarded semipermanently at the East
Port Inn. Steve, Jerry, and Bob vaguely described their work at a
plant in Yellow Creek, west of Iuka, as "building weapons." They
had tidy military haircuts and Steve and Bob wore simple, round
glasses.

As Bernard brought out the food and we began dishing up, Steve
turned toward me apologetically.

"I don't know how you feel about guns," he said, passing the
chicken, "but I love them."

Caught off guard, I said, "Well, I do have an 1861 Springfield
musket."

He seemed not to have heard and began telling us about a new
military device called a "personal combat weapon."

"This gun is so awesome. You hold it with outstretched arms,
and it doesn't point straight ahead but rather to the side. That way,
a person can aim it around the corner of a building without expos-
ing his whole body. The helmet the soldier wears has a panel that
shows where the gun is pointing. Kind of like a video camera. Then
the bullet explodes at a certain distance, killing everything within a

specified area from pieces of metal stored in the bullet!"

"Kind of like the canister and grapeshot used during the Civil War," I said. Now Steve seemed impressed that I knew something about weaponry.

"Yes, exactly, only this is much more accurate."

"Wonderful."

"Yeah, isn't it?"

To this I had no reply and, fortunately, because Steve's enthusiasm for the personal combat weapon made me uncomfortable, the rest of the evening unfolded around Bernard's food, the cooling southern evening, and the calls of cardinals and mockingbirds.

A few days later, having given up my investigations into the forgotten Doctor More, I visited the Shady Grove Cemetery on Iuka's southeastern limits. Crispy, curling maple and sweet gum leaves crackled under my bike tires as I toured the cemetery, and a warm breeze swirled the smell of pine trees around me. Near one edge, I found a barely discernible trench—the final resting spot for 263 unknown Confederate soldiers. Killed during the Battle of Iuka in 1862, their names now are lost to the winds of time that eventually erode everything. Again, I was confronted with the fact that so much of the past is unknown, and what is not written down is often lost forever. I wondered who these men had been, these soldiers whose bones now lay beneath my feet, and I wondered what they had felt while dying on the battlefield. I thought of my father and Darsie coping with death and killing and the fear of the unknown and of being captured. It was fear that came through from the journals and it was fear that I often encountered when remembering my own past, and now as I considered three people's histories, I knew that looking straight at what made me most afraid was what some of my journey was about. Despite my childhood fantasies of surviving in the wilderness and of being tested, I usually avoided situations of vulnerability. I hated being afraid and uncertain. Yet, if I looked hard enough at my own past, I could see how my greatest fears, for better and worse, had shaped the person I'd become.

Chapter 18

Descent

Your pain is the breaking of the shell that encloses your understanding.

—Kahlil Gibran, mystic, poet, and artist (1883–1931)

August 1996, southwest Oregon

THE SMALL COMMUNITY OF AGNESS, Oregon, sits at the confluence of two powerful coast-range rivers, the Rogue and the Illinois. Twisting through the vertical country of the Siskiyou Mountains, the green, aquarium-like water of the Illinois meets the murky Rogue, and together they flow for thirty-five miles before pouring into the Pacific Ocean. Forest Service Road 33, a gray serpent in a green landscape, hugs the mountainous hillsides in a series of sharp turns and blind corners from Agness Pass, elevation 2,354 feet, south to the village of Agness. The upper portion in particular is a section of road where one should never daydream while driving. The drop to the bottom varies, but at one point the slope tumbles two thousand feet in a quarter mile. There are no guardrails. There is little traffic, and few people would notice a car that had gone over the edge.

By late summer 1996, one month before my mother died, I had worked on the Siskiyou National Forest for seven years, minus two spent in Argentina on a leave of absence with the Peace Corps. After my time in South America, I'd returned to southwest Oregon and become the wildlife biologist for the Powers Ranger District, a slice of the forest north of the Rogue River. I loved working in the woods and designing the wildlife program, a combination of species surveys, habitat improvements, and area planning. I felt content, mostly, despite the fact that life wasn't perfect. I'd undergone several hundreds of dollars worth of medical tests that spring to determine why I'd started having trouble breathing. The doctors initially thought it was asthma. Then they thought something might be on my lungs. After many scans, they decided the problem was stress. I vowed to get out into the woods more, where forest breezes calmed my worry over my mother's deteriorating health, my anger and regret over my father's death, and a concern growing inside of me about my drinking.

Never having been a "good sleeper," even as a child, my challenges in this regard had multiplied after my father's death. Drinking alcohol every night didn't help, but it made me feel better while I was awake. During my years on the Siskiyou, I lived in a small logging town called Powers, thirty miles north of Agness Pass. Though the inky skies and tomblike quiet couldn't have been better for sleeping, many nights I would find myself wide-awake and nervous, even after a few drinks. I'd get in my car and drive up to the pass, then down the other side to Agness. Screech owls flew in front of me. Deer bounded across the road. Raccoons ambled along the edges. Every trip I hoped to see the mountain lion that was often spotted on the road to Agness—but I never did. Nonetheless, the darkness, so often a backdrop for fear in my life, calmed me. Driving twenty-five miles per hour on the sinuous road, the side of which fell like a curtain to the river, took my mind away from my worries.

One weeknight I drove to Agness after work to meet a friend for a drink. Jeremy, a British biologist, had spent the summer working for the Forest Service and was soon to embark on a road trip around the States. "Come on over to the pub for a last few beers, hey?" he had invited. The pub was Cougar Lane, a bar/restaurant/grocery store on the banks of the Rogue River that served as Agness's social center. Knowing that I had to work the next day, I told myself that this would be a short visit.

Jeremy was chatting with the bartender as I walked in. I suspected this friendly, good-looking young man had charmed all the middle-aged Agness women during his few weeks here. His accent, thin build, and dark, straight hair were probably welcome changes from the usual clientele of balding, beer-bellied, tobacco-chewing, good old American guys.

"Hey, Betsy," he said. "Beer, huh?" I nodded and sat down on the barstool. We talked about his upcoming trip and the Volkswagen he'd bought here to travel around the West. We also talked about the waning summer. Jeremy had worked on a different district so I had seen him only a few times, during amphibian and peregrine falcon surveys. I liked his relaxed manner and sense of humor. He told me he'd been working on loosening up Connor, his boss.

"It hasn't been easy," Jeremy said, finishing his beer, "but I believe I'm having an effect on the bastard. Hey, Judy, two more, eh?"

"Damn," I said, "you're a fast drinker." He shrugged.

"Why not, hey? You Yanks finally got some decent beer." It was true. Even a backwater like Agness had microbrews.

After a few more, I don't remember how many, Jeremy bought a six-pack to go and suggested we head to the guard station a half mile away where he'd been staying for the summer. Forest Service guard stations typically accommodate seasonal employees working on fire crews, but sometimes there is also room for a summer biologist. I followed Jeremy in my car. When we arrived, we found the crew having a party.

"Hey, man!" one guy shouted at Jeremy. "Have a beer!" He offered a can from an open case of Miller Genuine Draft.

"Jesus, ya call that beer?" Jeremy sneered, and they all laughed. I vaguely recognized a couple of the guys from wildfire assignments we'd been on together. We said hello and continued the party.

From that point on, the evening is almost a complete blur for me. I don't remember anyone's name. I don't remember how many people were there. I don't remember what the guard station looked like or how long I stayed. The only two images I *do* remember are the increasingly empty case of beer, and later, a ring of guys around me begging me not to leave.

"Betsy, really, you shouldn't drive," said Jeremy. "Come on, you can sleep on the couch. It's not a big deal." The others agreed, adding that I couldn't possibly navigate the road over Agness Pass in my condition.

"Listen," I said, waving my arms and weaving down the steps of the porch, "I've driven this road a million times. I go out at night looking for the cougar. Really, I'll be fine!"

Jeremy looked worried as we hugged at my car. "Don't worry!" I shouted. "I'm fine!"

"Right, then."

After crossing the bridge over the Rogue River, I began climbing the gravel road to the pass. It's beyond my imagination now how I navigated this route without making a fatal mistake. I remember thinking at the time that it was like I was walking on a high wire, and I knew that I could fall—but I also remember not caring. I tried to drive slowly, but ended up skidding around curves that were deep with soft gravel. Once or twice, the road blurred into two roads. Once or twice, I stopped the car to refocus.

Two hours later, by some miracle, or perhaps only luck, I arrived home. The next morning, a very bad hangover descended over me. I made it to work, but didn't stay long. I sat at my desk and knew I'd crossed a line. My coworker and friend Steve walked by and casually asked how I was.

"I'm hung the hell over," I said, staring straight ahead, hoping my boss wasn't around. Steve laughed.

I went home sick that morning and knew I was in trouble concerning alcohol. In fact, everything that was hard for me—my father, my mother, my drinking, myself—seemed to be converging. I sensed that something big was about to happen.

Early 1980s–early 1990s, Tacoma, Washington

"Mom, Dad won't stay in bed," I complained, walking into the kitchen behind my father. He careened to the dinner table in his pajamas and sat down next to his cousin and our other guests, all of whom were still playing cards. My parents had invited several people over to eat dinner and spend the night.

"James, come on," Mom said firmly. "You've got to go to bed." Dad turned her way but did not open his eyes.

"I don't *got* to do anything," he said. "Bets, get me a snort."

"Pop, please," I grabbed his arm.

"Hey, now, knock it off," he said, snatching back his arm. I let go.

My father's behavior while intoxicated was always congenial, yet, I remember times when he would *almost* get angry.

"Oh, leave him alone," said Patti, my father's cousin. "He's fine. Aren't you, hon?" Though I was fond of Patti, I hardly felt she was in any condition to accurately assess the situation. Dad looked at her.

"I'm a good boy, ain't I?" Everyone laughed.

Disgusted, I gave up and sat down. No one seemed inclined to go to bed anytime soon, and I would never get to sleep with all the shouting and laughing. *Oh well*, I thought and shoved fifty cents on the table in front of me. "Deal me in."

These "quiet family gatherings," as my father referred to them, happened every few weeks during my teenage years. They always began great, with lots of storytelling, joking, and sharing. If it was Saturday night, *The Lawrence Welk Show* would be on TV in the living room while both of my parents prepared dinner. One weekend when I was fifteen, Patti and her husband George came over. Lawrence was doing a special on big bands. Dad and Patti danced in the living room and later they sat on the couch and told me about seeing "the maestro" in Santa Monica, California, before he hit the big time.

"Lawrence played at this little club and you weren't allowed to bring in booze," said Dad. "But we snuck some in anyway. Hid the flasks in our coats. The problem was we had to mix the drinks under the table and, of course, we couldn't see so they came out pretty strong!" Patti laughed.

"Remember Aunt Tom?" she asked. "Tom," or Nina, her real name, was Darsie's granddaughter, my grandmother's sister.

"Hell, yes!" he laughed, then looked at me. "Aunt Tom got so drunk once we had to carry her out and let her sleep it off in the car."

"Those were great times," said Patti.

The good old days sounded better than ever to me. They came to me as stories of parties, fun, and family. I never heard about the troubles of "those times." I never heard about my father's first wife and her infidelities. I never heard about the affidavit I would later find that stated he had hit her on two different occasions, "bruising and injuring her and causing her to have a black eye." I never heard about his drinking that was obvious as alcoholism even in the 1950s, as described in an e-mail message to me by Dad's former comrade Joseph Schwan:

> He was quite down in spirit in 1957 when I saw him again.
> I slept over in his home. I was on a re-hab type tour trying
> to get over a nervous breakdown and I think he was also
> down because of his demotion because of the army's
> drawdown. I think it is wonderful that you respect your
> dad, even tho he was an alcoholic, which I first saw in
> 1957, but that did not lessen my respect for him.

No, these were not the stories passed down about the good old days.

In April 1982, during my junior year of high school, I went to Mexico with students from my Spanish class. It was a seminal event for me. Though I had friends, I almost never participated in group activities. After one season of track in the seventh grade, I gave up sports. After three years of viola lessons in elementary school, I gave up music. Competition agitated me. Group dynamics made me feel isolated. I preferred solitude.

In Mexico, however, I spent every waking minute for nine days with ten other people. We tested our Spanish and laughed at the mixed results. We worried about the water and suffered through diarrhea. We laughed at pigs' heads in the market and gawked at the filthy streams. Apart from confirming my desire for foreign travel, the Mexico trip also launched another sort of journey.

Upon our return to Tacoma, none of us wanted to break our special connection. A few weeks later, the parents of one boy in our group, Jason, left for the weekend. Jason decided to throw a fiesta.

One of the few sophomores who had gone to Mexico with us was a girl named Debi. Before our trip, I had known Debi only from afar. She was cute, popular, and a cheerleader. She knew how to wear makeup, had all the right clothes, and went out with the best-looking guys. In other words, Debi and I had nothing in common. In Mexico, however, we instantly became friends. I was surprised that she was not stuck-up. Perhaps she was surprised that I was not such a dork after all.

I picked Debi up on Friday night to go to Jason's party. She wore a pink ribbon in her hair that matched the color of her eye shadow. She had curled her thick, blond mane into a golden splendor that framed her face like a protective collar. *She's beautiful*, I thought, and I knew then that I would do anything Debi asked.

Jason had talked his older sister into buying us beer. He also got ahold of tequila and some margarita mix. Though this was my first party with alcohol that didn't involve my parents, I knew exactly what to do. I mixed drinks, passed them around, drank several, and told jokes. People paid attention to me and they thought I was great.

"Hey, Betsy, ya wanna smoke?" Debi asked as we sat on the living room floor laughing at our tongues turning green from the margarita mix.

"Sure!"

She handed me a lit cigarette. I inhaled and didn't cough.

"This is the first time I've ever smoked," I said. Debi eyed me with a grin.

"Yeah, right."

That night, I threw up green margaritas and passed out. Through a haze I heard Debi say, "She can never drive. Someone take her keys."

"No, no," I garbled. "I have to get up early tomorrow. Gotta take the SATs...going to college, ya know ..."

"Well, whatever, ya still can't drive," Debi said, and took the keys from my pocket. I spent the night at Jason's after calling my mother and asking if I could stay at Debi's, the first of many lies to come. I also made it to the test, the first of many tasks I would accomplish hungover.

Back at school the following week, I found I had garnered new respect and attention for my antics. Casey, another Mexico traveler and my soon-to-be boyfriend, slapped me on the back at lunch saying, "You were hilarious, Howell! When I got there, you were

doing the breaststroke on the floor! I didn't know you were a par-
tier!" Well, in fact, I hadn't been, but I had been raised for the role.

That summer, my life changed at an exponential rate. In the
space of a few weeks, I smoked my first joint, threw *my* first party,
went to bed with a boy for the first time (fortunately missing the
sex because he was too drunk), and got very drunk for the first time
in front of my parents. The joint, party, and tête-à-tête happened
largely because of Debi's encouragement. The fourth I accomplished
on my own.

My cousin had a gathering at his house. My parents and the other guests were all tipsy by the time I arrived and no one commented
as I helped myself to several cans of Coors and Budweiser. Soon,
I couldn't talk or walk right. Weaving around the house, I began
shouting. My cousin steered me out to the front porch to calm me
down. I nearly fell over the railing.

After a few more beers, someone carried me into the guest room
to sleep it off. I didn't stay there. Soon, I was up again, weaving my
way back to the party. I plopped down in the middle of people sitting on the couch and pretended to read the comics page of the
newspaper. I have no memory of my parents' reactions to my behavior. My father was most certainly drunk at the time, and my mother
likely on the verge. Perhaps they didn't even notice. I slept at my
cousin's, making my way home the next morning. My parents never
said a word about what happened.

That autumn, as my senior year began, I started smoking more
pot. One night, I came home very stoned and went right to bed. The
next thing I knew I was standing over my parents watching them
sleep. Apparently, I had gotten up, gone to their room, and turned
on the light. As they began to move, I awoke from this fugue state,
turned off the light, and ran back to my bed.

After this incident, I realized that my life had slipped out of control. It felt like I was moving further away from myself. I blamed
Debi. With her good looks and persuasive personality, I'd had no
defense. Now, as I look back, I realize *my* choices could hardly be
blamed on her. She had provided entry into a world of acceptance
I had not experienced growing up as a shy, insecure individual, but

Debi certainly had nothing to do with the family I was born into or the fact that I had become comfortable with the culture of drinking as a young girl. She was merely a gardener tending very fertile ground where seeds had been planted long before. After college and my twenty-first birthday, I drank openly with my parents. By this time, Dad was sixty-seven and Mom sixty-two. There seemed to be more of a moderation in their habits, though not in mine. However, on my father's seventieth and final birthday, we all, once again, drank too much.

My half brother Jimmy had flown out from Illinois for the occasion. I drove up from Powers. Dad didn't want a big party, so it was just the four of us. Lime green buds were just popping out of the apple and cherry trees in our backyard, and with the long-absent sun streaking down during this April evening, Dad decided the weather was good enough for grilling. He lit the charcoal and we stood outside drinking wine. Dad showed Jimmy his latest outdoor projects while I visited with Mom about her garden. As usual, the evening began well.

We finished the wine by dinnertime and moved on to a bottle of scotch. When that was gone, Dad found a half-bottle of crème de menthe. The liqueur, not an appropriate beverage for drinking in large quantities, was finished as well. My mother finally went to bed, but Jimmy, Dad, and I kept drinking.

"I'm so envious of you two," our father said. "You have your whole lives ahead of you. So much to do! So much to experience! It's a great thing to be young. You just ..." He searched for the words, then punched a fist into the air, "you just have to go for it! Do what you want. Don't ever sit around wondering what you *might* have done."

I smiled. My father seemed to have such enjoyment for life. He loved puttering around. He was waiting anxiously for my mother to retire from her job at my old elementary school so they could travel. I couldn't imagine him feeble and I could never imagine him being "old." Unfortunately, Jimmy didn't share our father's enthusiasm.

"What am *I* gonna do?" he asked. Aside from two years in the military, Jimmy had worked in a box factory all of his adult life. "I'm thirty-seven, no college. I can't do anything else but what I'm doing."

"I don't give a shit," Dad said harshly, surprising me with his vehemence. "You find what you want to do, and you do it."

Suddenly, the atmosphere changed. Doubt, disappointment, and fear replaced laughter, zeal, and encouragement. We found our conversation stripped down to a rawness that none of us was comfortable with. I glanced at Jimmy. He looked like a softer version of our father, with short hair that stood up on top, a mustache, and a beer belly. Jimmy was good-looking and a kind, sensitive person, yet he had often seemed sad, or maybe just uninspired. Both of my half brothers had always been mysteries to me. Their connection to our father seemed strained and uncertain. When I was younger, we had all spent more time together, but as an adult, I had not interacted much with Jimmy, and I had not seen John since I was twelve.

As we drank more, the evening became less pleasant. Jimmy's doubts about his life inflamed my own. I had just received an application for the Peace Corps, but felt nervous about going through with it—and my parents didn't yet know about my plans to go overseas. Finally, I also went to bed, leaving Jimmy and Dad in the kitchen.

Several hours later, I woke up and heard my mother's angry voice.

"James, you've had too much," she was saying. "Now, get out of there and get into bed." Dad mumbled something. I opened one eye to see the bathroom light on, and heard banging against the toilet. My head pounded while the rest of my body seemed frozen in ice. Apparently, my father had fallen into the bathtub, and sometime later Mom found him there. She eventually got him into bed.

After all the lights were out, I settled into the darkness of my own thoughts. Feeling sorry for myself, I wished that my family were different. I wished that we didn't drink to excess like we did, that we didn't fall into bathtubs, that we didn't detach from each other through alcohol. But these were all wishes that were as delicate as the strands of a spider's web, and though heartfelt, were quickly gone.

On New Year's Eve 1991, nine months after my father's death, I got very drunk and said good riddance to what I thought would be the worst year of my life. That night fourteen of my friends and I tried to break a record for hot tub occupancy. We squeezed in like tomatoes in a crate, then grabbed a few more party attendees who still had their clothes on. We laughed and drank and the water in the tub flowed over the sides. Then suddenly, it didn't seem funny anymore and I felt like I was being suffocated. Too drunk to think clearly, I imagined that I was sliding down a greased path toward that tangled ball of string from my childhood. The next morning I vowed to stop drinking—and I kept my promise for the next nine months.

In August 1992 I joined the Peace Corps and went to South America. A fresh start seemed the best thing, despite my concern over leaving my mother. I sold most of my possessions and looked forward to being with people who didn't know the "old Betsy." Unfortunately, my sobriety didn't last long in the Argentine culture. People drank red wine during lunch and dinner, and I finally decided there was no harm in a drink now and then. "Now and then" soon became every day, and "lunch and dinner" extended to in between meals. During my tour, I lived in three different houses in my small pueblo and each had a neighborhood *kiosko* that sold cheap but good *vino tinto*. I kept to myself, often drinking an entire bottle in one evening. I justified this behavior by saying I spent a lot of time alone anyway and I needed a break from speaking Spanish.

After the Peace Corps, I returned to Powers and my Forest Service job, visiting my mother as often as possible. Though we never discussed the difficult things—her accident or Dad's death—our relationship was better than it ever had been. I remember thinking that perhaps events had worked out for the best. While my dad was alive, there had never been enough room for my mother in our familial trio. I had never really known her, though for many years I hadn't wanted to know her. But now, in the wake of our shared loss, she and I had become friends. I never considered bringing up the past to clarify it, though, since I couldn't be sure of the outcome.

October 1996, southwest Oregon

One fall day in 1996, I rode my bike along the South Fork Coquille River, the waterway that flows through Powers and empties into the Pacific Ocean fifty miles north of the Rogue. My friends Dave and

Vivi had invited me to dinner at their log home on the banks of the South Fork. Autumn was just beginning to brown the hills surrounding Powers and the grass had withered, opening up numerous views along the Coquille where the trees were losing leaves. I breathed deep. Life didn't get any better than a cool fall day. It felt like the time of year when the earth was remembering how life used to be. The shorter, darker days and colder weather made me think of endless wilderness, of wolves and cougars and grizzly bears, of living by rivers and sitting next to popping fires. The energy of summer stimulated me, but I was a person of autumn.

That evening, while Dave grilled steaks and Vivi and I chatted, the phone rang. *That's for me,* I suddenly thought, surprised I would think a phone call at a friend's house would be for me.

"Hi, Sue!" Vivi said, and I knew that my best friend was on the line. As Vivi began listening, I watched her face simplify, the lines from her smile relaxing, her lips becoming narrow.

It is for me and it's about Mom.

Vivi handed me the phone without a word and put her arms around me.

"Sue?"

"B," she choked after a few seconds. "Your mom's passed away. Oh God, I'm so sorry."

It's not surprising that I had anticipated the phone call. My mother had known her life was nearing its end. She had tried to tell me. She had tried to make a good death. But I hadn't wanted to listen. During one phone call that summer she said that she had something to tell me.

"I've been to the doctor. I have an aneurysm on my stomach." My own stomach knotted.

"What's that?"

"I guess it's a spot where the wall of an artery is weak. It's...well... it's not a great situation."

The knot in my stomach turned into butterflies. *Please don't take Mom too,* I pleaded to the universe. I felt like I'd been left at the station, watching the train pull away with her waving from the window. I was five years old again and needed my mother. I was eight again and she was lying on the asphalt unconscious. I was thirty-one and did not want to be an orphan.

"Anyway," she continued, trying to sound cheerful, "the doctor wants to see me again in January."

I felt better. If the doctor didn't want to see her for another six months, maybe it wasn't so bad.

During the next two months, however, Mom did not sound good when we talked on the phone. Her voice seemed small through the lines and she sounded tired. Though I didn't realize it then, now I can see that my mother had slowly faded from life over several months. She had grown thin and had seemed to shrink in height. Her fine, white hair and gaunt face bore little resemblance to the painting in her bedroom of the 1940s-era woman with the long, curly red mane and smooth skin.

The Sunday before she died we talked on the phone as usual. She knew then, I believe, that this would be our last conversation.

"How are you feeling?" I asked her.

"Pretty good. Just really cold. I can't seem to get warm."

"Well, the days are getting cooler. Maybe you just need to take a hot shower and bundle up."

"Yeah, maybe."

Then we had said good-bye.

"I love you, Bets."

"I love you too, Mom."

Tears came to my eyes as I hung up the phone. I did love my mother. It was not like the relationship that I had shared with my father, which had been an easy and natural one between two people who were so much alike. I still didn't feel like I knew her. What had developed between us, however, was genuine. It had come out of fire and been melted down to something mysterious but invaluable. I would never have guessed that our time alone together would be so short.

Two hours before I rode my bike downriver to Dave and Vivi's, my cousin found my mother dead on the living room floor. The coroner said she had probably died the night before, and listed the cause of death as congestive heart failure. She was still in her pajamas, the TV on and the curtains closed.

———◆———

For the next three months, I lived in a fog of disbelief, sleeplessness, and mania. Tasks associated with wrapping up my mother's life required that I stay in Tacoma for three straight weeks. It was during this time that I became unable to sleep. Having *trouble* sleeping never surprised me. A sudden inability to sleep *at all* scared me. I saw a doctor who prescribed Valium. It helped, but I feared taking it every night, so my sleep remedies alternated between pills and alcohol—with some nights requiring both. Then my lower back began aching. I thought it was just from sleeping on the living room floor, but it didn't go away.

I returned to the Siskiyou determined to carry on as if nothing had happened. The district began a forest carnivore survey that winter using remote infrared cameras. The project involved setting up the cameras on the highest peaks of the forest. I slogged through snow with a backpack heavy with camera equipment, hand tools, and dead animal carcasses to be used as bait. My back throbbed. The pain I experienced when getting in and out of vehicles felt like sharp knives slicing into me. I walked bent over at a forty-five degree angle. Most of the time my mind felt like a forest fire ablaze, sweltering and filled with so much smoke I couldn't see or breathe clearly. Only the bitter-cold winter air calmed the flames of grief and confusion.

As the weeks passed and my sleeping didn't improve, I began to feel like I existed in a separate universe from everything and everyone around me. I couldn't concentrate. I couldn't get to work on time, and when I did, I was often too hungover or tired to do anything. Driving frightened me. Being alone frightened me. I thought of killing myself but was too afraid to do it.

Feeling like a failure, I asked my boss for the month of January off. Up until this time, I had adamantly refused to see a counselor, believing, correctly, that such a person couldn't change what had happened. And, in fact, after going to Portland to stay with my friend Sue and starting therapy, I found the discussions rarely focused on my parents' deaths. Perhaps this was because my grief came more from the memory of their lives, which I soon realized could never be wholly discarded. *Our* lives. *My* life.

I began meeting with Doss, a retired therapist in his early seventies. Doss had a full head of trim, military-like white hair; apart from his mustache, he resembled my father. We met in his home, and the first few visits I sat in frozen exhaustion. My eyes felt like they contained sand. After I explained the situation, Doss nodded. He told me that he, too, had been an only child. He understood my feelings of aloneness.

"I think you're probably suffering a serious case of depression," he said, matter-of-factly. "What I'd recommend is that you begin taking an antidepressant for sleep. You'll have to quit drinking, at least for awhile, and stop the Valium. As your body withdraws from the drugs, you will start sleeping again, but the next few days may be rough."

And they were. Another week passed before I made it through four hours of uninterrupted sleep. Once I got there, though, I couldn't stop sleeping. Feeling safe in the home of my best friend allowed me to relax in a way I hadn't since the previous October. As I sifted through the emotional pain, my backache gradually left. Doss had been right about the sleeping, but wrong about the drinking. As we uncovered the story of my family, a story I'd been so close to that I hadn't been able to see it, it became clear to me that I could never drink again.

Chapter 19

The Iron Cross

Everybody writes about the big battles like the Battle of the Bulge. You need to write about Wöbbelin. Watch the film. You're walking in your father's footsteps, face to face with reality.

—Joseph Schwan, private with the 82nd Airborne, 505th Parachute Infantry Regiment (April 1945–November 1945), during a phone call in December 2003 regarding a videotape he had sent me, *The Liberation of the Wöbbelin Concentration Camp*

Autumn 2002, Port Townsend, Washington

I OPENED MY FATHER'S SCRAPBOOK and turned to the page with the medal. My friend William's eyes grew big.

"Do you know what this is?" he asked, almost in a whisper.

"Well, it's a German medal of some sort. I mean, you can see the swastika."

"This is not just *any* German medal. This is *the* Iron Cross. It was only awarded to the top soldiers in the Third Reich. Where did you get it?"

"This is one of my father's scrapbooks. *He* got it somewhere." I touched the black and silver flared wings of the cross. The medal hung from a black, white, and red ribbon, which had been stapled to the yellowing page. From years of the scrapbook being closed, the Cross's outline had worn itself into the paper affixed underneath, a letter of commendation to First Lieutenant James W. Howell for "exemplary conduct" from the colonel of the 505th.

The history of the Iron Cross, I soon learned, stretched back to

1813, the year King Friedrich Wilhelm III of Prussia first instituted the award during the War of Liberation against Napoleon. Originally a campaign medal, the Iron Cross saw rebirths during the Franco-Prussian War and World War I. Germany's defeat in 1918 didn't diminish its stature. In 1939, the Third Reich, perhaps largely because Adolph Hitler himself had received the award twenty years before, reinstituted the medal with four grades: 2nd Class, 1st Class, Knight's Cross, and Grand Cross. The 2nd Class Iron Cross, the one in my father's scrapbook, was awarded for single acts of bravery. It is made of three pieces, an iron core and a silver frame on its front and back, which has been soldered together firmly holding the iron core in the center. The original design had a spray of oak leaves image in the middle. During World War II, the Nazi swastika replaced the spray. The year "1939" is etched on the bottom arm of the Cross in my father's scrapbook. On the reverse side is the year of its original inception, "1813." The black, white, and red ribbon represented the colors of the new Reich. Though I think William had mistaken the Iron Cross I showed him for the Grand or Knight's Cross, this one was actually by far the most widely distributed—it was bestowed upon Nazi soldiers as well as Axis allies and German civilian uniformed organizations, such as police, firemen, and Hitler Youth. An estimated five million 2nd Class Iron Crosses were awarded, one of which now stared back at William and me.

"Do you know where your dad got this?" he asked. I shook my head.

"My father only told a few stories from the war. I'd never even seen these scrapbooks until long after his death."

On September 17, 1944, the 505th Parachute Infantry Regiment, including my father, made their fourth combat jump—this time, into Groesbeek, Holland. After two months of training and absorbing replacements, the regiment was again at full strength. Everything about Operation Market Garden promised to be different than what the men had experienced in Normandy. The 505th's sister regiment, the 504th, which had stayed in Italy until late April and had been in no shape to join the D-Day invasion, would participate this time. And, because this jump would take place during the day, a ten-mile-wide corridor would be cleared by the Eighth and part of the Ninth American Air Force divisions before the C-47s carrying paratroopers began flying over enemy territory. The optimists of the 505th, the "old men" who had already made three combat jumps, believed these all to be good signs. Perhaps there would be little fighting and more processing of prisoners. The pessimists felt otherwise. Allen Langdon writes in his regimental history of the 505th, "Ready," that these latter individuals "noted that nothing had ever gone right in an airborne operation so far, so there was no good reason to believe that things would be any different in this one."

Yet Holland was different. The pilots didn't encounter a cloud bank, the paratroopers hit the drop zone (for the most part), and none of the C-47s carrying the 505th were shot down before the paratroopers jumped. The men said the sandy Dutch soil provided the softest landing they'd ever had. Within an hour of hitting the ground, all the companies were accounted for and the order to move out was given.

For the next nine days, the regiment fought Germans, captured prisoners, and liberated Groesbeek. The 505th would spend a total of two months in Holland, patrolling, guarding bridges, and making friends with the Dutch people. In "Ready," Allen Langdon writes:

> The people themselves were always friendly and cheerful even under the most adverse conditions. Generous housewives fed troopers whenever they could, washed and mended their clothes, and voiced no objection to the muddy boots that tracked mud and worse over their spotless floors.

Cam Anderson, the paratrooper with the 101st Airborne, had told me that the Dutch people really appreciated the Allied soldiers: "When we were there, we'd go in and eat lunch, get a cup of coffee and a sweet; they wouldn't charge us for it. We stayed in the homes, they paid for the transportation, everything."

In mid-November, after being relieved of duty in Holland, the regiment traveled to Camp Suippes, France. Expectations of returning to England were quickly dashed as the two-story, masonry barracks became the 505th's new home. Camp Suippes, near Reims, had been located along the Western Front during World War I. Approximately sixty miles to the east ran the Meuse River, along which two of the final Allied offensives of that conflict, the battle of St. Mihiel and the Meuse-Argonne offensive, had happened. I Company occupied the entire second floor of one building, and for the next three weeks the regiment assimilated more replacements, completed daylong training exercises, and stretched its abilities by solving new field problems.

On December 17, 1944, the British Broadcasting Corporation reported a "minor penetration" in the Allied lines. The breach had occurred in the Ardennes region, an area of extensive forests and rolling hill country in Belgium, but few soldiers knew where the Ardennes was and most of the men paid little attention to the news. That night they went to the movies. At 2:00 a.m., barrack doors banged open, whistles blasted, and platoon sergeants shouted to get the squads ready with full equipment. The 505th would move out at 8:00 a.m. For the next several hours, the men scrambled to find ammunition, winter clothing, and a day's supply of K rations (which provided three complete meals) and D rations (emergency rations such as chocolate bars and other high-calorie items). Allen Langdon describes in *"Ready"* that at 10:00 a.m. on December 18, "the regiment was off to its fifth campaign and [the] one that was destined to be the death knell of the old 505."

William Tucker, one of the veterans I interviewed, wrote in his memoir *Parachute Soldier*:

> *It was an all-day trip that took us through World War I*
> *battle grounds. I even noticed there was still some debris*
> *from it in the fields, together with many monuments along*
> *the road.*

At midnight, the 505th arrived at its destination: Werbomont, Belgium. Two days later, the regiment (and the 504th and 508th)

began fighting the Germans along the Salm River and, except for a two-week break in January, they didn't stop until returning to Suippes two months later on February 20. With snow and below-zero temperatures, the troops faced nearly as much danger from the cold as they did from the enemy. On Christmas Eve in 1944, orders had arrived from Field Marshall Montgomery to withdraw from the Salm, a position for which many men would later die as they strove to take it back. On the return, I Company ran into Germans who were also withdrawing. Most of the company made it through without serious casualties, but one platoon on rear guard lost over half its men in the fight that ensued. Whether or not this was the Third, my father's, platoon, I don't know.

During my phone conversations with the soldiers of I Company, one man, John Levitsky, told me he remembered my father in Belgium.

"Yeah, I was a private, Third Platoon," John shouted into the phone. "I didn't know Lieutenant Howell well. I mean, hell, he had his officer friends and I had my private friends. He was the one, though, that sent me up on top of that hill on December 24. 'You and Patino, go up there and check things out,' he said. So, of course, me and Patino go up there. The snow was four goddamned feet deep. Everybody was drunk as hell."

I wanted to ask what hill and who was drunk, but never got a chance. John spoke fast and didn't hear too well.

"Yeah, your dad," he continued, "he was a good officer. When I got shot up, he gave me some coffee. He did his job."

On January 3, 1945, the 505th, along with several other regiments of the 82nd Airborne, began an attack to retake the line along the Salm River that they had held on Christmas Eve. Allen Langdon writes:

> In taking these positions, the 505 was destined to suffer
> more casualties in one day than in any other single day in
> its combat history.

Colonel James Kaiser assigned I Company to take Fosse, a small village west of the river. All apparently went well until the company emerged into an open area in front of the town. Small-arms fire arrived in such volume that it quelled the advance, but not before leaving the captain, a lieutenant, and several men dead. As the survivors pulled back into the woods, artillery fire burst the trees around them. More men died or were wounded. Those left in I Company dug in around Fosse that night. It snowed and the temperature fell. Water froze in their canteens, and because there were few roads in the area, supply trucks would not be arriving with overcoats and sleeping bags.

It is fascinating to me that the combat experiences of my father, a man I knew, are in some instances more puzzling than those of Darsie Heath, who died thirty-five years before I was born. Perhaps the vital difference is simply that of a personal journal. I would have assumed Darsie fought at Franklin, Tennessee, were it not for his own words that put him on the expedition to Williamsport. A small event perhaps, but not to one trying to assemble the full picture of an experience. What a person looks for as she tries to understand history are documents that corroborate an event—a soldier's actions, times, places—all the details of the period. When those documents don't align or don't exist, one has a mystery. This was the case with my father's experiences in Fosse, Belgium. His certificate of service lists the Ardennes as one of the campaigns he participated in, so he was obviously there. John Levitsky remembered him, and William Tucker had told me on the phone, "Lieutenant Howell took over the platoon when Clark went home after Normandy."

The certificate also states that he was never wounded in action. Yet, according to Allen Langdon's regimental history:

When [January 3, 1945] was finished, so was "I" Company. Every officer was either dead or wounded and two-thirds of the men were casualties. "I" Company remained at Fosse, in battalion reserve, and waited for Lieutenant Joseph W. Vandevegt to come up from the Regimental Headquarters and take over the company.

I wondered why another officer was called up to take over. Why wouldn't a lieutenant already in I Company be asked to assume command? Nowhere in Langdon's *"Ready"* is my father's name mentioned.

This omission and seeming error in Langdon's statement about every officer being either killed or wounded on January 3, coupled with the fact that so few of the men I spoke with remembered much about my father beyond his good looks, made me feel like I was dealing with a ghost. Both William Tucker and George Clark, my father's platoon leader, had told me on the phone how quiet the new lieutenant had been. *He was quiet all right*, I thought. *Too quiet.*

In March 1945, after returning to Camp Suippes, what was left of the 505th, as well as the large numbers of replacements that had just arrived, made its last wartime practice jump. The drop zone was an old World War I battlefield, the trench lines still visible. The following month the regiment moved into Germany. In addition to holding various defensive lines, the men performed duties such as screening the population for Nazis and "displaced persons." Everyone believed, even dared to hope, they might now survive. However, an order arriving at the end of April quickly dashed this expectation; the 505th would make an assault crossing the Elbe River near Blekede, southeast of Hamburg. Allen Langdon writes in *"Ready"*:

> *Of all the operations undertaken by the 505 in World War II, probably no operation was "sweat out" by the "old men" more than this one. With the war's end obviously just a few days away, and four combat jumps and two years of combat behind them, the thought of being killed or drowned at the 11th hour was just a little too bitter to contemplate. Since the civilian population had been hastily evacuated from Blekede and hadn't had much time to hide the family treasures (which included a bountiful supply of vintage booze), to be candid, it was not exactly a sober group of 505ers who formed up that evening to move*

out to the crossing sites. If some of the most unsteady were the "old men," perhaps they can be forgiven, or at least understood.

When I read this, I wondered if Blekede was where the "scotch incident," one of my father's war stories, had taken place.

"We'd taken over this village," he had told me, "and I took a few of the boys out on a reconnaissance with me. We must have been gone a few hours. When we got back, we found the rest of the platoon had discovered a stash of Black and White Scotch whiskey. Not wanting to be culturally indifferent, they, of course, had to try it. I found my troops smashed! They were so drunk, they forgot to address me as 'Lieutenant' or 'Sir,' and instead called me 'Jimmy!'"

Fortunately, the crossing was only lightly opposed and though there were many well dug-in Germans, they only offered token resistance. Even so, the fighting that followed the crossing resulted in several more 505 men being killed or wounded.

May 1, 1945, saw the end of fighting for the 505th Parachute Infantry Regiment. In the ensuing days, the men settled into the work of guarding thousands of German prisoners and displaced persons the Nazis had held in various camps. On May 2, the 82nd Airborne liberated the Wöbbelin concentration camp near the village of Ludwigslust. Although not technically classified as a "death camp," prisoners at Wöbbelin had been neglected and many had starved to death. Disgusted by what they found, Airborne command ordered the citizens of Ludwigslust to bear witness and acknowledge responsibility for their roles, active or passive, in the Nazi atrocities there. The Americans made town officials dig graves and prepare crosses for the dead. They forced the residents to pass by the bodies and attend a mass funeral ceremony. After the full horror was revealed, Ludwigslust's *Bürgermeister* and his wife committed suicide.

One weekend, I sat down to watch the HBO miniseries *Band of Brothers*, a chronicle of one company in the 506th Parachute Infantry Regiment. The scenes depicting the experiences of this paratroop unit brought World War II home to me in a visual way that I had not experienced with my reading. I pictured my father falling against the walls of a C-47 as bullets tore through the aircraft over Normandy. I saw him killing people, then staring vacantly and red-eyed after days of combat.

Yet *Band of Brothers*, however graphic and based on fact, is still an organized, Hollywood version of events. Those events were softened for me by the knowledge that the blood I watched pouring from bodies was not real, the lifeless bodies were not truly dead, and the suffering on faces was merely a product of fine acting and directing. *Band of Brothers* agitated me and I could not sleep the night I finished it, yet these feelings paled next to what I experienced watching an even more difficult video: *The Liberation of the Wöbbelin Concentration Camp.*

Liberation is a raw sequence of images shot with an 8 mm camera by a French war correspondent. There are no special effects to soften the view. Opera music plays in the background, coupled with the hiss of the period's recording technology. The images are black-and-white. The film is grainy. Sergeant Leonard Linton of the 82nd Airborne narrates, and his voice sounds hollow, as if it were coming from an empty room.

The beginning of the video documents the German 21st Army surrendering to the 82nd Airborne. The camera captures soldiers of both sides talking. An Iron Cross hangs from the left pocket of one Nazi officer. Then the story travels to Wöbbelin. One shot stays focused for several seconds on a skeletal figure who died just as the paratroopers arrived. Sergeant Linton's voice breaks through:

> Many inmates were too disoriented to leave the death
> camp. Some lost the will to live and looked through you
> with sad, big, beady eyes. Many were dying. Freedom came
> too late for too many of them.

The prisoners open their shirts to show their emaciated bodies. One man—who looks like a hawk with his large eyes and hooked nose—displays his deflated torso. He stares at the camera for several seconds.

The Americans had organized compulsory visits to the infirmary for the residents of Ludwigslust. In the video, men and women enter one of the brick buildings at Wöbbelin, then walk out, their gaits jerky like those in old movies. The film then shows the very ill being transferred to a hospital on the outskirts of Ludwigslust. Finally, comes footage of the reburial of prisoners who had died earlier and been placed in mass graves. The voiceover continues:

German civilians [were] ordered to open common graves to transfer the cadavers for reburial in individual graves.

People dressed in heavy overcoats extract dirt-caked, bony frames from the ground and encase each one in a snow-white sheet.

The entire civilian population of the small town of Ludwigslust was ordered to participate in this reburial.

Horse-drawn wagons transport the white sheets to the reburial site, the grounds of the Grand Duke of Mecklenburg. The bodies are lined up next to graves with large, white crosses at the head of each. Civilian men and women file past, some weeping, most looking ahead without emotion. During the ceremony, while "The Star-Spangled Banner" plays, the camera focuses on Major General James Gavin, commanding officer of the 82nd Airborne. The final images are of American soldiers saluting while "Taps" is played.

Later that summer, the 505th prepared to head for the war in Japan. Dropping the atomic bomb and ending the conflict before this happened came as a great relief to the men, who had had enough of fighting. At the end of *Band of Brothers*, Donald Malarkey, a soldier with the 506th Parachute Infantry Regiment and now a man with white hair and many years behind him, summarized his experience:

I withstood it well, but I had a lot of trouble in later life, because those events would come back and you never forget them.

Chapter 20

Spanish Fort

[Thursday, March 16, 1865, Dauphin Island, Alabama]

The Island is called Dolphins Island and is a beautiful one—the Beach is white sand looks like snow. I could not think it any thing else-there is also groves of tall pines this gives it more the look of some northern State in Midwinter. we all slept cold the First night on the Island. it was dark when we came in camp so we could not put up our tents or else did not want to I could not sleep much. I got up at midnight and sat by the Fire until daylight the next day we moved still further to the west and encamped in a grove of pines Water here was scarce the water in the Lake being to salty for use.

—From the journal of Private Darsie Heath,
72nd Illinois Infantry, Company A

December 2000, southern Alabama

THE SLASH AND LONGLEAF PINE trees swayed in the cold December winds. Species such as magnolia, oak, and tupelo gum made up the hardwood component of this barrier island off Alabama's coast, while palmetto bushes blanketed the ground. As I walked along the trails of Dauphin Island's Audubon Bird Sanctuary, I heard few birds. At the southern edge of the pine forest I stopped at Gaillard Lake, named for the sanctuary's founder. Only four and a half acres in size, the lake was as clear as a recently scrubbed window. A broken sign at one end read, "Watch out for Alligators," however, in this cold weather, the pied-billed grebes swimming on the limpid water were safe. I lay back on the dock and contemplated the approaching end of my journey. One hundred and sixty miles to the northeast lay Greenville, Alabama, the town where Darsie's Civil War chronicle ended on April 24, 1865. In a few days, I would be there.

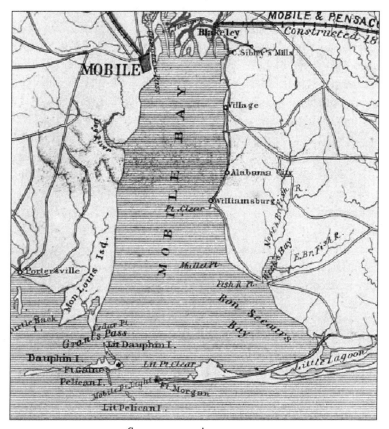

SOUTHERN ALABAMA
Courtesy of US Historical Archive

By 1865, the only Confederate landscapes not captured by the Yankees were the interior of the Carolinas and most of Alabama. The 72nd Illinois was assigned to General Edward Canby's Department of the Gulf Army with the task of invading southern Alabama through Mobile. After Iuka, the regiment had traveled back down the Tennessee River to Paducah, then to Cairo, and then journeyed once more down the Mississippi to New Orleans. From there, the regiment sailed on the steamer *Guiding Star* to Fort Gaines, Alabama, a stronghold on the east end of Dauphin Island. Fourteen miles long and only a scant one mile at its widest, this pencil-like stretch of land had been occupied by Union forces since August 1864 when Admiral David Farragut blazed into Mobile Bay past three Confederate forts and uttered his immortal words, "Damn the torpedoes! Full speed ahead." The Illinois troops landed at Fort Gaines and marched four miles west, making camp in the pine forest where today the Dauphin Island Campground welcomes travelers on all manner of pilgrimage.

Darsie didn't exaggerate about the snowlike sand. The fine, alabaster grains separated the semitropical forest and the salt water like a white satin ribbon. On this border between the two habitats, I watched two robin-sized, gray catbirds dressed in dignified colors of gray and black. One catbird darted around a bush, snatching red berries. I scooped up some sand to take home with me.

At my campsite, tucked beneath the coastal pines, I read more from Darsie's journal. After making camp, the men had decided that a welcome change of food could be found on the beach:

> *here we had a fine time gathering Oysters about 4 Oc*
> *in the Afternoon the tide went out then You could see*
> *hundreds of soldiers in water to their waists looking for*
> *oysters. I joined in the sport-for sport it was-the water*
> *was quite cold yet after I was in it a while I did not mind*
> *it even the officers might be seen in the water gathering*
> *Oysters too they were not plenty we had to hunt for an*
> *hour then could not find over 6 or 8 dozen.*

Around my tent lay dozens of broken oyster shells, bleached and smooth from years of weathering.

Closing the journal, I napped. A sadness had settled over me the last few days as my trip neared its conclusion. The loneliness of the road had caught up with me. The days of endless strangers, of faces that looked familiar but weren't, of living outside when no one else was, of a season that seemed to me more suited for reflection than propulsion—these all pulled me down. Sleep offered a respite where I still hoped to somehow see Darsie's face or find the comfort that I needed to live with my past, but both continued to elude me.

The next day, I learned that a Christmas reenactment was taking place at Fort Gaines. Figuring that a slice of reenacting culture would ease my loneliness, I rode my bike east. In 1821, construction had began on this fort, which is pentagonal in shape and built next to the land–water interface. There are bastions at each juncture, with cannons atop them that protect against invaders, and are connected to the interior via tunnels. Red ribbons and wreaths now hung from the brick walls, and four sutler tents had been set up for the event. Most of the people milling about were reenactors. Between the cold and the upcoming holiday, the general public probably had little time for living history.

I walked around the fort talking with the soldiers and civilians. The men from the Sixth Alabama Regiment offered me a cup of hot chocolate.

"You should come back on Mother's Day," one of them said. "The reenactment that weekend includes ships!"

"Mother's Day seems an odd time to have a battle," I said. The man shrugged.

"It's the only time the ships are available."

The coastal wind played havoc with reenactors trying to start fires. Women huddled near the tent openings and men stood shivering in their greatcoats, dashing pieces of outerwear that come down to the knees and have capes that extend to the elbow. This Civil War Christmas scene was having the opposite effect on me; I felt lonelier than ever. Finding a bench in the sun, I sat down, burrowed into my parka, and wondered if it had been this cold when Darsie was here. After a few minutes, a man dressed as a Civil War–era civilian hobbled up on crutches. He wore an all-black suit and top hat, which matched his black mustache and goatee and fit his nineteenth-century persona well.

"Hey, how ya doin'?" he asked, easing onto the other end of the bench.

"Fine."

"Cold, ain't it?"

"Freezing."

He stretched his leg out and I saw a long pin protruding from the side of his calf. It was held in place by a sturdy ring of metal around his leg.

"Battle injury?"

"Nah," he smiled. "Rollerblading. Hey, my name's Randy." He reached out a big hand.

"Betsy."

"What brings ya to the South, Betsy?" I told him about my journey, with as much enthusiasm as I could muster. My disappointment threatened to overwhelm me, and what made it worse was I didn't even know why I was disappointed.

"Ya know, the Confederate barracks used to be where you're camping right now," Randy explained. "Of course, the Rebels burned them before the fort's surrender."

"Huh," I managed, but thought, *Who cares? The 1860s aren't my time, much as I'd like them to be.*

My disappointment surprised me after experiencing the excitement and energy that had carried me through two long journeys along Darsie's trail. Ever since my childhood, I had wanted to live in the past, in the "good old days," with the wilderness and the wildlife and the simple world. Now, I couldn't be closer to that long-ago landscape, where the dead still lived, at least in my imagination, and all my mistakes and regrets were yet to come.

Unfortunately, my imaginings couldn't hug me or comfort me or tell me I would survive, and the past before I was born only seemed simple because I had not actually lived it. I suspected it was time to return to my own era, but I wasn't sure I wanted that either. Randy's voice pulled me out of this maelstrom of thought.

"What's that?" I asked.

"I's just saying that this fort is haunted. People say they see ghosts all the time. Soldiers walking the tunnels, marching on duty, cleaning weapons."

"Huh," I said, feeling even worse, *I never see ghosts.*

On March 18, the 72nd Illinois left Dauphin Island for the Alabama mainland. Four days later they arrived at the mouth of Fish River, southeast across the bay from Mobile, where they enjoyed more feasting on shellfish. Several days later, after traveling up the Fish River and then marching overland, the regiment arrived outside of Spanish Fort. The men began building earthworks and skirmishing with the enemy. Out in the bay, they saw Union ships moving toward the fort. As the North tightened its grip, Darsie wrote on March 24:

> it is reported [General] aJ. Smith said he intended to
> take [Spanish Fort] in seven minutes by his watch this
> we don't like much when we know it is not a.J. Smith that
> takes the Fort but the men & there will be many lives
> sacrificed to gratify an Idle whim of the Genls when a little
> maneuvering would serve the same purpose.

The March days melded into April. The weather turned warmer, the cannonading continued, Confederate deserters left the fort for the Union lines, and the 72nd soldiers dug trenches. On March 28, Darsie's chronicle continued:

> we wanted to advance our line of works. the other
> regiments in our brigade were already far in advance of
> us. Corporal Felsing of Co B. Volunteered to take a spade
> and his gun and work his way to the Front. he succeeded
> well and then I followed him I had to cros an open space
> of about 300 yards wide here I was exposed to the fire of
> the enemy all the way and while I crossed they poured
> shots thick and fast around none hurt me though when
> I reached Felsing he had commenced to dig; we worked
> quite briskly for a while. we had to get on our knees to dig,
> as we were to much exposed when standing

At this point, the soldiers on both sides had to know the war was ending and must have been considering the possibility of actually surviving. Like the "old men" of the 505th who worried over their last mission across the Elbe River in Germany, the Union troops around Spanish Fort must have wondered about risking their lives so close to the war's end. Yet, Darsie's descriptions of crossing open ground as a "volunteer" sounded like he was not finished taking chances. I wondered if he had simply let go of any expectation of survival, and if letting go had, ironically, saved his life.

"Would ya like a reservation for this place?" the woman at the tourist office in Mobile asked me. "It's only $29.99."

I hesitated, then mumbled something about needing to save money and that I should really be camping.

"Camping!" she shouted. "Ya can't camp in this weather! It's too cold!" I could hardly argue with that, so I booked a single room at the Eastern Shore Motel. Then I queried "Flo" about visiting Spanish Fort. She shook her head.

"It's all private property now. No public access. You could visit Fort Morgan to the south if you wanted."

No, I wanted to say, *Darsie wasn't at Fort Morgan. I don't care about Fort Morgan. I want to be where he was.* Instead, I told her, "I'm only visiting certain sites. Spanish Fort was the last battle my ancestor participated in." Flo looked thoughtful.

"There are a couple local historians who have permission to visit what's left of the earthworks on private lots. Why don't you call them?"

After a brief telephone conversation where I barely got a word in edgewise, Edward Cox agreed to meet me at nine the next morning. That night I slept well and awoke to the anniversary of Pearl Harbor, feeling hopeful. Perhaps learning about Spanish Fort would cheer me up.

For the next five hours, unfortunately, I learned more about Ed Cox than Spanish Fort. Ed, dressed in a red button-down shirt with a pocket full of pens and eyeglasses, a ball cap, blue jeans, and Nike tennis shoes, looked like he belonged in a mall rather than on a battlefield. While we drove on neighborhood streets called General Canby Drive, Rebel Road, and Artillery Range Street, I learned all about his diabetes, Civil War ancestors, two previous wives, four kids, fifteen grandkids, Confederate flag bedspread, and retirement from Scott Paper Company. He confessed to lacking a college education, but also concluded, "I must be pretty smart because I have a column in the weekly *Spanish Fort Bulletin.*" He took a breath and I nodded, jumping at the chance to change the subject.

"So, there are some earthworks left from Spanish Fort?"

"Yeah, a few." He looked me over. "It's not easy hiking, but we'll get ya back in there." Suddenly, Ed shouted, "Aigh! There's a lot I missed!"

We were driving by a house under construction. Ed had told me that he took his metal detector everywhere and had found all kinds of treasures over the years. "Once I found an unspent box of ammunition under a magnolia tree," he bragged. Everywhere we went, he either squealed in consternation or boasted about his findings.

Ed finally parked along General Canby Drive, adjacent to a stand of trees that had not yet been replaced by homes. We walked down a gentle slope a few hundred yards toward Bay Minette, a body of water woven into the tapestry of the Mobile delta landscape.

"Hey, you do pretty good out in the woods," Ed said.

"Thanks. Do you have any idea where the 72nd Illinois might have been?"

"Sure. Here's a map for ya of the battlefield. We're right here." Ed pointed to some squiggly red lines with the words, "Minette Bay Battery" next to them. "This is where the Illinois Battery was." My enthusiasm waned.

"I'm not looking for the artillery," I explained. "My ancestor was in the infantry," but Ed seemed not to have heard.

"Hey, let's get a picture of ya on these earthworks," he said. "Right where your grandfather was." I handed him my camera and, kneeling down, smiled perfunctorily. Too much of the past had been covered over at Spanish Fort. Similar to my experience in Iuka, I knew that too much would never be known.

Later, I thanked Ed as he dropped me at the motel. He handed me a plastic bag containing several spent bullets.

"Here, have these. I got 'em at Spanish Fort. At least you'll have a little something from your time here."

———

Two days after the end of the war, the mail arrived. Darsie wrote of a great surprise:

> *I received a letter this morning from Jacob Galley he*
> *is now in V[icksburg] until I received the letter I fully*
> *believed he was killed.*

Since the Battle of Franklin, Jacob had been imprisoned at the Southern prison in Andersonville, Georgia. The brothers would not meet up again, I presumed, until they walked among the swaying grasses of the Prairie Peninsula.

The last two pages of Darsie's journal are missing pieces in the center. The first of them described some excitement, the full explanation for which has vanished:

> *Evening I was out Foraging*
> *was chased by some Guerrillas*

This was followed by:

> *We came to a house where the man had gone out to shoot*
> *Yanks as there was plenty of Evry thing we needed there*
> *We confiscated all we wanted told the negroes to Give our*
> *compliments to the owner.*

On the final torn page, something happened with a mule. The fragments read:

> *we spied two mules in a corner of the wood we took them*
> *put our load on them. as I was helped on mine he gave*
> *evidence by bowing his back the Load was not to his liking.*
> *no sooner had*
> *loosened them he made a*
> *leaving me stretched*
> *took it all in good humor*
> *I wouldent try it again*
> *we took only one loaded*
> *all he could carry on him and left for the road.*

The next morning, the 72nd started early for Montgomery, Alabama, the first capital of the Confederacy. Darsie's last words from his journals on April 24, 1865, are "to be continued."

PART III:

Home

home, *noun*

1. a dwelling place; the place in which one resides
2. the members of a family
3. the grave; death

The Soldier, early 1960s

Chapter 21

The Return to Illinois, 1865

The past is never dead. It's not even past.

—William Faulkner, from *Intruder in the Dust*

ON APRIL 19, 1865, an officer riding his horse at a full gallop came storming up toward the column of soldiers marching north. Lieutenant Colonel Joseph Stockton halted his 72nd Illinois, the rear regiment, south of Greenville, Alabama. According to Stockton's memoir, he called to the breathless rider, now stopped, "What is the matter?"

"Lee's army has surrendered to General Grant!" the officer shouted. "The war is over!"

At this moment, Stockton wrote:

> *The flags were unfurled, drums beat and all were exulting at the news as it meant the ending of the war and our getting home. The people along the route had out flags of truce made of anything white they had. One house had a flag with these words "The United States they shall be preserved."*

Some days after the war's end, the men received ten months' back pay. According to Adjutant George Heafford in *Chevrons and Shoulder Straps*, a few of the soldiers sat around the campfire that night planning what do with their money. Many ideas revolved around practical matters, like what business to go into: grocery, horses, or blacksmithing. Upon such foundations of commerce, men could buy homes and build families. Finally, a little Irishman had had enough of the common sense talk. Heafford recounts the man saying:

> *Byes, I tell ye what I'm going to do when I get home. I'm going to buy the best bugle I can get in Chicago. I don't mind if I have to pay forty dollars for it. Then I'm going to hire a good bugler for three weeks—I'm willing to pay him as much at three dollars a day—and every morning at four o'clock I'm going to have him come to the front of my house and blow reveille, and thin I'll get out of my bed and go to the open window and say, 'go to hell with your old bugle, I'm going back to bed.'*

On April 25, just outside of Montgomery, Alabama, word reached the regiment that President Lincoln had been assassinated. No one believed it. William Mohrmann wrote that it was "unanimously voted to be a rebel lie." Joseph Stockton said, "Men swear that if it is true they will reenlist and fight the thing out to the [bitter] end." Darsie's journal ends the day before this news arrived, so I have no idea of his thoughts. When the president's death was confirmed, commanders in the Union regiments had to take measures to control the men, who were ready to wreak vengeance on the Southern people.

In late May, the 72nd Illinois was ordered to Union Springs, Alabama, forty miles southeast of Montgomery to "take possession of the town." There they remained for six weeks, as Mohrmann wrote:

> [We are waiting] *more or less patiently for the time when Uncle Sam should tell us to go home, for the war was over sure enough. In the absence of duty and under the "laisse[z] faire" policy of our regimental commander the last vestige of discipline vanished until we were little more than an armed mob.*

In mid-July orders finally arrived to return to Montgomery in preparation for traveling to Vicksburg, Mississippi, and being mustered out of the service. With most of the Southern railroads destroyed, the soldiers had no choice but to march the 330 miles to Vicksburg. Having spent a summer in the South myself, I knew that marching across Alabama and Mississippi during the hot and humid days of July had to have been a daunting task. Two weeks after setting out, they arrived in Vicksburg and completed the necessary paperwork. Darsie mustered out as a corporal. The regiment then headed up the Mississippi for the last time. Despite the war being over, however, the 72nd wasn't through taking casualties. When the steamer in which they traveled landed on the Arkansas shore at a spot called Yerger's Landing, the regiment encountered a group of Southerners having a dance. According to William Mohrmann:

> One of [the Southerners] *who had but one leg (probably an*
> *ex-soldier) calmly mounted his horse and then emptied his*
> *revolver into the crowd at the landing killing one outright*
> *and wounding Charley Blake of Co A seriously in the*
> *shoulder. All that could be done was to send a detachment*
> *to his farm and utterly destroy all his possessions.*

The war may have been over, but it would be a long time before the fighting ended.

Arriving in Cairo once again, the 72nd Illinois disembarked and awaited transportation via railcars to Chicago. Joseph Stockton wired the Chicago Board of Trade office of the regiment's arrival and the need for transportation. The Board wired back they would send a special train the following day. No one wanted to wait. Sergeant William Sparks of Company I wrote fifty years later in a letter of reminiscences:

> *Col. Joe (Stockton) called us together on the levee and read*
> *to us the telegram and also informed us that the railroad*
> *company could furnish us with stock cars at once if we*
> *preferred to go at once that way. He put it to a vote and we*

decided not to wait but would take the stock cars and not
wait for the special train to come from Chicago.

In this way, three hog cars carried the remaining 332 men of the 72nd Illinois home, whereas exactly three years earlier, seventeen passenger coaches had taken 967 men to war. Despite this less-than-illustrious arrival, the Chicago Board of Trade threw a grand party for its regiment's return. As the cars pulled into the station of the Illinois Central Railroad on Saturday, August 12, the Dearborn Light Artillery fired a thirty-six gun salute. The men marched through streets lined with thousands of citizens cheering and waving handkerchiefs and hats. According to a document with the lengthy title of *The 72d Regiment Illinois Volunteers. (Board of Trade First Regiment.) Their Return Home. – Banquet at Bryan Hall. – Addresses of Welcome – Toasts, etc. Sketch of the History of the Regiment. – Their First and Last Rosters, etc*, upon arriving at Bryan Hall, where the Board hosted special gatherings, Colonel Stockton made a brief announcement.

"Gentlemen, after dinner today you will be given a leave of absence until 8:30 a.m. Monday, which will allow you to visit your families and friends. However, on Monday morning, everyone should punctually assemble here. We will parade through the streets and organize your final payments."

The men broke out in applause. They had expected to be cooped up in Camp Douglas all weekend. Now, they were almost free!

Next, the Board marched them into a banquet room filled with meats, fruit, flowers, pastries, and other delicacies. Ladies with various connections to the 72nd Illinois arrived to wait on the men. According to a document describing their return home:

Fair faces and lovely forms flitted hither and thither
about the soldiers, who seemed bashful of accepting
their ministrations; brilliant eyes looked softest entreaty
or command, as they flashed blue or black, upon the
bewildered veterans; and the bronzed heroes, used to
war's alarm, seemed timid and shy of the magnetism of

a flowing sleeve or a stray curl (even an artificial one) of
the Houris who bent over them. That army modesty will,
however not be a lasting or dangerous complaint.

I wonder what these days were like for Darsie. Did Margaret
Heath Galley travel to Chicago from Toulon to meet her returning
son? How did he feel about saying good-bye to his constant companions of the past three years? Darsie's journals are not very reflec-
tive, however on April 8, he had penned:

only three months and a piece say the Boy's—The piece
is about 28 days—then we will be bound to Uncle Sam
no more. Save by our Patriotism I don't think I am very
patriotic

Then, a few lines later:

I am not over anxious nevertheless to charge the enemies
works and risk my Coacoanut to end the war—when It can
be done without If it takes a little longer Perhaps when I
go home and can sit by the fire my feet a trifle higher than
my head reading the morning paper and smoking my pipe
(no I'll smoke cigars then) my patriotism will return

He may not have felt patriotic and he may not have even felt
much like a fighting man, but one thing seems certain: Darsie's life
had changed forever. He would never really be a civilian again.

I know only a few highlights of Darsie's life after the war. He
returned to Stark County in western Illinois and began an appren-
ticeship as a painter and decorator, a profession that entailed painting houses, signs, and carriages. In 1870 he moved to Annawan and
in May 1871 he married my great-great-grandmother Maria Louise
Sturm. The following year their first child, my great-grandmother
Alberta Mae, was born. "Allie," a big woman with thick hands and
forearms and substantial hair always swept up in a bun, was the one
who told my father, "We were put on the earth to suffer."

Darsie and Maria had four more children, including two boys, Edward and John. As his children grew, Darsie was greatly involved in the Annawan community, becoming a member of the local Grand Army of the Republic post and serving as a school director, notary public, census taker, and as a police magistrate for twenty-two years. A lifelong Republican, Darsie cast his first presidential vote for his former commander, Ulysses S. Grant, in 1868.

In 1901, John Heath, Darsie and Maria's youngest child, was thirteen years old. One day in February he was playing on a straw pile in the street near their home in Annawan. According to the coroner's record, John accidentally fell upon the sharp point of a hay knife, a scythe I presume, and subsequently died. He would be the first Heath buried in the Annawan Cemetery. Four years later Maria would pass on at the age of sixty and Edward too would soon be buried, dead at twenty-two for reasons I could never find. Darsie would live another quarter of a century and see the birth of his great-grandsons, as well as the world erupt into a colossal war. According to reports submitted to the Bureau of Pensions, his health had deteriorated since shortly after the Civil War, from rheumatism and dyspepsia, and in 1923 Darsie became paralyzed following a stroke.

As I uncovered what I could from a life that was quickly fading into the forgotten, I saw more clearly the myth of the long ago and my own desire for something that didn't exist. It's no good to long for the good old days when they passed with pain and regret just like the present.

Chapter 22

The Return to Illinois, 1945

Remarkably, the survivors who could, at best, regis-
ter fragments of what was happening to them, somehow
decades later communicated the feelings and thoughts
about what had happened to them to their children. It
was their children who would testify as to what hap-
pened to their parents.

— Louise J. Kaplan, on survivors of the Holocaust and
the transmission of their experiences to their children,
from *No Voice Is Ever Wholly Lost*

IN SEPTEMBER 1945, First Lieutenant James Howell returned to Geneseo, Illinois. I assume that he knew, or quickly learned, that his mother, Blanche Howell, had died in June. Blanche, a school teacher with "Coke-bottle glasses" and black hair pulled tight behind her head, had been diagnosed with abdominal cancer several months before. The doctors had treated her with radium, which burned her body black, and in the end she would die anyway. Alberta must have told her grandson what had happened but my father never spoke about his mother's death. He was just twenty-five, the same age I was when he died in 1991. Maybe he had needed to escape. In June 1946, he left for the West Coast, and for the next four years the new civilian worked at five different jobs in Illinois, Alaska, and California. He was only at these jobs between two and sixteen months each, with a five-month period of unemployment in early 1947.

In Alaska, he worked at an engineering plant at Fort Richardson. After my mother died and I began looking at photo albums and scrapbooks I had never seen, I found pictures of my father in the northern wilderness. One labeled, "Fishing on Montana Creek" shows him standing on river stones, dressed in dark clothes that look like military surplus, pants tucked into tall boots, and a long outdoor coat that comes down below his knees. A Western hat with a brim adds the perfect touch to this "man of the woods." The background—a river channel, piles of river wood, and angled trees—all radiate in a blur from Dad. The rocky gravel bar in the foreground also extends out in a muddled way. He is clear, however, walking toward the camera, hat tipped back, a smile just beginning to curl at the corners of his mouth. It's the picture of where, and who, I always wanted to be as a child.

Perhaps it was during this time that Dad started scribbling notes in the little books I would find a half century later: the notebooks where he shared his idea for the title of a travel book, "Life is a Happy Trip"; where he wrote his favorite quotes, "Courage depends on how willing you is to use it," and "You ain't learning nothin' when you're talking"; and where he wondered, "What's left in the world to be explored?"

In early 1947, my father returned to Illinois, and in June he married his first wife. One year later, he reenlisted and, except for a few months after the Korean War, stayed in the military until the year after I was born. Looking at the list of jobs he worked in the late 1940s—the jumping from place to place, the resignations—I wondered if he had a hard time finding his footing on civilian ground. From my own experiences, I know it's hard to survive in a world where no one around you shares the same experiences. That's why groups such as Alcoholics Anonymous, Veterans of Foreign Wars, and other "survivor" organizations are so successful. People find strength in shared struggle. It gives one hope that others have suffered similarly and survived. My theory is that the military—ironically, the vehicle that took him to war—also offered my father this connection and support.

In 1999 when I had begun the first of my road trips following Darsie's path, I went to the city park in my father's hometown of Geneseo, Illinois. Covered in a thick carpet of grass, with trees dating back to the last century, this greenway provides a safe haven for children to play, dogs to run, and lovers to stroll. It is cool when the summer heat arrives, and quiet when the autumn cold pulls the leaves off of trees. The park is a place to enjoy living in the present. It is also a place to remember the past.

On one end of the park, a circular sidewalk encloses a garden of shrubs and white rock. Along a portion of the loop is a three-paneled marble wall. Engraved names line the wall, up and down, left and right. They are the people from Geneseo who served in the armed forces during World War II, many dead from that conflict, some yet living. It took me only a few minutes to find "James Wayne Howell" as well as my uncle, "Kenneth William Howell," who had been a first sergeant with the 95th Infantry Division. Beneath an eagle with outstretched wings in the middle panel are the words:

THAT THEY MAY NOT BE FORGOTTEN
THEIR NAMES ARE HEREON INSCRIBED
THEIR DEEDS LIVE FOREVER

The alabaster wall seemed so clean, so peaceful. I had wondered then if it was the right monument to represent the cost these people had paid for their service. Shouldn't a monument show the whole picture? Shouldn't we see the blood and the death that every veteran has to live with? Shouldn't there be some depiction of the alcohol and drug abuse and sorrow and regret and nightmares that afflict some individuals for the remainder of their lives? And where is the pain of the children and wives that live with them? What good is remembering if we clean up the past to where it's sparkling and silent? What good is a war if it doesn't prevent us from having another?

Later, I went to the Geneseo Historical Museum and mentioned to the docent that my father had been a World War II veteran. She asked his name.

"My neighbor was married to a Howell," she said. "He retired from the military and then died shortly thereafter. That was about thirty years ago." I knew my dad's brother Kenny had died in the early 1970s.

"What's her name?"

"Georgiana."

Georgiana, or "Jana" as my parents called her, was my aunt—and someone I had never known. When I called her, she remembered me immediately. "Betsy Howell! I haven't seen you since you were a baby!" We talked for an hour on the phone about family. Jana told me about my great-grandmother Alberta fixing toast for Darsie when he was bedridden. She told me about my father riding his motorcycle and being a bit "crazy," an adjective never fully explained. She told me how he came over to her house one night, drunk, and sat on her record albums, breaking them in the process. But we mostly talked about my father's and uncle's alcoholism.

"You know, everyone blamed me for divorcing Kenneth," she said, beginning to cry. "But I just couldn't take his drinking anymore. I don't know why he drank so much."

Chapter 23

Descendants' Reunion

Maybe we die twice. Once when our heart stops.
Again when the living stop telling stories about us.

—Phil Cousineau, from *The Art of Pilgrimage:*
The Seeker's Guide to Making Travel Sacred

M Y QUEST TO UNDERSTAND my family legacy had taken me down various paths: my two road trips in which I'd retraced Darsie's movements during the Civil War, my experiences as a Civil War reenactor, and my exhaustive research into both Darsie's and my father's military service. One more piece of the picture fell into place in the autumn of 2000, when I attended my first Battle of Franklin Descendants' Reunion.

It is still hot in Franklin, Tennessee, in October. By then the land has bronzed and the rivers are low, but the days heat up like a small cabin with a large woodstove. Sitting in the banquet hall of Franklin's recreation center this Friday evening with more than a hundred other people, I felt grateful for the air conditioning. We had traveled from thirty-two separate states to participate in the Battle of Franklin Descendants' Reunion. Sponsored by the Carter House Historical Association, this event is held every two years and includes a weekend of eating, singing, reflecting, and sharing stories, photographs, and letters. After signing in at the registration table, I'd been given a name tag with "Darsie Heath, 72nd Illinois" at the top and "Betsy Howell" at the bottom. Descendants from both sides attend these reunions, but Confederates typically outnumber Yankees. I hadn't yet seen anybody else from Illinois.

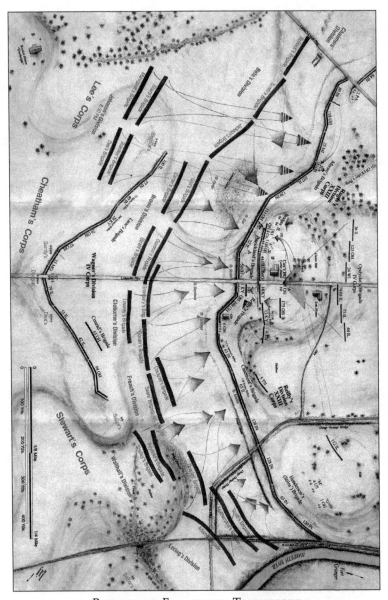

BATTLE OF FRANKLIN, TENNESSEE

Courtesy of The Carter House Association, Inc.

While Darsie and the envoy of twenty men from Company A made their way from Williamsport to Nashville on November 30, 1864, the Battle of Franklin began on the south side of this small, rural town. After an all-night march from Columbia, Tennessee, the Union army "beat" the Confederates to the southern edge of Franklin. The 72nd Illinois was deployed two hundred yards southwest of the Carter family's residence, an area that would soon become the heart of the battle. William Mohrmann wrote:

We arrived about 8 in the morning, hungry and tired out, half dead with want of sleep. We drew rations, made coffee, were given an allowance of whiskey (ominous sign) and then set to fortify.

By late afternoon on the 30th, the Union army was prepared for battle. They had added to fortifications begun in 1863, and in some places along the crescent-shaped defensive line, the walls rose six to eight feet high. Wood from barn buildings, plows, and branches from the nefarious Osage orange trees helped to make the barrier almost impenetrable. Wide ditches on each side would consume the offenders as well. Many Union soldiers believed the Confederates would never attack. The men in gray would have to cross two miles of open ground and engage with a well-fortified enemy. It would be folly.

At 4:30 p.m., the sun began to set, painting the sky a blood red and blurring the air into a golden haze. The Northern soldiers must have been surprised to see their foes moving forward from Winstead Hill, across the valley floor. Awed, Mohrmann wrote:

Behind [the Confederate skirmishers] *came in splendid order, banners flying, drums beating, the enemy in line of battle, as beautiful an array in active war as I have witnessed.*

For the next several hours, the battle raged as the temperature dropped below 30°F and a faint sliver of the waxing moon appeared in the southeastern sky. The fighting was intense, characterized by hand-to-hand combat and the prodigious use of bayonets and clubbed muskets by the men, and revolver fire by the officers. Colonel Joseph Stockton was wounded in the back of the neck and more than half the 72nd's officers were killed or wounded. Command of the regiment fell to Captain James Sexton of Company D. Forty-three years after Franklin, Captain Sexton wrote of the hell he witnessed that night:

> *I recollect seeing one man, with the blood streaming down his face from a wound in the head, with a pick axe in his hands, rushing into a crowd of the enemy and swinging his pick with the strength and desperation of a madman.*
>
> *It was at this time that a rebel colonel mounted our breastworks, and in language not choice, but profanely expressive, demanded our immediate surrender. In the frenzy of the struggle, Private Arbridge, of Company D, Seventy-second Illinois, thrust his musket against the abdomen of the rash colonel, and with the exclamation "I guess not" instantly discharged his weapon. The effect of the shot was horrible and actually let daylight through the victim. The doomed warrior doubled up, his head gradually sinking forward and downward until he finally plunged head foremost into the pit below, at the very feet of his slayer.*

By the morning of December 1, almost ten thousand men, out of approximately thirty-six thousand involved, lay dead or wounded on the fields of Franklin. When the citizenry went to see what the night cataclysm had wrought, they found bodies, mostly dead, stacked eight feet deep in the trenches beside the Union defenses. Some had been so riddled with bullets that they appeared cut in two. One Franklin teenager observed a Yankee soldier who had died standing up, leaning against a locust tree. In the ensuing days, forty-four hospitals would sprout up around town, forty-one of which were designated for the Confederate soldiers (presumably because they had suffered the most casualties, at seven thousand, and perhaps also because this was Southern territory).

This is what we, on an autumn weekend in the early twenty-first century, had come to Franklin to remember.

After helping myself to a plate of roast beef, mashed potatoes, green beans, and cherry cobbler from the buffet line, I sat down at a table occupied by two gray-haired men. Robert and Henry Fonville, farm boys and World War II veterans, were from Belzoni, Mississippi, a village along the Yazoo River, forty miles south of Greenwood, Mississippi. Robert, the stouter, more talkative brother, told me they had five ancestors in the fight at Franklin.

"Now, I got a story for ya," he said, leaning my way, the words rolling out of his mouth like windblown cotton. "My great-grandfather, James Putnam, of the Fourth Mississippi Infantry, was captured at Fort Donelson and sent to the prison at Camp Morton, Indiana. He died there, leaving behind a wife and five small children. Some months later, Union troops ransacked my great-grandmother's home, taking nearly all her food and usable items. She was sitting on her porch, pretty down about it, when a captain from the 113th Illinois named Harvey Hosmer came by. Grandma explained the story, and he ordered his men to return some of the goods. After the war, Captain Hosmer returned to Belzoni and married my great-grandmother!"

"You know what that means, don't ya?" I asked Robert. He shook his head.

"At the next reunion, you have to wear a name tag for your Yankee ancestor!" Robert looked shocked and leaned way back, smiling.

"No, ma'am! He wasn't blood!"

"Who was your ancestor?" he then asked me, scrunching up his nose and looking down his glasses at my name tag. With a mouth full of cobbler, I told him.

"I see," Robert said. "Your ancestor was down here fighting the war of *Southern rebellion*. Mine were fighting the war of *Northern aggression*."

Next, Thomas Cartwright, director of the Carter House (now a nonprofit museum and interpretive center located on the grounds of the Carter family farm where the battle reached its zenith) addressed our gathering. Thomas—a man with a salt-and-pepper mustache and goatee, and round glasses that looked as if from the nineteenth century—stressed the importance of keeping the past alive.

"Even ten years ago, many Civil War maps did not show the Battle of Franklin. It's important that the men who fought here be remembered. They are *your* ancestors. These Southerners and Northerners have earned the right to not be forgotten. Every day we remember that courage knows no uniform."

The next speaker was David Fraley, a historian at the museum. David, a man in his thirties with a round, serious face and beard, talked about the Tennessee Campaign and what the Confederate soldiers had been through as they moved closer to battle. He told us how one-quarter to one-third of the men were barefoot and how they had suffered for months with threadbare clothing and little food.

"They didn't have the luxury of thinking, 'How will I do it?'" David said. "They just did it. Think about what your ancestors were feeling 136 years ago, in October 1864."

After the speeches came the music. The first performer sang "Dixie," which brought the crowd to their feet, clapping and singing. I felt self-conscious, not knowing the words and very aware this was a Southern song. Noticing one other man still seated, I felt better, but quickly realized this was only because he was crippled. I stood up and clapped. The next singer's rendition of "Marching through Georgia," a bouncy tune about Sherman's army bringing "the jubilee" to the South, elicited less enthusiasm.

Our Franklin ancestors had served in every level of the military establishment. I saw name tags of men I knew to be colonels, generals, corporals, and privates. One man in the group, recognizable by his near-perfect resemblance to his ancestor, was O.C. Hood, great-great-grandson of General John Bell Hood, the man who led the Confederates into defeat that November day. O.C., a tall man with a steely stare and thick, wavy hair brushed back from his forehead, closed the evening with a poem he'd written entitled, "Reload":

lyin' on a dirt road
eye'n down the sight
pick out the lead man
shoulder the musket
fire

the driftin' smoke slowly clears
and there! he lays
face-up, wide-eyed, and still
I took his life away
he fell right where he fell
fightin' for his cause
I wonder what his name was

here they come a runnin'
ain't nothin' gonna stop 'em
hold your ground
fire another round
do what you can to drop 'em
horseback man runnin' me down

now wilson takes 'em down at
three shots in a minute
at a hundred yards he cuts 'em down
like standing corn, fallin' every which way
but I know his heart ain't in it

and they say that it gets easier
day by day
man after man
to send a man out of this world
but I ain't found it so
I got to face that man that fell
everywhere I go

On Saturday morning, we boarded two school buses and began the daylong field trip to the sites of the Franklin engagement. Most of the battlefield has been paved over with neighborhoods and businesses; the land had not been preserved by those who set aside park space in places like Vicksburg, Mississippi, and Shiloh, Tennessee, in the late 1800s. Though the toll on human life was astonishingly high for a relatively short battle, Franklin has never attracted much attention from historians or the public. Thomas Cartwright told me that even at the beginning of the twentieth century, the suburbs of Franklin were already encroaching upon the fighting ground.

"By 1915, the community had built houses on parts of the battlefield. It wasn't a rural area, like Shiloh, and therefore not easily preserved. The feds also weren't interested because Franklin was in the west. Let's face it, the focus was in the east! Also, Franklin happened toward the end of the war and the Battle of Nashville followed it, which was a decided Union victory, whereas both sides claimed victory at Franklin. And last, it was such a horrible massacre in a small area; a lot of people didn't want to remember. Many locals felt the men died in vain. I personally do not think *anyone* died in vain."

Our first stop was Fort Granger, occupied by the Union during the Battle of Franklin and located approximately one mile northeast of the Carter House. Union cannons from the fort bombarded the Confederate army as it crossed the open ground around the Lewisburg Pike, until darkness shrouded the fight. Built upon Figuer's Bluff, a precipice that rises forty feet above the Franklin valley, this earthen fort was neglected for more than one hundred years until the city purchased the property in the 1970s. Hackberry and scrub oak have now locked their roots into the ten-foot-high earthworks that, excepting the vegetation, look the same as they did in 1864.

We walked around the base of the works. Shadows resembling spiderwebs moved slowly over the ground as the wind blew the treetops back and forth. David Fraley walked behind me.

"All of this is original," he said as I tripped over one of many bricks lying along the path. "The bricks are from the powder magazine. It was constructed from the basement of a house which was here. The soldiers stored ammunition and rations in the magazine."

Inside the fort, we gathered around the grassy mound where the magazine had been. Thomas told a story about hardtack, the square cracker made of flour and water issued to the soldiers.

"Hardtack was famous for getting to the soldiers infested with weevils and being hard as a rock. Sometimes the soldiers would have to break it with their fists or soak it in water to make it chewable. The story goes that one man was eating his hardtack and suddenly winced, saying, 'I just bit into something soft.' His buddy asked, 'Was it a worm?' 'No,' the man replied, 'A ten-penny nail.'"

Everyone laughed, and Robert Fonville said, "The government saved the leftover hardtack and issued it to us in WWII!"

On the south end of the valley is Winstead Hill, our second stop and the place where the Confederates began their march into battle. During the Franklin fight, six Confederate generals died, and stone monuments are erected on the hill to their memory. On the bus I sat next to Hunt Armistead, the great-great-grandnephew of General John Adams, one of the six. Hunt, a quiet man, wore sunglasses that resembled a patrol officer's and carried his video camera everywhere, documenting the voices and faces of the weekend.

Thomas and David painted the scene for us as we gazed across a valley now filled with roads, cars, and buildings: a crimson sun setting in the west, a crescent moon rising in the southeast, 45°F temperature, Confederate bands playing "Dixie" and "Bonnie Blue Flag," and nineteen thousand Southern soldiers stretched across both sides of the Columbia Pike, now State Highway 31. On November 30, 1864, only three cottages stood between Winstead Hill and the Carter House, two miles north.

Many on John Bell Hood's staff thought it unwise to attack Union troops so well entrenched behind lines near the Carter House. David told us Hood would not listen.

"He said, 'We will make the fight. We will go in at right shoulder shift. We will drive the enemy into the river, with bayonets.' The men knew they would be slaughtered. Several took their possessions to the priest to keep for them, but he refused. 'I'm going in with you,' the man said."

Patrick Cleburne, one of Hood's generals, told Brigadier General Daniel Govan, "Well, Govan, if we must die, then let us die like men."

Sam Watkins, a private with the First Tennessee, wrote in his memoir, Co. Aytch: A Confederate Memoir of the Civil War, "I had made up my mind to die—felt glorious."

On the way back to the buses I walked next to a small, older woman who wore a belt with the different flags of the Confederacy engraved into the leather.

"My great-great-grandmother sent four sons to war," she mused. "Only one came home."

Before getting on the bus, I walked over to David, who was standing by himself.

"Even though it's nothing like it used to be," I said, "I'd like to make the march the Confederates did across the valley."

David nodded. "Come back after the reunion. We can walk it together."

Our next stop was the Carnton Plantation. Built by a man named Randal McGavock in 1826, this antebellum mansion two miles from the Carter House served as a hospital for the Franklin wounded. It was not long into the night of November 30 before the beds and floor space were completely filled with broken and bleeding bodies. It was also not long before four Confederate generals, including Hunt's great-great-great uncle, were laid out on the back porch to await transportation home. It was not long before the pine floors upstairs where the surgeons worked were saturated with blood. These dark stains—in the shapes of circles, the ring of a bucket, and a footprint—are still visible below the south-facing windows and near the fireplace.

"The McGavocks tried to scrub the stains away," a guide explained, "but they never came out. The smell of blood lingered for weeks. Years later, the wife of a tenant farmer, who lived in the house, found the stains disturbing. She asked her husband to sand them out. Fortunately, he never got to the upstairs rooms."

Many of the men who died on the Franklin battlefield were hastily buried where they fell in shallow graves. The Union army was retreating to Nashville to hook up with the rest of General George

Thomas's troops, and Hood's battered ranks followed. Two weeks later, when the armies passed again through Franklin, this time with Hood in retreat, the soldiers saw the feet and hands of their fellow men covered with just a few inches of dirt. Darsie had written only:

> *We pass throug Franklin about dark and encamp on the*
> *Battle Field that night. It rained all night and we got a*
> *complete wetting.*

William Mohrmann described the scene in detail:

> *We marched beyond Franklin to camp but next morning*
> *before we started I could not resist the temptation to go*
> *over to the scene of our night struggle. I never want to see*
> *another battlefield like that. The rebels had buried their*
> *own dead* [in] *separate graves, but ours after having been*
> *stripped of some articles of clothing as were needed, had*
> *been piled into* [the] *trenches we had made and some*
> *earth thrown on them. With true southern slovenliness*
> *they had merely covered* [them] *and the rains had washed*
> *most of the earth away, leaving hands and legs exposed, a*
> *horrible sight.*

What happened to many of these Union men is unknown, but after the war, the McGavock family donated two acres of the Carnton property for the reinterment of almost fifteen hundred Confederate soldiers. The cemetery is a narrow strip of grassy field surrounded by a wrought-iron fence. The graves are organized by state, most marked by square, blank stones. Our group spread out along the path. One young girl, whose name tag read, "31st Mississippi, Jemma Bevelle," asked her father, "What are all the stones?"

"There's a person buried underneath each one," he explained.

"Why are some bigger?"

"They know the names of those."

"Consider that nearly fifteen hundred men rest in this two-acre piece of ground," David Fraley began. "Imagine each one standing above his grave. Now imagine their wives and children or parents standing next to them. It's becoming crowded around each headstone. Now imagine each man's grandchildren...and great-grandchildren, some of you now enter the scene...and great-great-grandchildren, more of you appear. The effects of war reach far beyond the individual life of the participant.

"These are not unknown soldiers," David continued, addressing the blank headstones. "They were not unknown to their families or friends or sweethearts. They are not unknown to God. We simply do not know their names."

Next to one of the small headstones a man had placed a Confederate flag and a soldier's picture. Stanley Cichowicz was telling people about finding the grave of his ancestor, a thirty-one-year-old man in the 12th Louisiana.

"I'm Colonel Nelson's oldest great-great-grandson," he said. "As far as I know, I'm the first person in the family to visit his grave at Carnton." Then Stanley began to cry.

"What happened to Colonel Nelson?" I asked.

"He was wounded at Franklin and brought here to the McGavock house. He died upstairs."

———◆———

At the Carter House we ate a lunch of fried chicken, ribs, coleslaw, and cornbread and listened to a local musical duo sing "Johnny Has Gone for a Soldier." Thomas Cartwright kept encouraging us, like a track coach rallying his long-distance runners, to "keep the memories alive and green." I had no doubt of the worth of this endeavor, but I also wondered about persistently living so close to such pain. Is it healthy to taste the poison day after day? Sometimes, at home with my reading, research, and writing, I had felt overwhelmed. Sometimes I'd had to leave behind these experiences of war and replenish myself with the best of my life in the present, walking through a forest or sitting next to the soft, steady glide of a river. However, this weekend there would be no break.

The original 1864 buildings of the Carter estate are set upon nine acres of lawn, beneath sprawling oak and pecan trees, and include the family home, a farm office, a smokehouse, and a kitchen.

The south sides of the office and smokehouse are riddled with bullet holes, some finger size, some as big around as my fist. The office, now painted a deep red, has earned the distinction as "the most battle-scarred building left standing from the Civil War." By virtue of their survival, these buildings attest to General Hood's impatience to engage the Union troops without benefit of his artillery. By virtue of their scars, they attest to the determination of men.

One block southeast, the Carter cotton gin had stood. Some of the fiercest fighting had occurred around the gin. The men were so close together that there was no time to reload, and they had killed each other with their bare hands. A Domino's and a Pizza Hut now occupy the site.

"Eleven Union soldiers received Congressional Medals of Honor for the fight at Franklin," David told us. "So many medals earned during such a short period of time is unprecedented in American history."

"It's a bane!" Thomas then shouted, waving his arms toward the corporate dining culture that had usurped the landscape of memories. "The only possible benefit of this tragedy is if we learn what can happen when places where American blood flowed are not preserved." Everyone clapped and cheered.

"I'm sorry, ladies and gentlemen," he apologized. "I tried to hold back."

Saturday night after dinner, Thomas dimmed the lights. Each of us lit a votive candle and said something about our ancestor.

The descendant of Otto Strahl, one of the six Confederate generals killed said, "He gave his horse to Bishop Quintard to save the animal."

The descendant of Dennis Todd, a private in the Tenth South Carolina Infantry: "He came home without any shoes and was murdered when he was mistaken for a raider."

I stood up. "Darsie Heath, private, 72nd Illinois. In my ancestor's journals, he wrote twice that he would 'delete things from his memory.' I think I am a lot like him because ever since my father died, I have been trying to forget the past, because many memories are so painful. In truth, however, it is much better to remember than to forget."

At the time I said these words, I'm not sure if I really believed this last part. As the years went by, however, and I learned more about my father's battle experiences, the nightmares I'd had for so long (where he was always drunk or I'd be hitting him for ruining all our lives) began to be less frequent and then, finally, stopped altogether. It was at that point that I truly believed that remembering is better than forgetting.

When O.C. Hood spoke, a strange thing happened. He held his candle and began to explain what had happened to General Hood after the war. After a couple of sentences, he stopped.

"Most of you know the story anyway ..." Then O.C.'s candle went out as if a wind had entered the room. One hundred pairs of eyes looked at the smoking wick, then at their own. Everyone else's candle continued to burn.

Six months later I called O.C. to ask him about his own quest to learn more about his family's past. He said that growing up he had known that John Bell Hood was his ancestor, but had never thought the connection affected him personally.

"It wasn't until ten years ago that I began to delve into the past," he said. "I went to see my father, who was dying. I landed in Nashville and at the airport happened to find the book, *John Bell Hood and the War for Southern Independence* by Richard McMurry. I bought it. Then I found my father reading the same book. I said to him, 'This is about us, isn't it?'"

"You bet it is," he replied.

"Since then," O.C. continued, "I've become obsessed with the general, the war, the battlefields. I feel close to John Bell Hood in a way that I can't explain. After I began to read about his life, I realized how much we had in common. We both were the same kind of student, had the same problems, both our fathers were doctors."

"You certainly look alike," I said.

"When I'm out on a battlefield, I feel like I'm recovering something. But it's like a mirage; I can't ever really get to it. At times, I wonder what it is that's unresolved.

"Franklin moves me more than any place I've been to," he continued. "Sometimes I go to the McGavock Cemetery and Winstead

Hill at night. Once I found a piece of purple cloth in the ditch off the Columbia Pike. I don't know what it was, but it felt like a glimpse of something I couldn't quite comprehend. Something bigger than me."

After the reunion, David Fraley and I walked from Winstead Hill to the Carter House. The October heat had turned to a light drizzle. The two-lane Columbia Pike (State Highway 31) is a hazard to walk along, with no sidewalks and a tremendous amount of traffic. As cars rushed past and buildings blocked my view, I had trouble imagining an empty valley. David and I passed an antebellum rock wall, now nearly consumed by foliage. To the west of the pike we found seventy-two acres of grassy field and copses.

"These seventy-two acres are selling for 7.2 million [dollars]," David said dryly. "This is why battlefield preservation is so difficult."

As we neared the Carter House, we passed a building under construction. I asked David what it was.

"*That* is the new library, built literally over a burial spot for those who died during the battle. We wrote letters to senators and others in high places, but we couldn't stop it. The city council voted for the library 19-2. Even a decorated Vietnam veteran voted in favor. Later I told that man he had just pissed on top of the brave soldiers of Franklin."

Later, during lunch, David and I talked about World War II. He told me he had an uncle who had been a paratrooper.

"One day I received this package in the mail, and it was his airborne patches. I was surprised. Later I asked him if I could videotape him talking about his experiences. He said no. He told me, 'As I get older, the memories get harder.' I used to thank my uncle for his service, but he finally asked me not to do that."

David's energy, like Thomas's, seemed solely dedicated to bringing the past to life, but his heart seemed heavy. His serious eyes never lightened despite an occasional smile, and though I did not know David's story, he seemed to suffer a deep sadness. As we finished our burgers, he shared that he was going through a difficult time.

"It's been stressful and causing me some heart problems, so I've been treating myself to massages. My massage therapist has suggested I carry more than just my own pain." He shrugged. "The blood of war is in our DNA. We have to remember."

Before leaving Franklin, I walked along Strahl Street, just south of the Carter House, where the Union main line had been—now a quiet, suburban neighborhood with one-story houses. Over the course of my two Civil War road trips, I would walk over several battlefields. Like O.C. Hood, I felt like I was chasing after a mirage. I kept getting closer to *something*, but it was like groping in the dark for a mystery prize, and sometimes I wasn't sure if I really wanted to find it. As the months and years went by, and I kept writing and reading about war and thinking about my own life and the person I'd become, I suspected that I kept "tasting the poison" just to keep my own demons close to me. At least then I could keep an eye on them. I didn't enjoy their presence and I didn't like the dark thoughts they conjured up, but at least they couldn't sneak up on me.

In the autumn of 2002, I attended another Battle of Franklin Descendants' Reunion and another two years after that I marched down Highway 31 as a Union private at the Battle of Franklin Anniversary Reenactment. Spending so much time with the memories of war continued to take its toll on me, but one aspect of my investigations represented a bright spot: I had begun to forgive my father. Like the disappearance of my nightmares about him, I couldn't pinpoint where or when this happened, but my own losses began to diminish next to the whole of his life. The drinking, the withdrawals, my resentment at his embarrassing behavior, and the taciturn way in which he'd died—all now paled beside what I understood of the war experience. He would always be an alcoholic and a soldier and a casualty who had survived, but I could now also remember who else he'd been.

Chapter 24

The Flower Deliverer

Survival when others have perished brings its own suffering. The question inevitably poses itself, Why was I chosen to live? In the wake of this question, it is a comfort to discover something unique one might give to the world.

—Susan Griffin, from *A Chorus of Stones: The Private Life of War*

March 2001, Tacoma, Washington

THE MANAGER OF CRANE'S CREATIONS, a florist's shop near where I grew up, wrapped the two roses and two lilies with baby's breath and ferns, centering the flowers among the greenery as if she were styling hair. Her nametag read, "Sophia." As I paid for the arrangement, I asked Sophia how long she had worked there.

"Seven years—why?"

"My father used to deliver flowers for Crane's. I thought you might have known him."

"What was his name?"

"Jim Howell. But, he died ten years ago."

"I'm sorry. That was before my time."

March 13, 2001, marked ten years since my father's death. For the previous several weeks, I had been composing a letter to read at my parents' graves. Using a fountain pen on heavy bond paper, I had written five pages about the anger, love, guilt, and regret I had felt over the past decade. I planned to read this missive into the wind above their graves. Then I would burn every page. My hurt and disappointment would evaporate into nothingness, setting me free—or so I hoped.

But when I arrived at Mountain View Cemetery in Tacoma, the weather turned against me. It hailed and rained and the wind blew tree branches every direction, the previous autumn's leaves spiraling in funnel shapes across the ground. Untethered flower arrangements tipped over and spun in half-moons across the grass. Weather like this in the Pacific Northwest could last for days.

Ten minutes passed. An hour. A crippled Canada goose hobbled along on the grass, dragging one useless foot behind it and probing the sodden ground for tidbits. Maintenance workers wore dark green rain suits with pointed hats that resembled small mountains. I leaned the car seat back and thought about how many times Dad must have come to Mountain View bringing flowers, messages from the living to the dead.

———

In 1978, my father retired from the post office, bought a supply of white shirts and black pants, and began attending food preparation classes at the local community college. Though he was accomplished at barbecuing and made colorful, delicious Sunday morning breakfasts, he could also be a bit Dr. Frankenstein-like in the kitchen. For example, whenever I heard him say, "The world could live on soup!" I knew he was about to toss every leftover from the fridge into the Crock-Pot, and that I was not going to like it. Given this background, I knew we were in for a lot of experimentation when his classes started, and though I don't remember any disasters, I do recall feeling doom when Dad would come home announcing, "We're eating gourmet tonight, girls!"

I don't know if my father ever planned to get a job as a chef or not. Perhaps the classes had just been about learning something new and not a means to an end. Two years after retiring, he had accepted a part-time job delivering flowers for Crane's Creations.

Dad's decision to retire and change direction in his life came during my early teenage years when being well-regarded among my peers didn't just mean having a good-looking football star for a boyfriend (which I lacked completely) and the most "in" clothes (which I mostly lacked). It also meant having parents that were similar in age, profession, and demeanor to my friends' parents. I didn't want mine being too weird or different, but it was too late.

In 1980, my father turned sixty and my mother fifty-five. As a teenager, they seemed really old to me. Their primary careers were over. My mother still worked part-time at my elementary school, and now my father wanted to deliver flowers! I was mortified. What was I going to tell my friends? In explanation, I said only that he was retired from the military.

Dad only wanted to work part-time, but he was so cheerful and dependable that when the company opened new shops, he soon found himself working every day. By the time I began college, I had gotten used to his third profession and worried a little less about Dad's status. The summer after my sophomore year I returned home and had no job of my own.

"Do you want to come with me delivering flowers?" he asked one afternoon. I surprised myself by accepting the offer.

Early the next day, we drove to the main store in a suburb of Tacoma. Dad wore slacks and a nice shirt and jacket, as well as a baseball cap with the Crane's emblem on it. His thick, white hair, trimmed military-style above his ears and across the back of his neck, contrasted well with the dark cap. I met "the girls" who arranged the flowers, including Yuko, a Japanese woman who had married another soldier named Howell.

"This is Yuko," Dad said, chuckling, "my Japanese sister." Yuko also laughed, shaking my hand.

"Your father," she said, "he great."

We collected the arrangements and loaded everything into a white van. As we entered the first neighborhood, Dad looked around and smiled.

"You know, Bets, I'll bet I could come here early one Saturday morning and blow a bugle and fifty old soldiers would fall out of the trees." We laughed at his old joke.

I had never seen my father in his "public" personality. I had no idea how he looked to the world outside my small family and group of friends. Consequently, I felt nervous as we pulled up to the first house for a delivery.

"I'll just stay here," I said. The intoxicating smell of the roses, carnations, and other flowers made me feel like I had gone to sleep inside one of them.

He smiled and nodded, grabbed an arrangement from the back of the van, and walked up to the door. I had to admit my father was a handsome delivery man. He was not tall at five feet eight inches, and he had a beer belly, but the rest of his body still looked hard and fit. Dad's face was beginning to bronze as the cloudy, rainy days of spring gave way to the fresh, golden sun of the Pacific Northwest. The van windows were down on this warm summer day, so I could hear everything. A small older woman cautiously opened the door.

"Good morning!" my dad shouted. "How are you today, ma'am?" I slumped a little lower in the seat. *You don't have to shout*, I thought.

"Good morning," the woman replied. Dad continued to grin and asked her if she was so-and-so. She replied affirmatively.

"Well, I have this beautiful bouquet of flowers for you! Somebody is thinking of you today!" He handed her the basket and she thanked him in a soft, almost timid, voice.

"You're very welcome! Happy birthday! Have a good day now!" Dad walked away. She thanked him again, and he raised his arm to wave, smiling all the while. As he started up the van, I said, "You certainly are animated," hoping that maybe Dad would tone down his presentation a bit.

"If you can't have fun delivering flowers, when can you have fun?" he replied.

And so it went throughout the morning and afternoon, my father bringing exuberance and color into people's otherwise ordinary days. After a few deliveries, I got used to his shouting. Dad kept the radio tuned to an oldies station that played Glen Miller, and at midday Paul Harvey came on.

"I used to be socialist as hell," Dad mused, as we weaved through Tacoma's traffic and Paul Harvey droned on. "Something for everyone, the government taking care of us, sharing the wealth, but now I don't believe that system works. Capitalism works! Rewards have to be available to those who *do*, and those who do *not* deserve their situation. I've been working since I was thirteen years old. Started doing yard jobs for Mrs. Waterman, who lived near us in Geneseo. She paid me a dime a day!"

Of course, I had heard this story many times, but I still loved listening to him talk about the good old days.

Late in the afternoon, we drove into a typical middle-class neighborhood above the bluffs that looked out over Puget Sound. Cultivated rhododendron and arborvitae surrounded dark chocolate-colored homes with large windows and expansive lawns. Dad searched for a house number while a story aired on the radio about a teenage boy who had committed suicide in Tacoma.

"That's the most selfish thing a person can do," Dad said, turning the volume down and looking at me. "You know what suicide is, don't you? It's a permanent solution to a temporary problem."

I nodded and said nothing. Dad didn't need to know that sometimes suicide crossed my mind, when Mom withdrew or when he drank too much. Even with our fraught family life, it was obvious that he believed that no problem was so big it couldn't be worked through. I wondered if I believed that too.

After two hours of constant rain, I decided my letter-reading ceremony would have to wait a day. I placed the purple and red roses and the yellow and salmon-colored lilies, as well as a small American flag, next to my parents' grave marker. "I'll be back tomorrow," I said, and drove to the house on Snowberry Circle.

I had not been back to my childhood home since I'd packed up my parents' things four and a half years previous. Selling the house had been accomplished via faxes and Federal Express. I had never spoken with the new owners and knew only that they were a young couple with kids and that the husband was a soldier stationed at Fort Lewis. The signatures on the paperwork had read "Erin and Christine Wilkins."

Ever since my mother's death I had been plagued by nightmares about the house, including these scenarios: I'd sold it, but my parents hadn't actually died; I'd sold it, my parents had died, but the new owners never moved in; and I'd sold it, the new owners had moved in, but I still had a key and would enter whenever it suited me. It didn't take an expert on dreams to understand my lack of acceptance about my situation. I'd decided that seeing the house, with its new occupants, would help my subconscious believe, and accept, the events of the past.

I drove into Snowberry Circle. The rain had stopped in this part of Tacoma. Puddles of black water dotted the cul-de-sac, and the ashen sky hung so low it seemed I could reach up and wave my hands through the clouds. I parked in front of the house, now gray with a darker gray trim. The Big Dipper and North Star images on the garage were gone, as were the arborvitae shrubs in the front yard. The Douglas-fir and western red cedar trees my dad had planted in 1969 now towered fifty feet above the house.

I rang the doorbell and a young woman with long, dark hair, who looked to be in her midtwenties opened the door. When I asked, she confirmed that she was Christine Wilkins. I told her my name and explained that I had sold the house to her and her husband.

"I remember you," she smiled, "or your name at least."

I explained my request, and to my surprise, Christine opened the door wide. "The house is a mess and one of the kids just threw a bowl of cereal all over the living room. But if you don't mind that ..."

Her three children were playing a video game. The oldest boy immediately turned around and asked, "Why are you coming in?"

"Well, I used to live in your house, and your mom said I could look around." This seemed to satisfy him and he went back to the game.

I tried to absorb everything at once: the colors, the carpets, the things on the wall. It was almost as if I were looking at a double exposure. I could see the Wilkins' home, but underneath a thin membrane of time, I could also see my family's home. Whereas my parents had packed the house with wall hangings, furniture, and knickknacks, the Wilkins' decorative impulses were austere. Where we had lived into the '90s with green carpeting from 1969, they had opted for a modern, gray version. Where almost every room in our home was painted a different color, the Wilkins' had covered every wall, except those in the bedrooms, in a light tan hue. They had replaced the linoleum in the entryway. The drapes in the living room, however, were the same ones my parents had purchased years ago.

Christine took me through every room except the garage. The swinging saloon doors my dad had installed to separate the living and dining rooms were gone. The old green linoleum in the kitchen and dining rooms remained, and I could still see all the black scars on the hearth where fire embers had burnt the floor. As foretold by the real estate agent, my father's map of the world had been removed and the wall painted over, but the breakfast bar in the kitchen was still there.

"My dad built this," I said, running my hands over the veneer.

"That has been such a godsend," Christine said. "You know, since there is so little counter space."

And so it went for each room. I tallied the differences, what was still the same, what had changed. My yellow room was now burgundy-colored on the upper half of the walls and gray on the lower half, and bunk beds sat where my bed had been. My parents' bedroom had been a lime green; Christine and Erin had painted it light silver. Their bed and dresser were in the same position as my parents' furniture had been. The bathroom was still the same mustard yellow hue, but at least the Wilkins had removed the blue and yellow beads that my parents had hung by the toilet in the early '70s. My father's den, once a place of books and photographs of soldiers, was now painted pink and belonged to Christine and Erin's little girl. I could still see the shelves where Darsie's journals had sat, and the books on war, and I remembered the day I had tried to read *A Stillness at Appomattox*.

In the backyard, the thin oak tree seemed to recognize me and its spidery branches waved "hello" while I remembered my family's life on this ground: the lawn Tiger had run across after stealing a pork rib from my father's grill, the spot where I had buried my rabbit Gray-Gray, the pool parties I'd had with friends, my mom's garden, my dad's toolshed. Big-Boy's dog pen was still there, as was my dad's wire compost bin, rusting in a quiet corner by the garden.

This ended the tour. Christine and I talked while she placed dishes in the dishwasher.

"I had heard that your mom had died in the house," she said. "It kind of worried me, you know, what with poltergeists and all."

"Oh."

"But, you know," she added quickly, "it hasn't been a problem. I've had nothing but good feelings since we moved in." She looked my way. "I think it's great you grew up in this house."

<hr />

The next day I returned to the cemetery. The storm had moved on, and my flowers had survived the rain and hail. I stood next to them and the flag, letting the damp seep into my bones, and began reading.

Exactly ten years earlier, I had woken up the morning after my father died and thought, "My life will never be the same." Now, I shared with my parents how my life had changed. I told them about my anger, how they had let me down, how they had died too soon, how they had drank and smoked too much. I told them about the guilt I felt for not being able to save them. Finally, I also thanked them for what they had given me.

"I know you loved me," I said, "and I also know you weren't perfect. I wasn't perfect either. I wish we'd shared more and drank less, but I guess we all did the best we could. My heart hurts every day. I just want you to know how much I love you."

I got out my matches and, as the maintenance men moved around like wraiths, I wondered if it was illegal to light something on fire in a cemetery. The fire wouldn't be able to catch on and spread in this weather, and these people must see all manner of ritual. I could always plead ignorance later.

The first and second pages burned easily. With the third, the flame consumed one corner then succumbed to the wind. I had only a few matches left and one after the other went out. I became nervous. If burning my feelings was symbolic of letting go of my pain, then *not* being able to burn the papers would represent being stuck. I resorted to using a napkin from my glove box as a torch, and the rest of letter finally erupted in an orange-red wave. Yet the last section at the bottom of the final page documenting my anger over the last decade fought the fire. This anger was so much a part of who I had become that even burning it figuratively would not prove simple. Eventually, however, the paper turned to ash and the wind took the fragments away.

Chapter 25

The Corporal

Please subdue the anguish of your soul. Nobody is destined only to happiness or to pain. The wheel of life takes one up and down by turn.

—Kalidasa, dramatist (ca. fourth century)

Autumn 2002, western Oregon

CAPTAIN CHRIS SCARANO of the 19th Indiana Infantry looked over his troops, standing at attention with rifles at order arms. Mist was rolling off the Columbia River at Fort Stevens State Park near Astoria, Oregon. It covered our wool clothing, and I, for one, felt it was far too early to be awake. The band hadn't agreed. At 6:30 a.m. sharp the bugler had blared reveille, which was quickly followed by the sounds of the fife and drum corps.

"Private Howell, front and center!" shouted the captain.

I marched forward and stood in front of him.

"Private, it is my honor to inform you that you have hereby been promoted to the rank of corporal. Congratulations." Chris handed me a certificate and corporal's stripes and gave me a sharp salute. I returned the salute, attempted to look pleased, then returned to my place in line. After three seasons and many roster changes, I had become one of the "old men." Being promoted didn't surprise me.

Everyone clapped, including the women who had come over from civilian camp to witness the ceremony. Patty, Chris's mother, took pictures. After we broke ranks, she congratulated me.

"Let's see those stripes!" she said. I handed them to her and she situated them around my coat sleeve where they would be sewn on. She laughed as the ends of the two chevrons nearly touched.

"Your arm is so small!"

"Hey! That's my bicep you're talking about!"

"It looked like you were about to cry," she went on. "Were you surprised? Are you happy?"

Private Rick Fitzgerald came up and shook my hand.

"When you gonna get those put on?" he boomed.

"Soon, but I'll start bossing you before that."

Everyone seemed so pleased with my promotion that I didn't have the heart to tell them I didn't want it. I liked being a private. I liked letting others worry about drill and reports and discipline, while I wrote in my journal or read. Now, all that was going to change. An hour later, I received my first order with the new rank.

"Corporal, have the men fall in for parade," said Captain Scarano.

"Yes, sir." I took a big breath and tried to make my voice deeper. "Okay, boys! FALL IN!"

"Boys! Boys!" shouted Rick, and I knew right away I would have trouble with him. "We're not boys! We're men!"

"I'll call you 'men' when I see evidence of it," I said. Rick looked at me slyly, then walked away to get his canteen.

The reenactment at Fort Stevens is the only event in the Northwest to occur at a fort built during the Civil War. Originally an outpost of earthworks, Fort Stevens (along with two forts on the Washington side of the river) was designed to prevent an English invasion from Canada, should England decide to support the Confederacy. This never happened, and in later years the fort was upgraded for use during World War II. Improvements in aircraft technology, however, quickly made defenses like Stevens of little use, and it was dismantled in the late 1940s. Some of the earthworks still remain but more prominent are the resonant, cement bunkers from the Second World War.

Due to a low-hanging fog during the morning engagement, the black powder smoke lingered around us, making breathing and seeing difficult.

"This feels more like a real battle," said a sharpshooter next to me. I nodded, aware that neither one of us knew what a real battle felt like.

"Load faster, boys, load faster!" shouted Chris.

My fingers fumbled as I retrieved a black powder cartridge from behind me. I ripped it open and some of the paper stuck to my lip. We fired at will, as fast as we could load. The Indiana men took hits and recycled back into the ranks.

"19th Indiana!" yelled Chris. "Stand! At the double-quick, march!"

We trotted to a low fence and hunkered down behind it. Soon enough we were ordered to fall back. First Sergeant Derrick Sturdivant's face glistened red with sweat and excitement. He howled at the top of his lungs.

"Give me a line, HERE! Corporal! Get the men into line!"

Sweat poured down my face. I continued loading and shooting, with my gun sometimes misfiring. The damp air descended into the barrel, coating the black powder sufficiently to where it would not ignite. I fired again and heard nothing but a soft snap as the hammer hit the blasting cap. At that moment, Brett Williams, a new recruit, cried out. I turned to see him pawing at his ear, blood flowing out of tiny hole in the cartilage at the top. Brett pulled a small piece of blasting cap, possibly from my gun, from the hole. The wound was not serious and the blood quickly clotted.

As the Union soldiers made their way closer to the audience, the 19th Indiana found its sister Confederate regiment, the Fourth Texas Infantry. We had rehearsed hand-to-hand combat with them earlier and now were ready to engage. The Fourth and the 19th had done this several times in the past. The two units generally coordinated specific partners and moves, however, on this day, like at the movie shoot, I didn't have a partner. The plan for me was to find any Texan who wasn't busy, and do some shoving.

In the melee I got excited and gave one of the Confederates a faux rifle butt to the chest and he went down. Just as I was about to whack him again, a big guy grabbed me from behind. He picked me up and tossed me down. I landed atop of the Confederate I'd laid low, and heard my spine cracking. My attacker, who was running around like a Tasmanian devil, looked surprised.

"Hey, are you okay?"

"Yeah," I gasped. "I think so."

After the battle, I heard that our hand-to-hand looked so real that Union command thought it was real and were ready to punish both companies. Captain Scarano explained everything to our colonel and we received kudos for our excellent impression. That night, I sat around the campfire with another new recruit, Niels Foley. Most of the 19th had gone to the civilian camp or the evening ball, and I reveled in the quiet. My first day as a corporal had been busy—shouting orders on the battlefield, then later making sure the privates carried out their water, firewood, and cleanup details around camp. After eating our dinner, Niels asked me how I'd gotten into reenacting. I told him, emphasizing my desire to understand the experience of the soldiers in my family.

"Like the fight this afternoon," I explained, "that brings me closer, but I actually want to know what it's *really* like to be in a fight." I paused, remembering how upset I felt after my experiences on the movie set and at the backwoods tactical. "At least, I think that's what I want." Niels, a blond-haired man my age with large lips and teeth and an opinion about everything, thought that was a ridiculous idea.

"How could anyone *want* to be in a fight?" he said. "A fight is not nice. It hurts and you bleed a lot and swell up like a pickle. Why would you want that?"

"I just want to understand..." I replied. He looked at me like I was crazy.

"I don't think you need a black eye to understand how awful combat was."

The fire sparked and shot flames upward. The sun had gone down over the Pacific Ocean and from our camp I could see massive freighters heading into the Columbia River. Someone in the camp suddenly shouted, "Attention to the colors!" Niels and I and everyone on the company streets immediately stood and saluted the flag. Waving in the offshore breeze, the mammoth banner flew atop a ship's mast pole just outside the original Civil War earthworks.

As I stood at attention, I knew that Niels was right. How far was I going to take my obsession with war anyway? I didn't need to get beaten up to understand the pain of battle. I didn't need to know every single thing that had happened to either my father or great-great-grandfather; in fact, part of me didn't *want* to know and I was finally accepting that. I also didn't need to compare myself to these soldiers in my family and pointlessly wonder if I could have been as brave in the same situations. My father had told me, "You do what you have to do," and I'd done that with the life I'd been given. After five years, thanks to Darsie, I knew James Howell better than I had known him while he was alive, and I didn't need any more information to forgive him. I couldn't change the pain he and Darsie had lived and died with, and I couldn't change the pain I now carried, but I could keep telling their story.

"At ease!" the soldier, who had called attention, yelled. We brought our arms to our sides. The flag snapped in the wind and the rigging on the pole clinked against the metal.

———•———

EPILOGUE

In rivers, the water that you touch is the last of what has passed and the first of that which comes; so with present time.

—Leonardo da Vinci, painter, engineer, musician,
and scientist (1452–1519)

NEXT TO THE NATIONAL CEMETERY at the Vicksburg National Military Park is a museum dedicated to the USS *Cairo*, the first ironclad boat sunk by underwater mines in the Yazoo River on December 12, 1862. The *Cairo*'s captain and crew were headed up the Mississippi tributary to destroy Confederate batteries and clear the channel of these mines, called "torpedoes" during the Civil War. Unfortunately, the *Cairo* accomplished neither of these objectives. Seven miles from the Mississippi, the ironclad hit two torpedoes, which tore huge holes in the ship's hull. Within twelve minutes, the 175-foot behemoth that carried thirteen large cannons had sunk to the murky bottom of the Yazoo.

As the decades faded and the Civil War generation died, knowledge of Cairo's location dimmed as well. In the 1950s, however, historian Edwin Bearss and two friends set out to determine its final resting place. Three years later the first items recovered from the ship, armored port covers, made it back above the surface, but getting the entire ship above water and intact would not be easy. More than a century's worth of Yazoo River silt had curled around the ship like a tight glove. In 1964, three-inch-thick cables used in an attempt to raise Cairo cut deeply into its hull and hopes of wresting the ship unbroken from its watery grave were dashed. As much as possible was salvaged, which included several white oak structural pieces, the pilothouse, an eight-inch smoothbore cannon and its white oak carriage, and many personal effects—such as belt buckles, cookware, glassware, mirrors, combs, and even scraps of cloth, which were preserved in the mud like fruit in a canning jar.

What was recovered of the USS *Cairo* is now on display at the park, underneath a huge canopy of metal beams and supports. Because so little of the original structure could be salvaged from the river, the restoration crew began a process called "ghosting." This process combined techniques of preservation and restoration; every original piece was mounted on a new glue-laminated wood support structure. These surviving components were linked by "ghosting," or constructing, the outline and form of the missing sections. The result has been a distinct combination of original and new, with much of the bow and intermittent locations along both sides consisting of wood the color of Mississippi mud and the rest of the structure appearing clean, white, and new-looking. And the entire ship is full of gaps where there is nothing. Walking along a reconstructed part of the gun deck (during my time in Vicksburg), I saw the original engines, boilers, pilothouse, and the armored port covers the divers had found. I could see through the framework into other rooms. Looking at a postcard of *Cairo* in the 1860s, only the outside was visible. It is possible that pieces found in the future will complete more of *Cairo*, but for now, the broken ship is open for all to see, hiding nothing.

I had one more thing to do. On a warm, sunny Northwest afternoon, I packed up my father's military decorations and went to see Sergeant Gary Hall at the Port Angeles, Washington, U.S. Army Recruiting Station. The sergeant greeted me with a smile and an enthusiastic handshake. Tall, with the usual military haircut, he looked like an everyman soldier with a uniform so perfectly pressed it might have been resting on a mannequin. His shoes glistened like a mirror.

"You say your father was a paratrooper?" he began. "They were a tough bunch. Let's see what you have. I don't know if I'll know all of them, but some at least." I had told the sergeant over the phone that

I wanted to know the meaning of Dad's medals. I tipped the bag and out rolled the remains of my father's military career, which in addition to the colored bars he'd worn on his uniform included two folded squares of silk, two airborne patches, and the cords that had encircled his shoulders. Sergeant Hall first examined the eleven bars.

"These are actually called 'ribbons,'" he explained, "which fit over a ribbon mounting bar. See? They slide off. As a soldier acquires more, he gets a longer bar. They are worn above the left pocket on the uniform."

"This red, white, and blue one is for the bronze star, an army decoration. These others represent service medals, including this red, black, and white one, which stood for the Army of Occupation, a World War II award. I don't know some of these but we have a poster with most of the recent medals on it." He walked to a brightly colored display of military grandeur. I soon learned that the blue and white striped ribbon represented "United Nations Service"; red and white stripes was for "Good Conduct"; and a mostly yellow ribbon with very narrow red, white, and blue stripes was for "American Defense 1939–41." One ribbon—brown and green with three bronze stars and an arrowhead—was for the "European-African-Middle Eastern Campaign."

"On this last ribbon, each star, as well as the ribbon itself, denotes a campaign he participated in." The ribbon and three stars must have referred to Dad's participation in Normandy, Holland, Belgium, and Germany.

"This dark blue rectangle with the gold border is a Presidential Unit Citation." (Later I would learn the 505th was awarded the citation twice, for its work in Normandy and Holland. This commendation is the unit equivalent of the Medal of Honor awarded to individual soldiers.)

Sergeant Hall continued. "This is a ribbon-only award without a medal."

"So, there are medals and ribbons?

"Yes. The awards come with a medal and a ribbon and the medal sits in a display box while the ribbon is worn on the uniform. Like his army commendation medals." He picked up the clear plastic box that held these; inside, against the blue-black velvet, were a lapel pin, a ribbon, and a bronze-colored medal hanging from an inch-and-a-half piece of material. All had the same design: a green background with five white lines down the center. "Generally, the award would be presented as a set, like this, along with a certificate."

I looked at the pile of ribbons sitting next to my father's silver paratrooper wings and a plastic name tag that read, "HOWELL." Where were the actual medals? They had never been displayed in his den. I didn't remember ever seeing them as a child. Sergeant Hall then looked at the patches.

"This airborne patch was worn on the dress uniform," he said, holding up the square of red with symmetrical A's in the center. This stood for "All Americans," a nickname bestowed on the 82nd Airborne during World War I, when it was just a conventional infantry division, because its members came from all forty-eight states of the country.

"What about the cords?" I asked, holding up the sky blue braid and two others, one green with red flecks, the other with green and red stripes.

"The blue one represents infantry. These other two, called "four-ragères," were awarded to units from the governments of Belgium and France."

"And this," he continued, unfolding one of the heavily creased silk squares with the design of a map, "is almost certainly what the paratroopers were issued before D-Day." He looked at the bottom left corner. It read, "March 1944." "Each man had a map of France in case they got lost on the jump."

I looked again at the ribbon bars. Sandwiched in between the Army of Occupation ribbon and the one with the three stars and arrowhead was a ribbon of rainbow design with a big splash of red in the middle, bookended by lines of purple, blue, yellow, orange, and white. This, Sergeant Hall told me, represented "World War II Victory."

When I got home, I looked for the one other "medal" from my father's collection, which I hadn't taken to Sergeant Hall because I'd been fairly certain it wasn't from the Second World War. Where this particular award had been during my youth I couldn't remember; it had just somehow made it into the bag with the other decorations. It had the same band of colors, however, as the World War II Victory design. Beneath the material hung a bronze circle inscribed with a winged figure resembling the Statue of Liberty and holding a sword in one hand and a shield in the other. On the reverse were the words, "The Great War For Civilization," with a list of the Allied nations that fought in Europe from 1914 to 1918. Three battle clasps had been attached to the rainbow material and read, "St. Mihiel," "Meuse-Argonne," and "Defensive Sector." This is the "World War I Victory" medal.

I held the medal and looked at the battle clasps. This could only have belonged to William Howell, my grandfather, whose occupation on my father's birth certificate had simply read, "Sergeant, USA Auto Repair."

SELECTED BIBLIOGRAPHY

Civil War

Avey, Michael Garland, ed. *The Civil War Letters of John Avey, 2/4/1822–1/31/1911.* Lakewood: Fort Steilacoom Community College, Department of Anthropology, 1986.

Blanton, DeAnne, and Lauren M. Cook. *They Fought Like Demons.* Baton Rouge: Louisiana State University Press, 2002.

Dickens, Charles. *American Notes for General Circulation.* New York: Penguin Books, 2000.

Foote, Shelby. *The Beleaguered City: The Vicksburg Campaign, December 1862–July 1863.* New York: Random House, 1963.

Giambrone, Jeff. *Beneath Torn And Tattered Flags: A History of the 38th Mississippi Infantry C.S.A.* Bolton, MS: Smokey Row Press, 1998.

Grabau, Warren E. *Ninety-Eight Days: A Geographer's View of the Vicksburg Campaign.* Knoxville: University of Tennessee Press, 2000.

Heafford, George H. "The Army of the Tennessee." In *War Papers Read before the Commandery of the State of Wisconsin, Military Order of the Loyal Legion of the United States,* vol. 1, pp. 308–23. Milwaukee: Burdick, Armitage & Allen, 1891.

Heafford, George H. *Chevrons and Shoulder Straps.* Chicago: Poole Brothers, 1895.

Hemingway, Anson Tyler. "Diaries of Anson Tyler Hemingway, Private, 72nd Illinois Infantry, Company D (Chicago Board of Trade Regiment)." Microfilm, Illinois State Historical Library, Springfield, Illinois.

Hicken, Victor. *Illinois in the Civil War.* Urbana and Chicago: University of Illinois Press, 1966.

Hood, Oliver C. *Millstream.* Oliver C. Hood, 2000.

Horwitz, Tony. *Confederates in the Attic: Dispatches from the Unfinished Civil War.* New York: Vintage Books USA, 1999.

McPherson, James M. *Battle Cry of Freedom: The Civil War Era.* New York and Oxford: Oxford University Press, 1988.

Miles, Jim. *A River Unvexed: A History and Tour Guide of the Campaign for the Mississippi River.* Nashville: Rutledge Hill Press, 1994.

Mohrmann, William. Journal, ca. 1880–1885. Clarke Historical Library, Central Michigan University, Mt. Pleasant.

Seacord, Thomas S. Private. Co. E. 8/8/62–1/28/63. Papers, 1862-1865. Illinois State Historical Library, Springfield.

The 72d Regiment Illinois Volunteers. (Board of Trade First Regiment.) Their Return Home. – Banquet at Bryan Hall. – Addresses of Welcome – Toasts, etc. Sketch of the History of the Regiment. – Their First and Last Rosters, etc. Milwaukee, n.d.

Sexton, James Andrew. "The Observations and Experiences of a Captain of Infantry at the Battle of Franklin, November 30, 1864." In *Military Essays and Recollections: Papers Read before the Commandery of the State of Illinois, Military Order of the Loyal Legion of the United States,* vol. 4, pp. 446–84. Chicago: Cozzens & Beaton Co., 1907.

Sparks, William. "Reminiscences of Sergeant Wm. Sparks of the 72nd Illinois Volunteers." *Illinois Central Magazine* 3:3 (September 1914): 17-21.

Stockton, Joseph. *War Diary (1862–5) of Brevet Brigadier General Joseph Stockton, First Lieutenant, Captain, Major and Lieutenant-Colonel 72d Regiment Illinois Infantry Volunteers – (First Board of Trade Regiment.).* Chicago: John T. Stockton, 1910.

Sword, Wiley. *The Confederacy's Last Hurrah: Spring Hill, Franklin, & Nashville.* Lawrence: University Press of Kansas, 1992.

Watkins, Sam R. *Co. Aytch: A Confederate Memoir of the Civil War.* New York: Simon and Schuster, 1990.

Wiley, Bell Irvin. *The Life of Billy Yank: The Common Soldier of the Union.* Baton Rouge and London: Louisiana State University Press, 1952.

World War II

Ambrose, Stephen E. *D-Day June 6, 1944: The Climactic Battle of World War II.* New York: Touchstone, 1994.

Gabel, Kurt. *The Making of a Paratrooper: Airborne Training and Combat in World War II.* Lawrence: University Press of Kansas, 1990.

Griffin, Susan. *A Chorus of Stones: The Private Life of War.* New York: Anchor Books, 1992.

Langdon, Allen L. *"Ready": The History of the 505th Parachute Infantry Regiment, 82nd Airborne Division, World War II.* Indianapolis: 82nd Airborne Division Association Education Fund, 1986.

Thompson, Leroy. *The All Americans: The 82nd Airborne*. Newton Abbot Devon: David & Charles Publishers, 1988.

Tucker, William H. *Parachute Soldier*. Harwichport: International Airborne Books, 1994.

Wills, Deryk. *Put On Your Boots and Parachutes! The Unites States 82nd Airborne Division*. Leicester: Deryk Wills, 1992.

Other

Ellsworth, H.L. *Illinois in 1837; A Sketch*. Philadelphia: S. Augustus Mitchell and Grigg & Elliot, No. 9, N. Fourth Street, 1837.

Kaplan, Louise. *No Voice Is Ever Wholly Lost*. New York: Simon and Schuster, 1996.

O'Brien, Tim. *The Things They Carried*. New York: Broadway Books, 1998.

Oliver, William. *Eight Months in Illinois: With Information to Immigrants*. Shawnee Classics edition, with a new foreword by James E. Davis. Carbondale and Edwardsville: Southern Illinois University Press, 2002.

ACKNOWLEDGMENTS

I WANT TO THANK SEVERAL PEOPLE for taking the time to read earlier versions of *Acoustic Shadows* and for providing invaluable suggestions and encouragement: Annie Callan, Cat Brown, Sylvia Grisez, Darla Hillard, Kevin Purcell, Lucia Meijer, Kristina Wilkening, Dan Greenman, Carolyn Latteier, and Laurie and Dennis Brooke. I also extend my gratitude to Pat Banks, Bonnie Phillips, and Jana Tines, members of my family who welcomed me into their lives and cheerfully answered my endless questions about the past and the people I never knew. Likewise, thanks to all the men of the 505th Parachute Infantry Regiment, William Tucker, Stanley Kulikowski, George Clark, John Levitsky, and Jack Hillman, for their willingness to share what they could with a stranger on a telephone. A very special thanks goes to Joe Schwan for doing this as well as becoming a friend.

From my life as Bertram Howell, I want to thank the reenacting communities of the 19th Indiana, 5th New York, and 7th Wisconsin, for letting me sign up, as well as for sharing their own reasons for being participants in a hobby that most people consider very strange.

To all the people I met during my travels, I cannot extend my appreciation enough for all their encouragment, willingness to tell their own stories, and help in uncovering mine: O.C. Hood, Bob Duncan, Cam Anderson, Jeff Giambrone, Mary Jane Hall, Cathie Buechler, and Ed Cox. Very special thanks go to Thomas Cartwright and David Fraley for living lives so dedicated to keeping the past within reach, as well as to John Ruskey who endlessly inspires me with his dedication to the journey.

Thanks to the *Clackamas Literary Review* and the *South Loop Review* for publishing essays from *Acoustic Shadows*.

I also would like to thank Sue Livingston for helping me so many years ago to survive the initial shock of the deaths of my parents and to begin the healing process. Additionally, many thanks go to Carolyn Swayze for her belief in *Acoustic Shadows* and my writing. And to that end, this book would not be as smooth or as understandable without the dedication of two very fine editors, Michele Whitehead and Karalynn Ott. Likewise, for the final trimming, I want to thank Julie Van Pelt, and for the beautiful cover that is exactly what I have been imagining for many years, my utmost thanks to Mike Watters.

Finally, I'm not sure *Acoustic Shadows* would have been completed without my partner Barbara's belief in my ability to write this book. Her advice and optimism helped me conquer my own self-doubts, and I will always be grateful for her presence in my life.

ABOUT THE AUTHOR

Betsy L. Howell is a writer and wildlife biologist for the U.S. Forest Service on Washington's Olympic Peninsula. Her essays have appeared in the *Oregonian, Clackamas Literary Review,* an anthology entitled, *The Back Road To Crazy, Stories From The Field* (University of Utah Press, 2005), Columbia College Chicago's *South Loop Review,* and two online journals, *Women in Natural Resources* and *The Apple Valley Review.* She lives in Port Townsend, Washington.